MOVING TEACHER EDUCATION INTO URBAN SCHOOLS AND COMMUNITIES

When teacher education is located on a university campus, set apart from urban schools and communities, it is easy to overlook the realities and challenges communities face as they struggle toward social, economic, cultural, and racial justice. This book describes how teacher education can become a meaningful part of this work by repositioning programs directly into urban schools and communities. Situating their work within the theoretical framework of prioritizing community strengths, each set of authors provides a detailed and nuanced description of a teacher education program re-positioned within an urban school or community. Authors describe the process of developing such a relationship; how the university, school, and community became integrated partners in the program; and the impact on participants. As university-based teacher education has come under increased scrutiny for lack of "real world" relevance, this book showcases programs that have successfully navigated the travails of shifting their base directly into urban schools and communities, with evidence of positive outcomes for all involved.

Jana Noel is an American Council on Education Fellow and is Professor of Education at California State University, Sacramento.

MOVING TEACHER EDUCATION INTO URBAN SCHOOLS AND COMMUNITIES

Prioritizing Community Strengths

Edited by Jana Noel

Routledge
Taylor & Francis Group

NEW YORK AND LONDON

First published 2013
by Routledge
711 Third Avenue, New York, NY 10017

Simultaneously published in the UK
by Routledge
2 Park Square, Milton Park, Abingdon, Oxon OX14 4RN

Routledge is an imprint of the Taylor & Francis Group, an informa business

© 2013 Taylor & Francis

The right of the editor to be identified as the author of the editorial
material, and of the authors for their individual chapters, has been asserted in
accordance with sections 77 and 78 of the Copyright, Designs and Patents
Act 1988.

Library of Congress Cataloging-in-Publication Data

Moving teacher education into urban schools and communities : prioritizing
community strengths / edited by Jana Noel.
    p. cm.
  Includes bibliographical references and index.
   1. Teachers—Training of—United States. 2. Urban schools—United
States. 3. College-school cooperation—United States. I. Noel, Jana.
LB1715.M68   2012
370.71'10973—dc23   2012027852

ISBN: 978-0-415-52807-8 (hbk)
ISBN: 978-0-415-52808-5 (pbk)
ISBN: 978-0-203-11865-8 (ebk)

Typeset in Bembo
by Apex CoVantage, LLC

SUSTAINABLE
FORESTRY
INITIATIVE

Certified Sourcing
www.sfiprogram.org
SFI-00555
The SFI label applies to the text stock.

Printed and bound in the United States of America by
Walsworth Publishing Company, Marceline, MO.

CONTENTS

PART VII
Grow Your Own—A Final Example of Prioritizing Community Strengths

ACKNOWLEDGMENTS

I want to thank Routledge, and especially Naomi Silverman, Publisher, and Julie Ganz, Editorial Assistant, for their assistance in preparing this book. Their assistance has been invaluable throughout the entire publication process, from providing feedback on the book's overall concept to helping navigate through the minute details of putting together an edited collection. I also want to express appreciation to the reviewers who helped improve the original proposal.

On a personal note, I want to give special thanks to my husband, David Powell, and to my parents, Jim and Jan Noel, who have all given me love, support, and encouragement not only in editing this book but in all my personal and professional endeavors.

PREFACE

Urban schools and communities face numerous challenges: Urban poverty; high mobility and displacement in and out of neighborhoods; inadequate funding to adequately cover the educational, social, and health needs of children and their families; and high teacher turnover are just a few examples (Noel, 2010). Too often, schools and teachers are inadequately prepared for the social, political, and economic conditions impacting the lives of their urban students, families, and communities. This is because, as Keyes and Gregg (2001) explain, "while an urban school is located *in* a community, it is not often *of the community*. Employees are rarely neighborhood residents. Many do not share the culture or race of their students" (p. 32). Koerner and Abdul-Tawwab (2006) add that "most teachers in urban classrooms . . . often teach in communities that they have never previously even visited" (p. 37).

Clearly, greater effort must be made to ensure that future teachers in urban areas learn to see themselves as part of a school's community. Indeed, such a movement has has been recommended for over a decade, as Murrell (2001) documents:

> A key component of the new national agenda is collaboration among institutions of higher education, the K–12 schools they work with, and a broad community constituency. The success of urban school reform will depend, in part, on how the new national agenda makes good on its enthusiasm for creating new "communities of learning," embracing diversity, and preparing teachers through community and collaborative partnership. (p. 2)

A number of socially transformative implications of connecting teacher education with urban schools and communities have been documented, including building trust with local communities (Murrell, 2001; Reed, 2004); creating a greater commitment to community through service learning (Andrews, 2009; Boyle-Baise & Sleeter, 2000); preparing culturally responsive future teachers (Ladson-Billings, 2006) who are more effective when working with community members to support classroom learning (Shirley et al., 2006); increasing the number of preservice teachers who choose to teach in an urban, low-income, or diverse school (Noel, 2006; Wong & Glass, 2005) and are more likely to continue teaching in an urban school (Quartz, Priselac, & Franke, 2009); participating in community organizing (Oakes, Rogers, & Lipton, 2006); and transforming the educational system (Au, 2002; Solomon, Manoukian, & Clarke, 2005).

Despite the successes of connecting urban teacher education with school and community, these efforts have also been criticized for having a university-led focus. There is often an inequality in roles, with university programs and faculty setting the tone for interactions. University knowledge, programs, and ideas for transformation are still privileged over those held by the schools and communities, even when our programs are in collaborative partnerships. As Zeichner (2010) points out, "even in the current wave of school–university partnerships in teacher education, colleges and universities continue to maintain hegemony over the construction and dissemination of knowledge" (p. 90).

To be a more meaningful part of the commitment to the development of teachers who value and prioritize community strengths, a number of teacher education programs have responded by transforming their focus and strategies to work more intimately with their urban schools, communities, and community-based organizations. Such programs have recognized that when teacher education is located on a university campus, set apart from urban schools and communities, it is easy to overlook the challenges inherent as communities struggle toward social, economic, cultural, and racial justice. This book describes how teacher education can become a meaningful part of this work by repositioning programs directly into urban schools and communities. The book is theoretically framed by theories that prioritize community strengths. Basing their work in these theoretical frameworks, the authors provide detailed and nuanced descriptions of teacher education programs repositioned within the urban school or community. Each author engagingly describes his or her program, providing (a) the theoretical base on prioritizing community strengths that frame the program, (b) the process of developing the university–school–community relationship, (c) a description of how the university–school–community became integrated partners in the program, and (d) the impact on participants.

This book presents 13 chapters describing teacher education programs that have moved either partially or wholly into urban K–12 schools and their surrounding communities. The chapters in this book represent a range of geographic locations, levels of schooling, and research methodologies. The programs described here are located in Washington, California, Boston, Chicago, North Carolina, Texas, New York City, New Jersey, Indiana, Ohio, and Washington, D.C. Some programs are at the graduate level, some are postbaccalaureate teacher credential programs, and some prepare undergraduate students. All chapters are descriptive; two present quantitative data; and the majority are qualitative in nature, including case studies, narratives, observations, interviews, and surveys. The book is organized into sections that focus on the impact on the various stakeholders. The book ends with a conclusion that provides a summary of the theories of prioritizing community strengths, the steps taken by authors to establish school–community-based urban teacher education programs, and a summary of key works that have formed the foundation for the programs described in the book.

Nearly half of the authors have published books on topics in teacher education, urban education, or educational partnerships, and all are known widely for their work in these areas. The majority of chapters are written by collaborative teams, demonstrating the collaborative spirit of the partnerships described.

Versions of some, but not all, of these chapters were earlier published in a special issue of the journal *Teacher Education Quarterly* (*37*[3], 2010) on the theme of "Moving Teacher Education Into Urban Schools and Communities," and those authors and I would like to acknowledge Caddo Gap Press, publisher Alan Jones, and former *Teacher Education Quarterly* editor Thomas Nelson for their permission to build on the base that volume provided as this book was being developed. This book is conceived of differently than the journal issue, as it proceeds under the specific theoretical framework of prioritizing community strengths and focuses on the impact of school–community-based teacher education on all stakeholders.

As several of the authors write, merely locating a teacher education program within a school or community does not equal having authentic relations with that community. Rather, as many of the authors describe, it takes time, effort, trust, and commitment to create truly collaborative partnerships that involve the work of all partners to develop future teachers that will value urban schools and communities and their efforts to educate children. Several of these authors point out the need to have preservice teachers engage in communities to better understand the lives of the children and their families in urban communities. Many of these articles describe efforts at transformation: transforming urban communities, urban schools, university students who will be teachers, and teacher education programs.

The book is organized into seven parts, each with a focus on the impact on a different set of participants in teacher education programs located in urban schools and communities. Part I, "Democratizing Knowledge and Prioritizing Community Strengths," contains two chapters that lay the framework for contextualizing teacher education within schools and communities that is the overall theme for the book. In Chapter 1, Kenneth Zeichner and Katherina Payne introduce several key concepts related to "Democratizing Knowledge in Urban Teacher Education" and give examples of how this works successfully in practice. They describe that the current focus in teacher education is on knowledge found within universities. They raise the question of "*whose knowledge* should count in teacher education." Zeichner and Payne argue that community knowledge "must inform novice teacher learning. Specifically, we urge teacher education to better connect its work with the social justice work occurring in local communities and beyond" (p. 4). Zeichner and Payne bolster this concept with discussions of "hybrid spaces" in teacher education, spaces where universities, schools, and communities come together to share equally valued knowledge. Based in cultural historical activity theory, "expertise is distributed across systems and that individuals develop into the ways of thinking and acting that are afforded by the cultural practices and tools made available to them in the settings of their development" (p. 6). They exhort teacher educators to draw on local community expertise.

Ronald David Glass and Pia Lindquist Wong also provide a conceptual understanding of the concept of knowledge in Chapter 2, "Learning to Produce Knowledge: Reconstructing Teacher Preparation for Urban Schools." Similarly to Chapter 1, Glass and Wong discuss how knowledge is not isolated in universities but, rather, is developed through social and cultural contexts, explaining that "knowing is embedded within dynamic historical processes that form the social and cultural capital of particular ways of life, expressed in the *habitus* of everyday action" (p. 21). They add that "power is always implicated in judgments of what counts as *knowing*" (p. 22). Glass and Wong develop the idea of "Teachers for Communities (Not Only Classrooms)" (p. 24), in which they urge teachers to develop collaborative learning communities that involve community. They describe the Equity Network, a system of professional development schools in the Sacramento, California, region that put these theories into action.

The book's focus on the impact of school–community-based teacher education programs begins in Part II, "Focus on Preservice Teachers." Andrea J. Stairs and Audrey A. Friedman describe the Urban Immersion program in Boston in their Chapter 3, "Urban Immersion: The Impact of Preservice Preparation in an Urban School–University Partnership." In this decade-long program, part of the university's teacher education program has been located in an urban high school, as the collaborative university–school team "determined that through course work and experiences in classrooms, participants should develop their knowledge of content and pedagogy, but more importantly, develop their knowledge of the urban context and how to balance the multiple demands so that all students might learn and improve their life chances" (p. 43). Through both qualitative and quantitative research, Stairs and Friedman find that Urban Immersion students have developed improved cultural competence and an increased commitment to urban teaching. The authors conclude that "Urban Immersion provides all of us a context for deepening personal ideological clarity and professional epistemology that truly prioritizes community strengths" (pp. 53–54).

In Chapter 4, "Beyond the Ivory Tower: The Role of Contextually Based Course Redesign in a Community-Embedded Urban Teacher Preparation Model," Robert E. Lee, Brent D. Showalter, and Lucille L. T. Eckrich describe a university-wide redesign of programs that created a community-embedded teacher preparation program in Chicago. They explain that "a teacher's knowledge of how culture is formed and sustained" (p. 56), is vital to urban teaching and can be gained through "cultural mapping" within communities of practice. The authors argue that "more opportunities for preservice teachers to challenge and inform their cultural maps through community-based urban school experiences are needed if the shortage of well-prepared, culturally competent, and critically minded urban teachers is to be addressed" (p. 59). The authors present findings from quantitative studies that demonstrate that teacher education students participating in the program showed increased "intentions to teach in an urban setting" as well as effects on "their perceptions of urban education, their attitudes toward diversity and multiculturalism, and their developing sense of self-efficacy toward urban teaching" (p. 68).

The focus on impact on participants shifts in Part III to a "Focus on Children." In Chapter 5, "The Poetry of Voice," Susan Catapano and Candace M. Thompson describe a partnership program in a North Carolina middle school that matches preservice teachers with sixth graders on a Language Arts project in a service learning model. In addition to university connections, the school's administration and teachers joined in to form a community of practice. As they describe the partnership from the perspective of the preservice teachers, "in engaging with adolescents working to express their world through poetry, they too are engaged in a process of developing their own voices as teachers and learners in relationship with students and each other" (p. 76). The outcome of the project is a sixth-grade student poetry night. Catapano and Thompson interviewed the sixth graders about working with university students and provide a sampling of the children's enthusiastic responses. The result: the development of students' voice.

Barbara Morgan-Fleming also focuses on the impact of a partnership on children in Chapter 6, "Listening to K–12 Students' Advice." Continuing the theme of children's voices, Morgan-Fleming writes that "K–12 students' voices also remind us that, while it might be comforting to invent simple, universal solutions to 'educate everyone,' to be successful, an educator must be able to view the world through a variety of lenses" (p. 90). She points out the importance of understanding "shared power in relationships" (p. 91), so that when teacher educators and their preservice teachers spend time in school partnerships, children's comfort level with adults increases, and they feel able to share their advice with adults in the partnership. In describing the impact on children in her Texas university–school partnership, Morgan-Fleming includes children's letters, drawings, and responses to the questions, What is in a good teacher's head? What is in a good teacher's heart? and How should teacher educators help people become good teachers?

Part IV, "Focus on Practicing Teachers and Schools," moves the focus to the impact of urban school–community-based teacher education programs on those practicing teachers and schools where the programs are located. In Chapter 7, "Transformations in Site-Based Teacher Preparation Courses: The Benefits of Challenges," Jill V. Jeffery and Jody N. Polleck examine the impact of a co-instructed teacher education course in a partnership school in New York City on the school-level participants. Jeffery and Polleck remind us of the critical importance of ensuring that a partner school benefits from teacher education's presence in that school. They describe the many nuances of co-instruction and ask the question, "How, then, might universities participate in the work of schools in ways that are, in the eyes of school stakeholders, transformational rather than burdensome?" (p. 105). They present both the benefits and challenges that schools and teachers have in working in a co-instruction partnership with a university. They present data from observations, interviews, and a survey. The results can be summarized by saying that having a co-instruction model of partnership in their school provided multiple forms of professional development, built professional learning communities, and served as a transformational experience for the school.

In Chapter 8, a team of faculty from Chicago and New York move the discussion directly into the arena of social justice in "Creating Intentional Partnerships in Urban Spaces: Schools, Communities, and Teacher Preparation Programs." Eleni Katsarou, Bree Picower, and David Stovall explain that "by taking the position that teaching for social justice is an act of necessity and solidarity, this chapter seeks to highlight two examples of teacher education initiatives that prioritize community strengths" (p. 121). The focus on collaboration is clearly seen as the authors describe an "intergenerational/interinstitutional community of teacher educators" (p. 125). They discuss the difficulties of urban education and urge "rethinking expertise for solidarity and empathy" (p. 129). They describe how communities for support of social justice teaching and curriculum develop as the result of intentional relationships between universities and urban "schools/spaces" that "are central in our developing teacher candidates that will engage in deeply caring, ethical, and socially and politically relevant teaching" (p. 128). They conclude by stating that "classrooms must be in and of the community, blurring the boundaries between who teaches and who learns and the borders between schools and neighborhoods" (p. 132).

The next two chapters describe the impact of school–community-based programs on the communities themselves in Part V, "Focus on Community Partners." Jana Noel describes the process of "Partnering in a Community's Efforts to Transform Urban Education" in Chapter 9. She describes the Sacramento, California, Urban Teacher Education Center's move to an urban school community, with a focus on the community's long-standing history in mentoring children from the neighborhood. She emphasizes the value of "being there" on a daily basis in the school, supporting the school's and community's educational efforts. Noel presents narratives from the program coordinator's journals; student teacher reflections; and results from a survey, interviews, and a focus group with the community's leaders. The results are summarized by the statement that "our daily presence within the school and community had begun to break through the layers of distrust the community held toward outsiders. UTEC became seen as a source of strength for the community's efforts to support the neighborhood children's education" (p. 149).

In Chapter 10, "A Community–University Partnership to Develop Urban Teachers as Public Professionals," Cynthia Onore and Bonny L. Gildin shift focus on a partnership with a community organization, the All Stars Project Inc. Teacher education students spent time in the community-based organization in after-school programs and the community, participating in such cultural events as churchgoing with community residents. A key purpose of the program is the reconceptualization of teaching as a "public profession," in which teachers "are citizens with special purposes—to work together with those outside of school to achieve common goals" (p. 165). As the authors write, if the focus of teacher education were to shift to the development of public professionals, then public schools "would not simply occupy spaces within a community, but they would see their work as embedded in the community and, thus, intimately tied to community values and goals" (p. 154). Impacts on the community include residents of the community serving as mentors to the university students and the development of a new after-school center.

Two chapters with a "Focus on University Faculty" can be found in Part VI. Francine P. Peterman discusses "Sustaining Teacher Educators Engaged in Partnering to Prepare Urban Teachers" in Chapter 11. Peterman lays out the immense complexity of the roles of teacher educators who work in collaborative partnerships with schools and communities, describing that "one need only to have lived the life of a partnering teacher educator for only a semester to understand the complexity of the roles and responsibilities involved and their competing demands upon one's time, resources, and intellectual and physical capacities" (p. 171). She presents interviews of teacher educators who leave the profession, as well as provides the story of those who stay. Peterman addresses the professional identity of teacher educators, the need to feel one's work is valued, and the importance of a focus on social justice. A key piece of the work of such teacher educators, according to Peterman's interviews, is "building and sustaining relationships with community" (p. 181). As Peterman writes in her conclusion, "because the work is public, authentic, and involves other professionals in inquiry and creative problem solving, it requires teacher educators to look closely at what they know, what they say, and what they do—and to seek the integrity of the alignment of these three aspects of their practice" (p. 183).

In Chapter 12, Deidre B. Sessoms describes "Teacher Preparation Faculty in Urban Partnerships: Learning and Leading." Similar to the previous chapter, Sessoms examines the impact on multiple faculty, in this case, the Equity Network (also described in Chapter 2). Sessoms discusses the web of university, school, and individual faculty efforts to develop meaningful partnerships. She lays out the "supportive conditions" (p. 186) that allow faculty to be able to engage meaningfully in school–community-based teacher education programs, and she discusses the complexities and challenges of such work. Sessoms lays out the paths of several teacher educators who have served as both learners and leaders through their work and how being fully engaged in these efforts can also lead to those same faculty leaders "leaving" to effect change at differing levels of the university.

Chapter 13, "Teacher Preparation With/In an Urban Community," by Elizabeth A. Skinner, comprises the final section, Part VII, "Grow Your Own—A Final Example of Prioritizing Community Strengths." This "grow your own" program began with a request from the community to bring the university into the neighborhood and draws from the urban neighborhoods' residents to enter the teacher education program. Skinner presents us with the lives of the members of this urban neighborhood through the lives of the students in the teacher education program. This article provides an example of truly community-oriented urban teacher education in that the idea for the program came from the community and the preservice teachers are residents in the community.

As university-based teacher education has come under increased scrutiny for lack of real-world relevance, the book offers a theoretically based set of programs that have successfully navigated the travails of shifting their bases directly into urban schools and communities, with evidence of positive impact on all involved. It is hoped that readers will build on their theoretical knowledge of community strengths, develop some practical strategies for developing and maintaining teacher education programs based in urban university–school communities, and most significantly, join in urban schools' and communities' efforts as they struggle toward social, economic, cultural, and racial justice.

Jana Noel

References

Andrews, D. J. C. (2009). "The hardest thing to turn from": The effects of service-learning on preparing urban educators. *Equity & Excellence in Education, 42*(3), 272–293.

Au, K. H. (2002). Communities of practice: Engagement, imagination, and alignment in research on teacher education. *Journal of Teacher Education, 53*(3), 222–227.

Boyle-Baise, M., & Sleeter, C. E. (2000, Spring). Community service learning for multicultural education. *Educational Foundations*, pp. 1–18.

Keyes, M. C., & Gregg, S. (2001). *School-community connections: A literature review.* Charleston, SC: AEL Inc.

Koerner, M., & Abdul Tawwab, N. (2006). Using community as a resource for teacher education: A case study. *Equity & Excellence in Education, 39,* 37–46. doi:10.1080/10665680500478767

Ladson-Billings, G. (2006). It's not the culture of poverty, it's the poverty of culture: The problem with teacher education. *Anthropology and Education Quarterly, 37*(2), 104–109.

Murrell, P. C., Jr. (2001). *The community teacher: A new framework for effective urban teaching.* New York: Teachers College Press.

Noel, J. (2006). Integrating a new teacher education center into a school and its community. *Journal of Urban Learning, Teaching, and Research, 2,* 197–205.

Noel, J. (2010). Weaving teacher education into the fabric of urban schools and communities. *Teacher Education Quarterly, 37*(3), 9–25.

Oakes, J., Rogers, J., & Lipton, M. (2006). *Learning power: Organizing for education and justice.* New York: Teachers College Press.

Quartz, K. H., Priselac, J., & Franke, M. L. (2009). Transforming public schools: A synthesis of research findings from UCLA's Center X. *Equity & Excellence in Education, 42*(3), 313–326.

Reed, W. A. (2004). A tree grows in Brooklyn: Schools of education as brokers of social capital in low-income neighborhoods. In J. L. Kincheloe, A. Bursztyn, & S. R. Steinberg (Eds), *Teaching teachers: Building a quality school of urban education* (pp. 65–90). New York: Peter Lang.

Shirley, D., Hersi, A., MacDonald, E., Sanchez, M. T., Scandone, C., Skidmore, C., et al. (2006). Bringing the community back in: Change, accommodation, and contestation in a school and university partnership. *Equity & Excellence in Education, 39*, 27–36.

Solomon, R. P., Manoukian, R. K., & Clarke, J. (2005). From an ethic of altruism to possibilities of transformation in teacher candidates' community involvement. In L. Pease-Alvarez & S. Schecter (Eds), *Learning, teaching and community: Contributions of situated and participatory approaches to educational innovation* (pp. 171–190). Mahwah, NJ: Lawrence Erlbaum.

Wong, P. L., & Glass, R. D. (2005). Assessing a professional development school approach to preparing teachers for urban schools serving low-income, culturally and linguistically diverse communities. *Teacher Education Quarterly, 32*(3), 63–77.

Zeichner, K. (2010). Rethinking the connections between campus courses and field experiences in college and university-based teacher education. *Journal of Teacher Education, 89*(11), 89–99.

PART I

Democratizing Knowledge and Prioritizing Community Strengths

1

DEMOCRATIZING KNOWLEDGE IN URBAN TEACHER EDUCATION

Kenneth Zeichner and Katherina Payne

One of the central issues underlying current debates about teacher education and teacher quality is concerned with the knowledge that teachers need to be successful in teaching all students to high academic standards. Although there has been extensive writing over the years about the so-called knowledge base in teacher education (e.g., Darling-Hammond & Bransford, 2005) and about the particular teaching practices that novices need to learn how to enact (Ball & Forzani, 2009), this work has focused on analyzing what teachers need to know to be well-started beginners. Similarly, over the years, a substantial literature has emerged in the United States and elsewhere on the question of who should be prepared as teachers to teach in democratic societies (e.g., Villegas & Irvine, 2010) and how this preparation should occur (e.g., Hollins & Guzman, 2005). Very little attention has been given, however, to *whose knowledge* should count in teacher education.

We argue that teacher education needs to make an epistemological shift in whose knowledge counts and whose expertise must inform novice teacher learning. Specifically, we urge teacher education to better connect its work with the social justice work occurring in local communities and beyond (e.g., Warren & Mapp, 2011; Watson, 2012). We also argue that this shift needs to attend to both the processes of teacher education, how and from whom teachers learn in courses and field experiences, and how those decisions are negotiated—as well as to the larger structures in which teacher education is embedded. Importantly, we are not defending the status quo in university teacher education, nor standing in rank with the new "reformers" who call for tearing down and privatizing teacher education. Rather, we argue for a transformation of teacher education as a public good that requires participation from colleges and universities, schools, and communities.

Currently, there are basically two general approaches to the preservice education of teachers in the United States, despite all of the specific program variations: "early entry" and "college recommending" (Grossman & Loeb, 2008). Even with the advent of "early-entry" programs in the 1980s where much of preservice preparation is completed by individuals while they serve as teachers of record, college and university-based teacher education programs that include significant course work and fieldwork prior to a candidate becoming a teacher of record continue to be the major source of teachers for our public schools (National Research Council, 2010). In the following sections, we summarize the current state of teacher education in the United States, and highlight the ways in which we believe its transformation based on democratizing knowledge creates new opportunities for teachers to learn to work with all students in urban schools.

College-Recommending Programs

The traditional model of college-recommending teacher education emphasizes the translation of academic knowledge into practice. Candidates are supposed to learn what and how to teach in their courses on campus, and then go out and apply what is learned during their field experiences in schools. Historically, very little success has been achieved in coordinating what is done in the course and field components of teacher education programs. Oftentimes, the teachers in P–12 with whom teacher candidates are placed for their field placements know very little about the course-based portion of the program, and the course instructors know very little about the placement sites and the work of the cooperating teachers (Zeichner, 2010b). Even in the current era of school–university partnerships, partner and professional development schools, colleges and universities continue to maintain hegemony over the construction and dissemination of knowledge for teaching in teacher education (Duffy, 1994; Zeichner, 2009) and schools remain in the position of "practice fields" where candidates are to try out the practices provided to them by the university (Barab & Duffy, 2000).

We are not suggesting that power can or should be equalized and that the goal should be to reach consensus on all issues. We are suggesting though that power hierarchies be lessened in teacher preparation programs in which colleges and universities are involved, that more participants and more perspectives be brought into the decision-making process, and that different views are seriously considered despite important differences that will continue to exist about what constitutes good teaching and how teachers should learn (Apple, 2008).

Although the reality of how and from whom teacher candidates learn to teach is much more complex than portrayed here, the way in which college- and university-based teacher education is usually structured is fundamentally undemocratic and largely fails to strategically access knowledge and expertise that exist in schools and local communities that could inform the preparation of teachers. Although most prospective teachers spend a substantial amount of time in schools during their preparation, there is typically very little planning that is done (e.g., a practicum curriculum) as to how they can access practitioner- and community-based knowledge to inform their preparation as teachers. Further, there is generally a lack of investment of resources and careful attention to the placement and supervision of teacher candidates during their clinical experiences (Greenberg, Pomerance, & Walsh, 2011; National Council for Accreditation of Teacher Education, 2010).

Early-Entry Programs

The rapidly expanding number of "early-entry" programs place teacher candidates in schools with very little preservice preparation and emphasize, and sometimes uncritically glorify, practice and practitioner knowledge while minimizing the importance of professional education course work that is not seen as directly connected to daily teaching practice. This kind of thinking leads to such things as the definition of social foundations content as "nonessential" in a teacher education program (Walsh & Jacobs, 2007), to teachers who can implement teaching scripts but who have not developed the professional vision and adaptive expertise they need to meet the changing learning needs of their students, as well as to continue to learn in and from their practice (Hamerness et al., 2005). Importantly, neither college recommending nor early-entry programs often give much attention to the role of community-based knowledge in teacher preparation (e.g., Murrell, 2001).

Neither of these two stances toward a "knowledge base" for teacher education (an emphasis on academic or practitioner knowledge to the exclusion of serious attention to other knowledge sources) is sufficient for preparing teachers to be successful in urban public schools. Despite the social justice multicultural content that is common in college and university teacher education programs across the nation, the hidden curriculum of teacher education (Ginsburg & Clift, 1990) often sends a very clear message about the lack of respect for the knowledge of P–12 practitioners and nonprofessional educators in communities.

In our view, the preparation of teachers in democratic societies should be based on an epistemology that in itself is democratic and includes a respect for and interaction among practitioner, academic, and community-based knowledge. Whether this can take place in newly created spaces within universities such as "Centers of Pedagogy" (Paterson, Michelli, & Pacheco, 1999) or whether new institutional spaces need to be created for teacher education with different knowledge histories (Gorodesky & Barak, 2008) remains to be seen. This is very different than the current wave of interest in teacher residency programs that place teaching practice at the center of preparation and that wraps course work around this practice (Duncan, 2009). Very few of urban teacher residencies involve the kind of ecology of expertise that we have in mind. What we are proposing is the creation of new hybrid spaces where academic, practitioner-, and community-based knowledge come together in new ways to support the development of innovative and hybrid solutions to the problem of preparing teachers.

Conceptualizing Hybrid Spaces in Teacher Education

We think the creation of new hybrid spaces in teacher education is needed where academic, school-based, and community-based knowledge come together in less hierarchical and haphazard ways to support teacher learning. To further theorize collaborations between university, school, and community-based sources of knowledge, we use some of the conceptual tools afforded by cultural–historical activity theory (CHAT). CHAT provides a way to think about bringing together the expertise that teacher candidates need that is located in schools, colleges and universities, and communities. Two of the key ideas in cultural–historical theories are that expertise is distributed across systems and that individuals develop into the ways of thinking and acting that are afforded by the cultural practices and tools made available to them in the settings of their development (Ellis, Edwards, & Smagorinsky, 2010). From a CHAT perspective, teacher candidate learning takes place in "a changing mosaic of interconnected activity systems" (Engestrom, 2001, p. 147).

The concept of "activity system " emerged from Leont'ev's (1978) and then Engeström's expansion of Vygotsky's (1978) zone of proximal development (ZPD), which Vygotsky defined as "the distance between the actual development level as determined by independent problem solving and the level of potential development as determined through problem solving under adult guidance or in collaboration with more capable peers" (p. 86). Vygotsky's development of the ZPD recognized the importance of tools, from language to physical objects, in mediating individual learning and development. Engeström expanded the ZPD into cultural–historical activity theory, which emphasizes the productive means of learning through joint mediated activity.

Importantly, Engeström emphasizes that human activity is simultaneously constrained by macrostructures and sociopolitical contexts, as well as transformed by individuals' actions, proclivities, and tendencies within their everyday activities. Specifically, activity theory acknowledges the community, distribution of work, and rules that affect both individual and collective activities. Engeström elaborated the ZPD from an individualistic account of learning and development toward a more expansive view of learning through participation with others within activity systems that are simultaneously enabling and constraining.

Engeström (1987; Engestrom, 2001) emphasizes the expansive aspects of learning that occur through engaging in the activity, particularly through the contradictions and tensions that are the "engines" of change and transformation in practices, tools, and activities. By centering the activity of teacher learning in the contradictory, conflictual spaces among the university, school, and community knowledge and practice, the possibility for collaborative efforts around these contradictions can lead to remediation of preservice teachers' learning. Further, through these tensions in learning how to work with diverse learners, and toward the goal of accessing both school and community knowledge, activity theory allows us to look at preservice teachers' learning in and across multiple spaces, to recognize how those spaces both expand and constrain learning opportunities.

Assuming that the knowledge and expertise needed by teacher candidates is located in schools, colleges and universities, and in communities, and that the key problem of teacher education is to figure out how to provide teacher candidates with access to this needed expertise from these different systems, the concepts of "horizontal expertise," "boundary crossing" and "boundary zones," and "knotworking" prove particularly useful in theorizing these hybrid relationships. These conceptual tools are rooted in Kerouso and Engeström's (2003) examination of work that occurs across organizations, such as healthcare providers. Of import, the tensions and contradictions that emerged for patients who navigated multiple types of healthcare providers (e.g., clinics, hospitals) were the impetus for the collaborative efforts. A major issue was that there was a disruption in the communications within and across providers, resulting in significant ruptures in the continuity of patient care. Moreover, multiple and different rules, tools, reporting systems, and patterns of interaction guide these organizations, which made the establishment of common goals difficult to pursue concurrently.

To work collaboratively to articulate new goals, practices, and tools, participants had to cross the boundaries of their own organizations and work with others to create new solutions to their common problems. By crossing these boundaries and creating new practices and tools, horizontal expertise emerged as "professionals from different domains enriched and expanded their practices through working together to reorganize relations and coordinate their work" (Anagnostopoulos, Smith, & Basmadjian, 2007, p. 139). In contrast to vertical notions of learning and expertise (i.e., "lower" and "higher" forms), these professional collaborative efforts relied on horizontal expertise. That is, the unique knowledge and understanding that each professional brought to the collective activity was treated as more equally valuable, relevant, and important. Each professional develops a range of expertise across work and organizational spaces, but working collaboratively, these forms of expertise serve as resources in joint problem-solving activity. Further, these collaborative processes reorganize the traditional hierarchies of expertise (vertical expertise), as they help individuals and groups find innovative solutions to the compelling dilemmas that characterize their everyday work life. Creating these innovative tools, practices, and solutions not only addresses the joint activity and dilemma, but also expands individuals' learning as they appropriate new tools and work languages that they could not have created on their own with access only to their particular languages, rules, and systems.

While originally developed in studies of workplace learning in Finland and later elaborated in studies throughout the world which depict a mixing of domain-specific expertise from different spheres of activity, these conceptual tools are useful for thinking about the more democratic political economy of knowledge that we believe is necessary to educate teachers well so they can be successful in the complex and underfunded urban public schools where many of them will teach (e.g., Edwards, 2010; Edwards, Daniels, Gallagher, Leadbetter, & Warmington, 2009; Ellis et al., 2010; Engestrom, 2008).

The task of bringing together expertise from the different activity systems of university, school, and community for the benefit of teacher candidate learning can be considered analogous to the problem of coordinating the work of health-care professionals who work in different systems but who all serve the same patients or the task of coordinating the work of a group of individuals from different education and social service agencies who are all serving the same children and families (Edwards, 2010; Edwards et al., 2009; Engestrom, 2008).

While boundary crossing serves as an initial image to understand the equalizing of institutional boundaries, it does not necessarily change the relationship between the various activity systems involved in teacher education. In other words, a boundary crosser can move between activity systems without ever changing the actual institutional relationship between the two systems. Max (2010) urges us to consider "boundary zones" (Konkola, as cited in Max, 2010) as a space where two activity systems meet; and similar to the idea of a "third space" (Guitierrez et al., 1999), a boundary zone is "polycontextual, multivoiced, multi-scripted, and shaped by alternative and often oppositional discourses, positionings and practices" (Max, 2010, p. 216). Ellis (2012) describes the boundary zone as "a relatively neutral space where different priorities are respected and new ways of thinking can emerge" (p. 5). Importantly, Ellis (2012b) also urges us to pay greater attention to "how cultural practices have become historically sedimented" in each activity system that is overlapping in these boundary zones. Yet, we must heed the caveat that no deliberation can ever truly be free of power differentials (Sanders, 1997). If we attend to these distinct and important histories of the university, school, and community, we at least begin acknowledging the role of historicity in shaping future collaborative work.

The concept of "knotworking" offers a way to understand the learning of teacher candidates that occurs when there is collaboration across activity systems (university, school, and community). The different interests, values and practices that exist in these different systems are mediated in the knots (Engestrom, 2008; Engestrom, Engestrom, & Vahaaho, 1999).[1] Insights from international research on the pooling of expertise in these knots, or boundary zones between organizations (e.g., Edwards, 2010; Engestrom, 2007), can benefit efforts in teacher education to build new hybrid or "inter-spaces" (Hartley, 2007) between schools, universities, and communities in ways that support teacher learning.

Norton-Meier and Drake (2010) argue that a hybrid or "third space" in teacher education is more than moving university courses to schools or bringing K–12 teachers to the university campus. There is substantial evidence that traditional knowledge hierarchies are maintained among universities, schools and communities even in situations that have been characterized as genuinely collaborative. Bringing P–12 teachers to the university campus or university faculty and staff and their teacher education courses to schools and bringing in community people to sit around a table with professional educators from schools and universities does not necessarily change anything in terms of undemocratic knowledge hierarchies (Popkewitz, 1975).

As we indicated earlier, we are not suggesting that it is possible to create a situation of democratic deliberation free of power differentials, the kind of "ideal speech situation" that has been suggested by Habermas (1984) and Rawls (1971). There are real dangers involved in merely rhetorically romanticizing a model of teacher education based on deliberative democracy (Apple, 2008). There is no question that the negotiations that will need to take place in the hybrid spaces that we are suggesting (e.g., over different visions of what makes high-quality teachers and how to prepare them) will be difficult to navigate (e.g., Bartholomew & Sandholz, 2009). As Klein, Taylor, Onore, and Strom (2011) have pointed out, "a third space is a continual construction, a utopian prospect that is never fully achievable" (p. 14).

Sanders (1997) has argued that efforts to deliberate in a democratic manner toward a common view often reinforce status inequalities. He calls for attempts to represent a fuller range of voices under conditions of mutual respect rather than trying to reach consensus and seeking to equalize power differentials. In creating hybrid spaces in teacher education that bring in school and community perspectives that are often marginalized in traditional university-based models, Sanders' goals of the inclusivity of voices and mutual respect are reasonable ones to strive for in the deliberation process (also see Zeichner, 1991). There is some evidence in recent studies of collaborative efforts in interorganizational spaces that achieving this inclusivity and reaching a situation where participants achieve "reasonable agreements" about certain elements of the situation at hand is generative of productive boundary work that results in new and creative solutions (e.g., Edwards, 2010).

In the following sections, we briefly examine how teacher education, and in particular preservice teacher education, can attempt to use some of the conceptual tools of CHAT to create more expansive learning opportunities for preservice teachers by creating spaces for the kind of boundary crossing and boundary zones, horizontal expertise, and knotworking that can lead to more democratic teacher education.

Examples of Hybrid Spaces in Teacher Education

Some examples of hybridity in preservice teacher education involve sustained efforts to involve expert teachers in all aspects of university-based teacher education, including program planning, instruction, and ongoing evaluation and renewal. Two examples are the Teachers' in Residence Program at the University of Wisconsin–Milwaukee and the Faculty Associate positions at Simon Fraser University in Canada (Beynon, Grout, & Wideen, 2004; Post, Pugach, Harris, & Hughes, 2006). Another example is the work done at the Carnegie Foundation for the Advancement of Teaching that led to the utilization of web-based documentation of the work of outstanding K–12 teachers in methods courses taught by university faculty (Pointer-Mace, 2009). Faculty members in several university-based teacher education programs have used these teacher websites in their courses to give their teacher candidates access to the thinking and practices of master teachers who were using the same practices and approaches promoted in the university courses (Hatch & Grossman, 2009). Also, Merryfield (2006) high-lights the possibilities of web-based tools used within a social studies and global education learning community to redefine authority, equity of voice, and partici-pation in teacher education. Who participated in the community—M.Ed. students, professors, and cooperating teachers—and how they participated, created more spaces for equitable sharing of knowledge and the testing of new ideas.

Another aspect of this work involves moving methods and foundations course work from the university into school-based sites. Merely moving courses does not create a knowledge shift; however, when instructors and teachers collaborate to strategically connect academic and school-based forms of expertise around par-ticular content areas, the possibility for a democratic construction of knowledge emerges (e.g., Campbell, 2008, 2012). For example, in practice-based methods courses, in addition to the usual practice of professors providing teacher can-didates with the theoretical basis for particular teaching strategies and showing them video examples of teachers using these practices, teacher candidates some-times have opportunities to observe a professor or a classroom teacher using the teaching strategy with students, to plan and rehearse lessons using these strategies that they then go and teach with students, and to debrief their teaching with their peers, and with the professor and teachers in the school (Kazemi, Lampert, & Franke, 2009).

It is our belief that this kind of more situated instruction in teacher education programs better prepares teacher candidates to successfully enact the research-based teaching practices that they are learning about in their programs and that are not commonly used in schools currently. There is a laser-like focus on building the capacity of teacher candidates to enact particular research-based teaching prac-tices in the complex world of high-need urban schools, and evidence is beginning to accumulate that this approach leads to greater enactment of the teaching strat-egies that focused in these courses (Campbell, 2008, 2012). Further, Campbell's (2012) study of the practice-based methods course in secondary mathematics showed that this approach helped disrupt candidates' deficit-oriented views of the students and helped them position their students as competent.

Despite the many logistical and resource issues involved in running these practice-based courses, other universities in the United States are also beginning to situate their courses more in the context of public schools and to strategically supplement their own contributions with the expertise among teachers in the schools where the courses are taught. Examples include Montclair State University (Klein et al., 2011; Onore & Gildin, 2010), Boston College (Shirley et al., 2006), New York University (Jeffrey & Polleck, 2010), and Texas Tech (Morgan-Fleming, Simpson, Curtis, & Hull, 2010).

Local Community Expertise

While the role of school-based expertise is essential in teacher preparation, the role of expertise based in local communities is also important. The idea of "community teachers" (Murrell, 2001) can guide the preparation of teachers who are working in and for an increasingly diverse democratic society. Murrell defines a community teacher as "one who possesses contextualized knowledge of the culture, community, and identity of the children and families he or she serves and draws on this knowledge to create the core teaching practices necessary for effectiveness in diverse setting" (Murrell, 2001, p. 52). Key to Murrell's definition and the argument we are making here is that the knowledge is contextualized; it cannot be learned in a university classroom away from the communities in which teachers will work. All preservice teachers must engage with diverse communities, both inside schools and outside of schools, as part of their preparation. Teacher education programs' collaboration with communities ought to aim for preservice teachers not only understanding but also utilizing community and cultural knowledge in their teaching.

Local communities have the possibility to serve as resources for teachers to access and learn about other forms and spaces of knowledge outside of schools. Teacher education programs must deal with the question of encountering difference in the classroom, not only for the benefit of student achievement but also because it is this diversity that makes public schools ideal places for cultivating democratic citizens (Parker, 2005). Allen (2004) argues that encountering difference, or as she terms it, "talking to strangers," is precisely what democracy in the United States requires to overcome the distrust that has fossilized patterns of mutual disdain among different groups. If schools are ideal places for cultivating democratic citizens, then teacher education programs need to emphasize the assets of this diversity in its curriculum to help teachers facilitate this cultivation. Creating mediated cross-cultural or community-based learning experiences is one way that teacher education can both work toward inclusion of multiple knowledge spaces in preservice education, as well as work toward a more democratic ideal in teacher education.

Cross-cultural community-based experiences represent one way in which teacher candidates can encounter and learn about social and geographical communities that were previously unfamiliar to them (Sleeter, 2001; Sleeter & Boyle-Baise, 2000; Zeichner & Melnick, 1996). Cross-cultural community-based experiences span a broad range, and often differ in their purpose and how they are situated in teacher preparation programs. These experiences can be short term in a single course and /or community that may be characterized as visiting a community, or experiences can also be longer and more intensive, which may be thought of as immersing preservice teachers in the community. Some programs are elective, such as Indiana University's Cultural Immersion programs, which allow student teachers to work in local schools in other countries and within diverse communities in the United States (Longview Foundation, 2008). Other community experiences are required portions of teacher education programs, such as University of Washington's community-based practicum experience (see McDonald et al., 2011).

Fostering more democratic relationships between universities and local communities attempts to value and access the knowledge that each holds that bears on preservice teachers' growing identities and pedagogy as multicultural, critical teachers. To leverage the benefits from these types of encounters, particular pedagogical efforts must be employed. These experiences must be mediated to facilitate candidates' recognition and articulation of culturally relevant teaching practices; otherwise, we risk losing valuable opportunities for learning (McDonald et al., 2011). Further, mediation must come through the joint activity of experts in both spaces (e.g., Seidl & Friend, 2002). This involves collaboration and joint problem solving regarding the design and selection of tools and pedagogies in co-mediation efforts.

The Future for Hybrid Spaces in Teacher Education

One potentially promising way to create the kind of shared responsibility for educating teachers that we think is needed is to create new structural and governance models for teacher education programs like the teacher residency programs that are expanding across the United States with help from the Obama administration (Berry et al., 2008). As stated earlier, though, merely establishing the structure for a teacher residency program does not necessarily mean that schools, universities, and communities participate in genuinely collaborative ways. Although teacher residency programs share certain general characteristics, they also vary both in terms of how the curriculum is structured and in the roles that are played by the various partners. From our observation and study of some of the existing teacher residencies, the power and influence of school, university, and community partners vary greatly.

Generally, we know very little as a field about the various ways in which these hybrid activities operate, and we need to be careful not to assume that merely bringing people together from the different spheres of universities, schools, and communities is necessarily any different epistemologically than what went on before, or is any more educative for teacher candidates or students. What is needed is a fundamental shift in whose expertise counts in the education of new teachers and in the work of college and university teacher educators. It is no longer adequate to implement special projects here and there that are funded on temporary money and to then see the innovations disappear after the money is gone and the conference papers are presented and the articles and books are published. It is no longer enough to have university academics alone framing the discourse and inviting school-based educators and people from the broader community in to "participate" in a university-owned teacher education program, or to have school-based teacher educators in early-entry programs shut out the potential contributions of university academics. It should no be longer be acceptable for teacher educators in both schools and universities to marginalize or shut out the perspectives of those who send their children to public schools and live in the communities that schools are supposed to serve.

Given the labor-intensive nature of building interinstitutional communities of practice in teacher education, the habits of those from schools and universities, and the low status of teacher education in many research universities, it is going to be difficult to achieve this cultural shift in teacher education. Figuring out how to achieve this shift is also complicated by the defunding of public schools and the continual decline of the percentage of state support for public universities, where most teachers in the nation continue to be prepared (Newfield, 2008).

Conclusion

Almost every week, a new report is released in the United States criticizing the quality of the contribution of colleges and universities to initial teacher education or praising one of the newly emerging alternative providers of teacher education programs. In 2010, the Obama government's education department distributed $263 million dollars on a competitive basis to promote innovation in various sectors of education. The only teacher education projects that were funded in this competition were those from two of the major alternative certification providers, "Teach for America," which received $50 million dollars, and "The New Teacher Project," which received $20 million dollars. None of the proposals for innovation in teacher education submitted by college and university teacher educators were funded.[2]

Although there continues to be some federal investment in recruiting talented individuals to teaching through various scholarship and loan programs, university teacher education is generally not seen today as worthy of investment by the federal government or many foundations, even though it still prepares most of the nation's teachers (see, e.g., Suggs & deMarrais, 2011). A situation has been framed in the United States where colleges and universities are seen as obstacles to reform and efforts are being made at the highest levels of government to figure out how to shut down university programs and to support the spread of non-university teacher education providers (Zeichner, 2010a).

Despite the weaknesses that have existed in university-based teacher education in the United States and elsewhere, including its lack of attention in educator preparation to the complexities of schooling, its failure to supply schools with enough fully qualified teachers in remote rural and urban schools in areas of high poverty, and lack of respect for the expertise that exists in schools and communities, the solutions to problems of inequality in public education are not to be found in the deprofessinalization and commodification of teaching and teacher education and by supplying schools with underprepared teacher technicians to teach the children of the poor (Tucker, 2011).

This is both a very exciting and dangerous time for university-based teacher education. There is a real opportunity to establish forms of democratic professionalism in teaching and teacher education (Apple, 1996; Sachs, 2003) where colleges and universities, and schools and communities come together in new ways to prepare professional teachers who provide everyone's children with the same high quality of education. There is also a real danger, however, that teacher education will be transformed into a pure market economy divorced from universities, where a constant supply of underprepared and temporary teachers will be sent into schools to teach other people's children. It is very important for university teacher educators to pay attention to what is happening around them in the larger policy context and to take it seriously. It is not going to go away. It is also very important for university teacher educators not to act defensively, to only protect their own position. It is our belief that attempts to defend college- and university-based teacher education that are isolated from the struggles for greater social justice in other sectors of societies will be seen as largely self-serving and will fail.

In this chapter, we have suggested that what is required for university teacher education is a political response and a paradigm shift[3] in how we think about whose expertise should contribute to and who should be responsible for the education of professional teachers for public schools. We believe that without the shift in power relationships and the formation of the kind of political alliances that we have suggested, the future of teaching as a profession and the university's role in teacher education are in serious danger.

The idea of multiple pathways into teaching has long been a part of teacher education in the United States except for a brief period of time (Fraser, 2007), and in our view, multiple routes into teaching should be maintained. Different models of teacher education and pathways into the profession can potentially stimulate innovation, generate research, and provide access to teaching to individuals in different life circumstances. Currently, it is clear that there is a range of quality within both early-entry and college-recommending programs (National Research Council, 2010), and that there are weak programs of all kinds that probably should be shut down, as well as practices in both college-recommending and early-entry programs that merit wider use.

We have argued in this chapter that neither schools nor universities can educate our nation's teachers alone, and that, even together, schools and universities cannot educate teachers well without accessing the expertise that exists in the local communities that are supposed to be served by schools. Both early-entry and college-recommending programs have a role to play in providing high-quality teachers to everyone's children.

For their part, schools, colleges, and departments of education need to reverse the "mission creep" (Ogren, 2005) that has drawn many of them away from a serious commitment to teacher education, and return to their central mission as professional schools (Clifford & Guthrie, 1988). Education schools must focus the intellectual expertise of some of its tenure line faculty and clinical faculty on working in new and more respectful ways with those in schools and communities to build and learn how to sustain over time high-quality preservice teacher education programs that draw on the expertise that exists in each domain.

Unless a college or university education school is willing to make a serious commitment to offering high-quality teacher education programs in which faculty invest their intellectual talent, then it should get out of the business of preparing teachers. Making a commitment to high-quality teacher education programs in research universities does not mean an abandonment of the responsibility for conducting research, including research on teacher education. On the contrary, a serious commitment to teacher education in research universities would involve utilizing their teacher education programs as laboratories for the study of teacher learning and development and effective practices in preparing teachers. We argue that by recasting who is an expert, rethinking how universities cross institutional boundaries to collaborate with communities and schools, and envisioning the creation of interinstitutional boundary zones, teacher education programs can more thoroughly interrogate its challenges and innovate with new solutions to prepare the teachers our students need.

Notes

1 The notion of a knot refers to "a rapidly pulsating, distributed, and partially improvised orchestration of collaborative performance between otherwise loosely connected actors and activity systems" (Engestrom, Engestrom, & Vahaaho, 1999, pp. 346–347).
2 The Boston Teacher Residency Program, which is a joint effort of the Boston Public Schools and the University of Massachusetts–Boston, also received $4.9 million in a project submitted by a local foundation.
3 A recent national report on teacher education in the United States has referred to the kind of paradigm shift that we are calling for as "turning the education of teachers upside down" (National Council for Accreditation of Teacher Education, 2010, p. ii).

References

Allen, D. S. (2004). *Talking to strangers: Anxieties of citizenship since Brown v. Board of Education.* Chicago: University of Chicago Press.

Anagnostopoulos, D., Smith, E. R., & Basmadjian, K. (2007). Bridging the university–school divide. *Journal of Teacher Education, 58*(2), 138–152.

Apple, M. (1996). *Cultural politics and education.* New York: Teachers College Press.

Apple, M. (2008). Is deliberative democracy enough in teacher education? In M. Cochran-Smith, S. Feiman-Nemser, & D. J. McIntyre (Eds.), *Handbook of research on teacher education* (3rd ed., pp. 105–110). New York: Routledge.

Ball, D., & Forzani, F. (2009). The work of teaching and the challenge for teacher education. *Journal of Teacher Education, 60*, 497–510.

Barab, S., & Duffy, T. (2000). From practice fields to communities of practice. In D. Jonassen & S. Land (Eds.), *Theoretical foundations of learning environments* (pp. 25–56). New York: Routledge.

Bartholomew, S. S., & Sandholz, J. H. (2009). Competing views of teaching in a school–university partnership. *Teaching and Teacher Education, 25*(1), 155–165.

Berry, B., Montgomery, D., Curtis, R., Hernandez, M., Wurtzel, J., & Snyder, J. (2008, August). *Creating and sustaining urban teacher residencies.* Hillsborough, NC: Center for Teaching Quality and the Aspen Institute.

Beynon, J., Grout, J., & Wideen, M. (2004). *From teacher to teacher educator.* Vancouver, CA: Pacific Education Press.

Campbell, S. S. (2008, March). *Mediated field experiences in learning progressive teaching: A design experiment in teacher education.* Paper presented at the annual meeting of the American Educational Research Association, New York City.

Campbell, S. S. (2012). *Taking it to the field: Teacher candidate learning about equity-oriented mathematics teaching in a mediated field experience.* (Unpublished doctoral dissertation). University of Washington–Seattle.

Clifford, G. J., & Guthrie, J. W. (1988). *Ed school: A brief for professional education.* Chicago: University of Chicago Press.

Darling-Hammond, L., & Bransford, J. (Eds.). (2005). *Preparing teachers for a changing world.* San Francisco: Jossey-Bass.

Duffy, G. (1994). Professional development schools and the disempowerment of teachers and professors. *Phi Delta Kappan, 75*(8), 596–600.

Duncan, A. (2009, October). *Teacher preparation: Reforming the uncertain profession.* Address given by Secretary of Education Arne Duncan at Teachers College, Columbia University, New York.

Edwards, A. (2010). *Being an expert professional practitioner: The relational turn in expertise.* Dordrecht, Netherlands: Springer.

Edwards, A., Daniels, H., Gallagher, T., Leadbetter, J., & Warmington, P. (2009). *Improving professional collaboration: Multi-agency work for children's well-being.* London: Routledge.

Ellis, V. (2012a, April). Promoting collaborative approaches to developing effective teachers: The contribution of cultural-historical activity theory. Paper presented at the meeting of the American Educational Research Association, Vancouver, BC.

Ellis, V. (2012b, April). The contributions of CHAT to studying teacher learning in practice. Invited lecture, College of Education, University of Washington–Seattle.

Ellis, V., Edwards, A., & Smagorinsky, P. (Eds.). (2010). *Cultural–historical perspectives on teacher education and development.* London: Routledge.

Engeström, Y. (1987). *Learning by expanding: An activity theoretical approach to developmental research.* Helsinki, Finland: Orienta-Konsultit.

Engestrom, Y. (2001). Expansive learning at work: Toward an activity theoretical reconceptualizaton. *Journal of Education & Work, 14*(1), 133–156.

Engestrom, Y. (2007). Enriching the theory of expansive learning: Lessons from journeys toward co-configuration. *Mind & Society, 14*(1–2), 23–39.

Engestrom, Y. (2008). *From teams to knots: Activity-theoretical studies of collaboration and learning at work.* Cambridge: Cambridge University Press.

Engestrom, Y., Engestrom, R., & Vahaaho, T. (1999). When the center does not hold: The importance of knotworking. In S. Chaiklin, M. Hedegaard, & O. J. Jensen (Eds.), *Activity theory and social practice: Cultural historical approaches* (pp. 345–374). Aarhus, Denmark: Aarhus University Press.

Fraser, J. (2007). *Preparing America's teachers: A history.* New York: Teachers College Press.

Ginsburg, M., & Clift, R. (1990). The hidden curriculum of preservice teacher education. In W. R. Houston (Ed.), *Handbook of research on teacher education* (pp. 450–468). New York: Macmillan.

Gorodesky, M., & Barak, J. (2008). The educational–cultural edge: A participative learning environment for co-emergence of personal and institutional growth. *Teaching and Teacher Education, 24,* 1907–1918.

Greenberg, J., Pomerance, L., & Walsh, K. (2011, July). *Student teaching in the United States.* Washington, DC: National Council on Teacher Quality.

Grossman, P., & Loeb, S. (Eds.). (2008). *Alternative routes to teaching.* Cambridge, MA: Harvard Education Press.

Gutiérrez, K., Baquedano-López, P., & Tejada, C. (1999). Rethinking diversity: Hybridity and hybrid language practices in the third space. *Mind, Culture, and Activity, 6*(4), 286–303.

Habermas, J. (1984). *The theory of communicative action.* Boston: Beacon Press.

Hamerness, K., Darling-Hammond, L., Bransford, J., Berliner, D., Cochran-Smith, M., McDonald, M., et al. (2005). How teachers learn and develop. In L. Darling-Hammond & J. Bransford (Eds.), *Preparing teachers for a changing world* (pp. 358–389). San Francisco: Jossey-Bass.

Hartley, D. (2007). Education policy and the "inter-regnum." *Journal of Education Policy, 22*(6), 695–708.

Hatch, T., & Grossman, P. (2009). Learning to look beyond the boundaries of representation. *Journal of Teacher Education, 60*(1), 70–85.

Hollins, E., & Guzman, M.T. (2005). Research on preparing teachers for diverse populations. In M. Cochran-Smith & K. Zeichner (Eds.), *Studying teacher education* (pp. 477–588). New York: Routledge.

Jeffrey, J. V., & Polleck, J. (2010). Reciprocity through co-instructed site-based courses. *Teacher Education Quarterly, 37*(3), 81–100.

Kazemi, E., Lampert, M., & Franke, M. (2009). *Developing pedagogies in teacher education to support novice teachers' ability to enact ambitious instruction.* Paper presented at the annual meeting of the Mathematics Education Research Group of Australasia, Wellington, New Zealand.

Kerosuo, H., & Engeström, Y. (2003). Boundary crossing and learning in creation of new work practice. *Journal of Workplace Learning, 15*(8), 345–351.

Klein, E., Taylor, M., Onore, C., & Strom, K. (2011). *Finding a third space in teacher education: Creating an urban teacher residency program with Montclair State University and the Newark Public Schools.* Paper presented at the annual meeting of the American Educational Research Association, New Orleans, LA.

Leont'ev, A. N. (1978). *Activity, consciousness, and personality.* Upper Saddle River, NJ: Prentice Hall.

Longview Foundation. (2008). *Teacher preparation for the global age: The imperative for change.* Silver Spring, MD: Author.

Max, C. (2010). Learning for teaching across educational boundaries: An activity theoretical analysis of collaborative internship projects in initial teacher education. In V. Ellis, A. Edwards, & P. Smagorinsky (Eds.), *Cultural–historical perspectives on teacher education and development* (pp. 212–240). London: Routledge.

McDonald, M., Tyson, K., Brayko, K., Bowman, M., Delport, J., & Shimomura, F. (2011). Innovation and impact in teacher education: Community based organizations as field placements for preservice teachers. *Teachers College Record, 113*(8), 1668–1700.

Merryfield, M. (2006). Electronic discourse, school/university collaboration and democratic spaces in teacher education. *International Journal of Social Education, 21*(1), 73–94.

Morgan-Fleming, B., Simpson, D., Curtis, K., & Hull, W. (2010). Learning through partnership. *Teacher Education Quarterly, 37*(3), 63–80.

Murrell, P. (2001). *The community teacher.* New York: Teachers College Press.

National Council for Accreditation of Teacher Education. (2010, November). *Transforming teacher education through clinical practice: A national strategy to prepare effective teachers.* Washington, DC: Author.

National Research Council. (2010, April). *Preparing teachers: Building evidence for sound policy.* Washington, DC: National Academies Press.

Newfield, C. (2008). *Unmaking the public university.* Cambridge, MA: Harvard University Press.

Norton-Meier, L., & Drake, C. (2010). When third space is more than the library: The complexities of theorizing and learning to use family and community resources to teach elementary literacy and mathematics. In V. Ellis, A. Edwards, & P. Smagorinsky (Eds.), *Cultural–historical perspectives on teacher education and development* (pp. 196–211). London: Routledge.

Ogren, C. (2005). *The American state normal school: An instrument of great good.* New York: Palgrave Macmillan.

Onore, C., & Gildin, B. (2010). Preparing urban teachers as public professionals through a university–community partnership. *Teacher Education Quarterly, 37*(3), 27–44.

Parker, W. C. (2005). Teaching against idiocy. *Phi Delta Kappan, 86*(5), 344–351.

Paterson, R., Michelli, N., & Pacheco, A. (1999). *Centers of Pedagogy: New structures for educational renewal.* San Francisco: Jossey-Bass.

Pointer-Mace, D. (2009). *Teacher practice online: Sharing wisdom, opening doors.* New York: Teachers College Press.

Popkewitz, T. (1975). Reform as a political discourse: A case study. *School Review, 84,* 311–336.

Post, L., Pugach, M., Harris, S., & Hughes, M. (2006). The Teachers-in-Residence Program: Veteran urban teachers as teacher leaders in boundary-spanning roles. In K. Howey & N. Zimpher (Eds.), *Boundary spanners: A key to success in urban P–16 university–school partnerships* (pp. 211–236). Washington, DC: American Association of State Colleges and Universities and Land Grant Colleges.

Rawls, J. (1971). *A theory of justice.* Cambridge, MA: Harvard University Press.

Sachs, J. (2003). *The activist teaching profession.* Buckingham, UK: Open University Press.

Sanders, L. (1997). Against deliberation. *Political Theory, 25*(2), 347–376.

Seidl, B., & Friend, G. (2002). Leaving authority at the door: Equal-status community-based experiences and the preparation of teachers for diverse classrooms. *Teaching and Teacher Education, 18,* 421–433.

Shirley, D., Hersi, A., MacDonald, E., Sanchez, M. T., Scandone, C., Skidmore, C., et al. (2006). Bringing the community back in: Change, accommodation, and contestation in a school and university partnership. *Equity and Excellence in Education, 39,* 27–36.

Sleeter, C. (2001). Preparing teachers for culturally diverse schools: Research and the overwhelming presence of whiteness. *Journal of Teacher Education, 52*(2), 94–106.

Sleeter, C., & Boyle-Baise, M. (2000). Community service learning for multicultural teacher education. *Educational Foundations, 14*(2), 33–50.

Suggs, C., & deMarrais, K. (2011, July). *Critical contributions: Philanthropic investment in teachers and teaching.* Atlanta: Kronley & Associates.

Tucker, M. (Ed.). (2011). *Surpassing Shanghai: An agenda for American education built on the world's leading systems.* Cambridge, MA: Harvard Education Press.

Villegas, A. M., & Irvine, J. J. (2010). Diversifying the teaching force: An examination of major arguments. *The Urban Review, 42*(3), 175–192.

Vygotsky, L. S. (1978). *Mind in society.* Cambridge, MA: Harvard University Press.

Walsh, K., & Jacobs, S. (2007, September). *Alternative certification isn't alternative.* Washington, DC: National Council on Teacher Quality.

Warren, M., & Mapp, K. (Eds.). (2011). *A match on dry grass: Community organizing as a catalyst for school reform.* Oxford: Oxford University Press.

Watson, V. (2012). *Learning to liberate: Community-based solutions to the crisis in urban education.* New York: Routledge.

Zeichner, K. (1991). Contradictions and tensions in the professionalization of teaching and the democratization of schooling. *Teachers College Record, 92*(3), 363–379.

Zeichner, K. (2009). *Teacher education and the struggle for social justice.* New York: Routledge.

Zeichner, K. (2010a). Competition, increased surveillance and attacks on multiculturalism: Neo-liberalism and the transformation of teacher education in the U.S. *Teaching and Teacher Education, 26,* 1544–1552.

Zeichner, K. (2010b). Rethinking the connections between campus courses and field experiences in college and university-based teacher education. *Journal of Teacher Education, 89*(11), 89–99.

Zeichner, K., & Melnick, S. (1996). The role of community field experiences in preparing teachers for cultural diversity. In K. Zeichner, S. Melnick, & M. L. Gomez (Eds.), *Currents of reform in preservice teacher education* (pp. 176–198). New York: Teachers College Press.

2

LEARNING TO PRODUCE KNOWLEDGE

Reconstructing Teacher Preparation for Urban Schools

Ronald David Glass and Pia Lindquist Wong

As university professors, we were trained to produce knowledge through our individual physical and intellectual labor, conducting research and gathering data in the library or in the field, analyzing the findings, and finally reporting the results in publications and reports. We hoped that someone might subsequently read what we had produced, and in turn that they would make a change or difference in their own particular context. Since we are education scholars, we hoped that our knowledge production would improve teaching and learning in schools; as critical, social justice-oriented scholars, we hoped to enable schools to improve the lives of low-income, racially, culturally and linguistically diverse (LI/RCLD) students who must contend with a variety of structural inequities in their schools and lives. This is not the model of knowledge production that we examine in this chapter.

Rather, we focus on public, collaborative, *learning processes* that constitute the ground on which knowledge production takes place; we emphasize the dynamics of knowing and the linkages between learning, knowing, and acting. We explore ways that university faculty members, student teachers, teachers, K–12 students, and parents formed communities of learners to produce knowledge in an equity-oriented, urban professional development school (PDS) network with specific commitments—to integrate community knowledge in the service of student learning, and to serve community needs through that same learning.

We begin with brief overviews about the nature of knowing (and of school knowledge) and about the PDS network that sought to produce knowledge that would enable public schools to better serve the needs and interests of LI/RCLD students and communities. We examine some PDS projects that demonstrate the transformative possibilities of learning to produce knowledge, concentrating on three in particular: elementary grades science curricula; a community mapping exercise with parents and teachers; and a lesson study project with teachers. We conclude with a discussion of how critical learning and knowing can produce the power needed to transform urban schools.

Learning, Knowing, and Acting

There are many ways of knowing, each with its particular phenomenology. For example, *knowing that* some fact or state of affairs exists or is true (*knowing that* carbon has an atomic weight of 12, or *knowing that* Ollier's Syndrome is a genetic mutation effecting bones) is different from *knowing how* to do something (*knowing how* to play a musical instrument, or *knowing how* to make a cake). These forms of knowing differ from others, such as *knowing right* from wrong; *knowing why* a phenomenon occurs or someone acts the way they do; or *knowing who* someone is or *knowing who* is the best person to consult about a problem. Each form of knowing may be integral to or implicated in the others to a certain extent, but they cannot be reduced to one another or to a singular form. Nonetheless, we can characterize some features of knowing in general, and we can note the relative importance of these different ways of knowing in the standard curriculum and in the relationships among the youth and adults who spend time in public schools.

A phenomenology of knowing first has to recognize that ways of knowing are historically and culturally situated; they undergo transformations, and are marked by the particular cultural frameworks in which they emerge and are deployed. The warrants for all forms of knowing, including scientific knowing, shift ground over time. What counts as true or as established fact, or what counts as the right thing to do, or what demonstrates the epitome of a skilled performance, changes in response to new insights and perspectives, to new developments and conditions. It is also the case that each form of knowing is embedded within a learning process that varies with the way of knowing and that is differentially susceptible to enhancement through explicit instruction or teaching. For example, *knowing how* to play a musical instrument skillfully depends on innate talents and the learning that occurs through coaching and practice, while *knowing that* the notes on a scale have certain mathematical relationships can be learned through direct instruction and is not at all dependent on one's playing a musical instrument at all.[1] We best understand knowing as a verb or activity rather than a noun (knowledge); as a noun it calls to mind an object or product, something that is wholly quantifiable, or that can be simply transferred from one person to another. Instead, knowing is a dynamic human process of engaging with the world, with others, and with the self. Knowing is a relational experience, not strictly a private and individual matter; it is a kind of doing, a way of acting, in which one is continuously re-creating and transforming experience (Dewey, 1929, 1933).

Knowing is embedded within dynamic historical processes that form the social and cultural capital of particular ways of life, expressed in the *habitus* of everyday action (Bourdieu & Passeron, 1990). The norms and standards that organize social and cultural capital also ground assessments of the value of various ways of knowing, and shape the dispositions, thinking, and performances that are measured and ranked in schools. Power is always implicated in judgments of what counts as *knowing*. Our ways of thinking, acting, and feeling, our ways of relating with others and engaging with our communities, are disciplined and aligned by political forces and discursive formations that establish the common sense by which we live (Foucault, 1972; Gramsci, 1992). The official knowledge of school is always in favor of some goals, and not others, and it privileges *knowing that* above all other forms of knowing (Apple, 1990). Moreover, forms of knowing are articulated with hierarchical judgments of the ethical and social worth of the knowers themselves.

Not only do teacher preparation programs and schools neglect to foster knowing about knowing and instead favor narrow and prescriptive domains of *knowing that*, they further reduce this knowing to what can be demonstrated on a standardized test (mostly of a multiple choice variety).[2] Teacher preparation programs themselves increasingly focus on training teachers to adhere to scripted, uniformly paced curricula in the perverse belief that only by increasing the quantity of *knowing that*–type facts in the heads of students can they raise test scores, which is the official legitimated marker of what students "know and can do" (according to No Child Left Behind [NCLB]). These historic constraints are significant, but it also must be noted that other forms of knowing (*knowing how, knowing right, knowing who*) have long received short shrift both in preparing teachers and in schools. Further, engaging with the forms of knowing of parents and other community members, let alone of the students being taught, has never been a priority in formal schooling. Clearly, crucial forms of knowing for successful teaching (and learning) get eclipsed.

Within the Equity Network urban PDSs, we focused instead on the variety of forms of knowing, and involved student teachers, university faculty members, K–12 teachers, community members, and K–12 students in learning communities. These learning communities explored a holistic understanding of the interrelationships among forms of knowing and the development of the sorts of skills and dispositions that contribute to knowledgeable action in multiple domains (including traditional standardized tests). The ethical and political dimensions of knowing and learning made additional questions integral to teacher preparation, such as who has what kinds of knowledge; how is that knowledge useful; who might want it and for what purposes; how is it developed; and what kinds of teaching can foster it?

The Equity Network

PDSs are one type of teacher education reform intended to address widely perceived failures to prepare teachers adequately for schools serving the poor and those without proficiency in Standard English. The major PDS programmatic goals aimed at improved pupil achievement and teacher preparation—professional development across the learning-to-teach continuum, action research linked to instructional practice, school-level reform, and reflexive teaching—require substantial changes in universities and schools. Most PDSs only partially reach these goals; they unevenly embody the standards set by the National Commission for the Accreditation of Teacher Education (National Council for Accreditation of Teacher Education, 2001) because of numerous constraints tied to existing institutional cultures and broader political forces (Hoffman, Reed, & Rosenbluth, 1997; Johnston, Brosnan, Cramer, & Dove, 2000). This irregular development was evident in the Equity Network's 12 PDSs (in five districts) serving the lower income neighborhoods of a greater metropolitan area in the California Central Valley (Wong & Glass, 2005; Wong & Glass, 2009). In all 12 Equity Network PDSs, students of color constituted a majority, with Latinos, Southeast Asians, and African Americans predominating. The White population included significant numbers of recent Russian and Ukrainian immigrants. At least 20% of the students were English learners, with over 40% in five of the schools. In seven schools, over 80% of the students qualified for the federal free/reduced lunch program, and in another four schools, over 50% qualified.

Established in 2001 from preexisting university–school partnerships, the Equity Network created a wide range of opportunities for both novice and experienced educators to collaborate to enhance the academic and social development of LI/RCLD children: cooperating teacher workshops, teacher research projects, lesson study, research reading clubs, co-instruction of teacher preparation courses, K–16 curriculum development projects, before- and after-school tutoring programs, and school–community events (Science and Literacy Days, Teaching Open House Days, Renaissance Fairs, and Community Health Fairs). Specific principles guided the network's instructional and pedagogical practices, and its curricular approach (Glass & Wong, 2003). Network teachers recognized the importance of understanding the particularities of their students' lives and the larger contextual issues impacting them, and they grasped how schools shape identity. Students' languages, historical and cultural backgrounds, perspectives, and emergent social formations were integrated with the core curriculum in whatever ways possible. Teachers implemented dialogical approaches that linked students' voices and ideas to actions, subject in turn to critical evaluation. The network fostered continuous professional reflection and development linked to classroom- and school-level reform, which entailed a more critical engagement with the selection and construction of curriculum that positioned students as co-constructors of knowledge, and that fostered multiple ways of knowing themselves and their world better. These commitments required teachers to pursue their own self-realization and knowledge building, and to transform their relationships with others having key roles in the lives of children and youth. They also required everyone involved in the network partnership, and not just university faculty members, to design and deliver an effective educational experience for the next generation of teachers.

These principles of "engaged pedagogy" provided the foundation for the multiple intersecting learning communities of the Equity Network. The learning associated with the various forms of knowing required for successful urban school teaching reorganized the relationships among the network partners; teachers, parents, student teachers, K–12 pupils, and university professors built on the funds of knowledge (Moll, Amanti, Neff, & Gonzalez, 1992) that each brought into the collaboration, and discovered that only through learning were new ways of knowing developed.

Teachers for Communities (Not Only Classrooms)

The Equity Network created numerous different communities of learners united around common academic interests and curricular content (Hammond, 2001, 2005). Every person in the learning community was actively engaged in learning, although projects and tasks varied based on age, skill level, and ultimate learning goal (Gabelko, 2000; Lave & Wenger, 1991). For example, learning goals in an environmental science learning community included standards-based academic mastery for pupils, instructional methods mastery for teacher candidates, and learning assessment strategies mastery for teachers. Even more deeply, the Network approach specifically integrated community funds of knowledge into the school curriculum not just in the service of student achievement outcomes, but also in the service of meeting community needs. For the preservice and in-service teachers, this meant learning to be a teacher for a community, not only a classroom.

The following principles guided this refocused approach to teaching: (a) Pupil learning is central, but collaborative learning by everyone connected with the school is valued; (b) all learning community members create content and pedagogical knowledge; (c) all ways of knowing that serve community needs are important; (d) community funds of knowledge are honored and integral to the official curriculum; (e) learning community members demonstrate respect and support for one another; (f) the dispositions of flexibility, risk taking, and reflexivity are fostered to enrich learning processes.

Network educators put these principles to work by beginning with a topic relevant to the students. The learning community of pre/in-service teachers, university faculty members, parents, and in some cases, community members, constructed units of study through an iterative review of what was needed to understand the topic and of the various state content standards, making obvious and not-so-obvious connections. These units of study provided fertile ground for integrating the ways of knowing of each participant, and for establishing deeper relationships among participants as they collectively stretched to connect school and community knowledge, and to address real community needs. The master teachers modeled the unit lessons for the candidates, who extended them into small group tasks that were observed by the university faculty members and master teachers. At the conclusion of this cycle, the learning community met to assess student work and behavior, aiming to understand and improve the efficacy of the lessons. Then, candidates developed additional constructivist lessons on the theme and continued to work with the same small groups to extend the learning and achieve the unit goals. The culminations of the instructional units were generally major projects or events, though many other benchmarks were completed along the way (such as lab reports, PowerPoint presentations, informational posters, and the like).

Health and Science Curricula

Two science education units—one focused on health and the other on a nearby river ecosystem—provide vivid examples of how two network PDSs developed teachers for communities and not only classrooms (see Wong & Glass, 2009, for more extended discussions of these and other examples). The neighborhoods surrounding these schools would be viewed from a deficit perspective as blighted, but our work built on the many resources present (Baker, 2003; Olsen, 1997). The health and science themes creatively incorporated community realities and funds of knowledge into standards-based units developed in the learning communities housed within the candidates' on-site methods courses in science, math, multicultural education, and technology. The organic integration of teacher preparation, in-service professional development, standards-based curriculum construction, and student learning connected everyone's teaching and learning with projects that met the parents' and communities' real and important needs.

At one PDS, a routine guest speaking engagement by a local nurse (friend of the teacher) revealed in personal terms the reality of the devastating health statistics for the community that had shaped the presentation. Holding up a glucose monitor and asking students if they could identify it, the nurse discovered that 80% of the fourth-grade students could do so. Suddenly, it was clear that the PDS could play a critical role in securing a healthier future for the students and their families. The learning communities set out to create a semester-long science unit for the fourth, fifth, and sixth grades. Community health indicators were investigated, and diabetes, heart disease, and drug and alcohol addiction were identified as major challenges. State content standards in English/Language Arts and Science were matched with relevant key vocabulary and content (*knowing that*) about endocrinology, cardiology, neurology, nutrition, and the social determinants of health to construct lesson plans. Assignments were shaped around skill development (*know how*) in public speaking, expository writing, and multimedia presentation development. Connections were made with community health care providers (*knowing who*); guidelines for healthy living (*knowing right*) were researched.

All of these ways of knowing were shaped and refined over a number of years into more and more effective constructivist learning experiences in an integrated health science curriculum for each grade level (Dobb, 2004). The culminating event each year, designed to combat and maybe reverse the health indicators for the community, was a community health fair at which the fourth, fifth, and sixth graders were the educators. Using performances, brochures, PowerPoint presentations, and video-taped public service announcements that they produced, the students conveyed their deep knowing about the body's systems (how they work, what they need, how they become sick and what keeps them healthy) to teach their families and community members, while local health providers conducted basic screening and connected with people who needed care. Over 300 community members attended this event annually. And just as important in this Title I school populated by learners of Standard English, science was part of the daily curriculum, unlike at any other elementary school in the area.

The community and science focus in our second example emerged in relation to the two major waterways that form the natural boundaries for this urban neighborhood. The river ecosystem abuts the school grounds, offering many learning and curricular opportunities. Yet teachers had mostly ignored the rivers or referenced them only to induce the children to fear them because of tragic (though infrequent) drownings and floods, or because of occasional criminal activity along their secluded banks. While maintaining every safety precaution, the learning community of middle school pre/in-service teachers, university faculty members, and community members created units of study that centered on the river ecosystem and also invoked some of the agricultural roots of the immigrant families of the majority of students (Hammond, 2000). For the first unit, students explored velocity and buoyancy, core concepts for eighth-grade science standards. After learning the meaning of the concepts (*knowing that*), the students tested some theories through a culminating performance assessment (*knowing how*) of a Small Boats Regatta. Teams of students had designed boats made of natural materials from the banks of the river, and the regatta would test their application of the concepts they had studied. On the big day, the "scientists" filled data tables with wind speeds, air and water temperatures, current flows, and boat weights, and avidly followed the progress of the boats down the river. After the grand experiment, the data were analyzed and discoveries were made about buoyancy and velocity and how they were related.

A second curriculum unit evolved from a serendipitous discovery on the riverbank of some mysterious scat that contained desiccated bones. Using their newly acquired facts about physiology, biology, and ecosystems (*knowing that*), and their skills in scientific inquiry (*knowing how*), the student scientist teams devised and conducted tests of their hypotheses to determine the animals belonging to the bones and the scat. Each team built its case from evidence and reasoning, developed PowerPoint presentations to convince a lay audience, and then heard an expert (*knowing who*) critique their analyses and reveal the solutions. The PDS community of learners developed this unit for newly arrived immigrants in their English Language Development class, so their provision of a complex science curriculum was also a means of addressing a persistent equity issue related to English learners lack of access to grade level content (a concern as well for the boat builders).

These examples clearly demonstrate that each community of learners was comprised of diverse members with different funds of knowledge to contribute, and that the instructional units they developed facilitated and assessed multiple ways of knowing in relation to highly complex curricular domains. At every level, learning processes were the foundation of knowledge production, and the creative approaches to these processes yielded exceptionally effective teaching–learning and real engagement with important issues of equity for LI/RCLD students and communities. While pre/in-service teachers were oriented by the state content standards, they had to learn the content and standards at far deeper and more dynamic levels to develop and facilitate the lesson units, and they had to have stronger relationships with community members to see the possibilities for making the units more meaningful for the students and families. These are the teachers for communities, and not only classrooms.

Community Mapping

Equity Network PDSs also demonstrated that *knowing who* and *knowing why* are important and necessary complements to *knowing that* and *knowing how*. One of the PDSs is a charter school that parents, teachers, students, and university faculty members co-created in response to pressure to convert a K–6 bilingual program into a K–3 early transition program. Securing a charter for their own free-standing K–8 public school in 2004, this coalition has provided a high-quality, dual-language (Spanish–English) school in one of the poorest neighborhoods in the region.

Central to the mission of the school was the transformation of the curriculum, not only regarding bilingual/biliteracy outcomes, but also in relation to the community. Drawing on Paulo Freire's approach in São Paulo, Brazil (Freire, 1993; O'Cadiz, Wong, & Torres, 1998), a team of pre/in-service teachers and university faculty members invited two parent groups to meet at the school to begin identifying themes for the school curriculum that would integrate parent goals for their children's education and also meet state-mandated content standards. The team divided the parents into groups by their predominant spoken language (English or Spanish) to facilitate ease of discussion, as the planned activities hinged on the free exchange of information. Each group had 10 or fewer members, and included men and women. They were asked to draw a community map on a large whiteboard and to identify the community's assets (Freudenberger, 1999).

As the educators observed the mapping, they learned more about *who* lived in the community, about what was expected of them as educators, and about the skills (*knowing how*) and knowledge (*knowing that*) the parents wanted their children to gain. The mostly immigrant Spanish-dominant parents mapped a community full of services. Intricately detailed, their map highlighted butchers, markets with good seafood, health clinics, and stores where money could be wired internationally. At the center of their map was the school. Their dynamic and spontaneous process kept adding to each person's contribution, with responsibility for naming places to map and for drawing freely shared, the pen rotating among scribes, who were both men and women. The English-dominant group produced a very different map through a markedly different process. They spent 8 min in discussion before making a mark, debating the community boundaries (our instructions had been deliberately vague), and determining the appropriate scale. They also placed the school at the center of their map; however, their map had very few details similar to the other map, but did note every other school within the boundaries of the "community" that they ultimately decided on. There was also one person clearly "in charge" of the mapping, though all group members contributed.

Our team was struck by many insights as we observed the mapping. First, the dynamics within each group were clearly shaped by prior relationships. The Spanish-dominant parents had connections outside the school and were evidently familiar with one another, while the English-dominant group lacked those relationships and interacted much more formally. Second, their perceptions of the community echoed larger race and class subjectivities that framed other school dynamics. The school's English-dominant parents tended to be professionals, many of whom were African Americans who had grown up in the immediate neighborhood but had moved to better housing nearby more consonant with their newly acquired social class standing. Like the African American parents, the European-descent professional English-dominant parents often lived outside the immediate neighborhood, but sought out this school specifically because they wanted its bilingual program for their children. For the Spanish-dominant parents, the community contained almost all the amenities and services they needed, while the English-dominant parents did most of their shopping, socializing, and recreating outside the neighborhood.

The distinct maps brought social class, citizenship status, and race into high relief, not only in relation to the parents but also in relation to our team of educators. We all had long-standing relationships with this school since before its charter conversion, and some of us worked with neighborhood organizations, yet none of us saw this community through the assets perspective of the Spanish-dominant group. Had we drawn a map, we would have missed almost every detail that they included, and even the English-dominant group's map identified more assets than some of us might have. Thus, each team member was prompted to reflect deeply (and, unfortunately, mostly privately) about our own still-entrenched deficit views of a community that we were strongly committed to and thought we knew well.

The mapping activity culminated with a discussion about what was missing from the community and what could be improved. A convergence emerged for both groups (and our team) around hopes and wishes. We all hoped for more safety—for pedestrians, at the local parks, and in general. We all wished that empty lots could be cleared of debris and rubbish. We all complained about absentee landlords that were egregiously remiss in property maintenance. The Spanish-dominant group also wished for a movie theater closer to the neighborhood. The list of improvements was incorporated into activities that shaped subsequent interviews with community elders; the interviews gave our team important historical knowledge and helped us to understand the community's path from cultivated orchards to city suburb to inner-city ghetto. Utilizing all these investigations, the team then worked with other pre/in-service teachers and parents to create curriculum for the intermediate grades that focused on social justice advocacy and safety. Students learned about local government, particularly how it was structured and which units attended to what aspects of city life. They studied different social justice initiatives, especially those led by youth. And from these areas of study, they delved deeply into the attributes and knowledge base required for effective advocacy, eventually put to the test by advocacy projects that they engaged in as teams.

As with the science education examples, these curricular units centered issues of importance to the community, integrated community funds of knowledge, and addressed mandated content standards. This curriculum also demanded more complex, sophisticated, and elaborate student products than are typical in schools serving LI/RCLD communities. In addition, our team of pre/in-service teachers and university faculty members gained a much deeper understanding about the school community, about how different parents engaged with the school, and what they wanted from the school. The mapping exercise by the two groups of parents contributed to the team's expanded *knowing who* about the community and gave the teachers, in particular, deeper insight into the tensions and difficulties, as well as points of mutual interest, that emerged in the school's decision making, planning, and policy development. Similarly, the *knowing why* within the team now encompassed understanding the importance to the parents of certain content and skills. By creating new lesson units on social justice advocacy, pre/in-service teachers and students co-discovered new and profound answers to a pivotal question of learning and knowing: for what ends? Or, as their students might ask them: why do we need to know this stuff?

Lesson Study

One of the most enduring and impactful professional development initiatives sponsored by the Equity Network was the development and support of lesson study teams. Lesson study (Lewis & Tsuchida, 1998), an iterative collaborative process of lesson development and modification, shows teachers how to "see" students and their learning so that lessons can maximize deep student engagement and learning. Lesson study originated in Japan, where it is the primary form of teacher professional development, and it is becoming more widely known in the

United States. The Equity Network selected it as its focal professional development activity because it emphasizes collaboration, student engagement, and building on teacher knowledge toward expertise.

The basic lesson study cycle begins with a collective identification of student development goals and content learning goals. These goals are compared with students' current profiles and a "gap" is identified (Stigler & Hiebert, 1999). The lesson study team then develops a research lesson designed to close the gap between where the teachers aim for the students to be and where they are. To create the lesson, the team researches key concepts and facts, identifies the most effective instructional strategies for the particular group of students, develops formative assessments that illuminate how students are engaging with the concepts and tasks, and creates data collection tools that are integral to the lesson. One team member then teaches the collaboratively developed research lesson, while the other team members observe and collect data on predetermined aspects of the lesson implementation (e.g., engagement by specific students, kinds of student questions). At the conclusion of the lesson, the team reviews and analyzes the data generated by the students and the team members, using insights gleaned to rework the lesson. Another team member teaches the revised lesson, and evaluative data is again collected. In Japan, though not yet in the United States, this process of lesson refinement leads to a published lesson for others to use; the Equity Network did, however, make research lessons available to other teams after at least two iterations of development.

The learning process of lesson study produced new ways of knowing for the teachers. Their *knowing that* associated with the content became substantially deeper. Their *knowing how* to foster student engagement through inquiry, discussion, and exploration became more skilled. Their *knowing why* certain lesson designs elicited the strongest student understanding led them toward more conceptual, flexible, open, and questioning approaches to teaching content. The teachers discovered their previous skills at teaching loosely connected facts, Jeopardy! style, were little help in fostering the kind of student learning for which they aimed. Through lesson study, they grasped both the content and methods of their teaching in far more sophisticated ways, and they developed much more adept approaches to assessment that enabled them to modify instruction to maximize student uptake.

The focus on creating tasks that fully engaged all students and the process of collecting data on levels of student engagement and content retention pivoted teachers' attention also toward *knowing who*: Who are the students, what are their interests, what accommodations do they need, what induces their attention to stray, what misconceptions are they likely to have? While these are all reasonable and important questions to consider when planning and tailoring instruction to yield deep knowing by individual students, they are not, regrettably, typically considered by teachers who are overburdened by crowded classrooms and demands for fidelity to standardized curriculum guides. Given the program improvement status of many of the Equity Network schools, and the district commitments to uniform curricula, these new ways of knowing challenged the lesson study team members to produce new knowledge, skills, and dispositions that they could demonstrate as effective.

Overall, the learning processes underlying lesson study grounded significant advances in teachers' *know how* and they became noticeably stronger teachers. They learned better how to teach particular students and specific concepts and subjects, how to structure effective lessons that allowed students to explore open-ended themes, how to create engaging tasks, how to meaningfully assess student learning, how to understand why a lesson was effective, and how to collaborate with colleagues. For our teachers, these ways of knowing proved especially powerful because they were founded on documented, authenticated, evidence-based approaches that were enduring and useful in multiple contexts. Further, the knowledge the teams were producing constituted a legitimate research-supported response that could counter state, district, and publisher mandates that seemed to have been deadening their classrooms. Moreover, even when lessons did not attain all of the desired outcomes, the ongoing iterative process of study and professional development positioned the teachers in starkly contrasting ways to the NCLB-dictated perceptions of them as inadequate, unqualified, and failing teachers. Lesson study helped pre/in-service teachers—in collaborative, transparent, evidence based, and reflective ways—to know better what they already knew, and to be professionals responsible for their own as well as their students' learning.

Learning to Produce Knowledge: Toward What End?

We have focused on certain aspects of the Equity Network school–university partnerships that were deliberately organized to produce and validate multiple forms of knowing. Our efforts do not negate the importance of *knowing that*. Rather, they make problematic the current stance and practice that situate *knowing that* as the singular type of knowledge to measure and as the only metric of a school's or teacher's contribution to student development (Orfield & Kornhaber, 2001). Our Equity Network projects substantiate that expanded, accelerated, intensified, and multifaceted learning and knowledge production occurs when collaboratives push beyond a goal of *knowing that* and attend to tasks that increase *knowing how, why*, and *who*. But while few would argue about the general benefits of the projects we described, the fact is that they emerged uneasily from their school contexts and were constantly threatened by both the local and national politics of knowledge and assessment.

The Network teachers' sense of responsibility led them to follow the drills related to raising test scores, but their ethical and political values and professional understanding compelled them to seek more for their students than the narrow education NCLB dictates. They recognized the necessity to develop reliable and valid measures of student learning that were more in accord with the multiple aims of their classrooms and schools. These measures definitely needed to attend to gains in knowing and understanding generated by activities focused on learning *how*, learning *why*, and learning *who*, and not only on learning *that*. Equity Network educators put considerable effort into creating assessments for students, pre/in-service teachers, and university faculty members that accurately measured changes in knowing and understanding resulting from the various PDS activities. These assessments helped to identify both strengths and weaknesses in our collaborative efforts. While their context- and assignment-specific nature reduced their generalizability, they addressed a need unmet by standardized tests: providing authentic and timely insights into what students knew and could do, and how they could be supported in learning more. This information about student learning was critical for making informed decisions for all the instructional variables we had to consider regarding students, preservice teachers, university course requirements, and more. It also layered new forms of knowing onto our increasingly robust professional learning communities.

Despite our inroads in creating tools that assessed multiple dimensions of learning and knowing, we consistently ran headlong into the barriers erected by the political, economic, and social contexts of our schools and their communities. We have to note the tragic irony that the NCLB emphasis on closing the test score gap pointedly does not seek to eliminate the causal precursor inequalities in school funding, in family income and child poverty rates, or in access to health care and nutritious food; yet these inequalities shaped the daily lives of the students in our schools. Similarly, psychological phenomena like stereotype threat (Steele, 2010) are ignored. Yet all these have been scientifically shown to affect student performance in schools and on standardized tests, and to produce related challenges that impact the performance of pre/in-service teachers. Moreover, repeated studies have shown that in-school factors explain less than 40% of student test scores, and the quality of teachers explains less than 20%, yet the political discourse around school reform and teacher preparation reform reflect none of this (Ravitch, 2010).

The PDS projects we highlighted are designed with these community and sociopolitical factors fully in mind. In fact, they were developed to support the very teachers that chose to stay in these difficult circumstances and to prepare future teachers to be successful in these contexts. Better-qualified teachers have incentives to leave these schools, particularly since creative teaching and learning tend to diminish as teachers and schools narrow the curriculum for LI/RCLD students to focus more and more on test prep and the "basics" (Jones, Jones, & Hargrove, 2003; McNeil, 2000). *Knowing that*, the type of knowing most readily embedded in standardized test items, increasingly comes at the cost of *knowing how, why* and *who*; these latter forms of knowing prove difficult to capture and measure, so curricula increasingly ignore them. Our experiences demonstrate that school and university partnerships can hold steadfast to a vision of education for LI/RCLD communities that provides rich opportunities to construct the kind of learning that yields development in all forms of knowing for students and pre/in-service teachers alike. Only multidimensional learning and knowing can sustain projects that hold real promise of improving the lives of LI/RCLD students and communities.

The Equity Network commitment to learning to produce knowledge points beyond questions related to measures of student learning to other equally compelling questions regarding accountability: accountability for what, and to whom? Why should schools only be accountable for test scores? Why should schools be more accountable to politicians and bureaucrats than to the parents whose children attend the schools? Why aren't politicians and bureaucrats made accountable for the inadequate resources available to schools serving LI/RCLD students and communities, and for their failure to address the entire range of proven causes of limits to learning, from inadequate housing and health care to insufficient nutrition?

The Equity Network's multilayered programs attempted to address as many of these deep structural issues about learning, teaching, and the politics of education as possible. While this made the tasks for its educators more complex and difficult, it made the rewards for its successes more profound. We know in every way possible that the challenges of learning to produce knowledge for communities and not only classrooms pushes us to know and serve our LI/RCLD students better, and to insure that their learning is bettering their lives and not just their test scores.

Notes

1 Standardized tests, which focus exclusively on *knowing that*, can yield an ironic inversion in cases where respondents actually *know how* to perform some task that utilizes the tested knowledge. That is, according to the test results, "those who have learned [*how*] do not know [*that*; i.e., the right answers], and those who have not learned [*how*] do know [*that*]" (McDermott, 2009, p. 280).
2 Ironically, schools focus on *knowing how* to take such tests since scores can thus be positively impacted, but there is little interest beyond "test prep" in other forms of *knowing how*.

References

Apple, M. (1990). *Ideology and curriculum* (2nd ed.). New York: Routledge.
Baker, S. (2003). *Anglo-American Anglophone bilingual teachers and teaching the "other": A look at the linkages between teacher discourses, teacher backgrounds, and teacher practice.* (Unpublished doctoral dissertation), Stanford University, Palo Alto, CA.
Bourdieu, P., & Passeron, J.-C. (1990). *Reproduction in education, society and culture.* New York: Sage.
Dewey, J. (1929). *The quest for certainty.* New York: Minton Balch.
Dewey, J. (1933). *How we think.* Boston, MA: D. C. Heath.
Dobb, F. (2004). *Essential elements of effective science instruction for English learners.* Los Angeles, CA: California Science Project.

Foucault, M. (1972). *The archeology of knowledge*. New York: Pantheon Books.

Freire, P. (1993). *Pedagogy of the city*. New York: Continuum.

Freudenberger, K. S. (1999). *Rapid rural response appraisal and participatory rural appraisal*. Baltimore: Catholic Relief Services.

Gabelko, N. H. (Ed.). (2000). *Toward a collective wisdom: Forging successful educational partnerships*. Berkeley, CA: ECO.

Glass, R. D., & Wong, P. L. (2003). Engaged pedagogy: Meeting the demands of justice in urban professional development schools. *Teacher Education Quarterly, 30*(2), 69–88.

Gramsci, A. (1992). *Prison notebooks*. New York: Columbia University Press.

Hammond, L. (2000). *Building a Mien American house: An inter-cultural dialogue*. (ERIC Document Reproduction Services No. ED441673).

Hammond, L. (2001). Notes from California: An anthropological approach to urban science education for language minority families. *Journal of Research in Science Teaching, 38*(9), 983–999.

Hammond, L. (2005). Digging deeper: Using reflective dialogue to illuminate the cultural processes inherent in science education. In G. Spindler & L. Hammond (Eds.), *Innovations in educational ethnography: Theory, methods, and results* (pp. 287–320). Mahwah, NJ: Erlbaum.

Hoffman, N. E., Reed, W. M., & Rosenbluth, G. S. (Eds.). (1997). *Lessons from restructuring experiences: Stories of change in professional development schools*. Albany: State University of New York Press.

Johnston, M., Brosnan, P., Cramer, D., & Dove, T. (Eds.). (2000). *Collaborative reform and other improbable dreams: The challenges of professional development schools*. Albany: State University of New York Press.

Jones, M. G., Jones, B. D., & Hargrove, T. Y. (2003). *The unintended consequences of high-stakes testing*. New York: Rowman & Littlefield.

Lave, J., & Wenger, E. (1991). *Situated learning: Legitimate peripheral participation*. New York: Cambridge University Press.

Lewis, C., & Tsuchida, I. (1998, Winter). A lesson is like a swiftly flowing river: Research lessons and the improvement of Japanese education. *American Educator,* pp. 14–17, 50–52.

McDermott, R. (2009). The superstition of necessity. In R. D. Glass (Ed.), *Philosophy of education 2008* (pp. 280–288). Urbana: University of Illinois at Urbana–Champaign and the Philosophy of Education Society.

McNeil, L. (2000). *Contradictions of school reform: Educational costs of standardized testing*. New York: Routledge.

Moll, L. C., Amanti, C., Neff, D., & Gonzalez, N. (1992). Funds of knowledge in teaching: Using a qualitative approach to connect homes and classrooms. *Theory Into Practice, 31*(2), 132–141.

National Council for Accreditation of Teacher Education. (2001). *Standards for professional development schools: National Council for the Accreditation of Teacher Education*. Retrieved from http://www.ncate.org/standard/m_stds.htm

Nieto, S. (2004). *Affirming diversity: The sociopolitical context of multicultural education* (4th ed.). Boston: Pearson.

O'Cadiz, P., Wong, P. L., & Torres, C. A. (1998). *Education and democracy: Paulo Freire, educational reform and social movements*. Boulder, CO: Westview Press. Portuguese translation: *Educacão e democracia: A praxis de Paulo Freire em São Paulo*. São Paulo: Corez, 2002.

Olsen, L. (1997). *Made in America: Immigrant students in our public schools*. New York: New Press.

Orfield, G., & Kornhaber, M. L. (Eds.). (2001). *Raising standards or raising barriers? Inequality and high-stakes testing in public education.* New York: Century Foundation Press.

Ravitch, D. (2010, November 11). The myth of charter schools. *New York Review of Books.* Retrieved from http://www.nybooks.com/articles/archives/2010/nov/11/myth-charter-schools/

Steele, C. (2010). *Whistling Vivaldi: And other clues to how stereotypes affect us.* New York: W. W. Norton.

Stigler, J. W., & Hiebert, J. (1999). *The teaching gap: Best ideas from the world's teachers for improving education in the classroom.* New York: Summit Books.

Wong, P. L., & Glass, R. D. (2005). Assessing a professional development school approach to preparing teachers for urban schools serving low-income, culturally and linguistically diverse communities. *Teacher Education Quarterly, 32*(2), 63–78.

Wong, P. L., & Glass, R. D. (Eds.). (2009). *Prioritizing urban children, teachers, and schools through professional development schools.* Albany: State University of New York Press.

PART II

Focus on Preservice Teachers

3

URBAN IMMERSION

The Impact of Preservice Preparation in an Urban School–University Partnership

Andrea J. Stairs[1] and Audrey A. Friedman

It is the second Thursday of the new school year. Sitting around the conference table at 3:30 are Andrea (the first author), a boundary spanner who was the full-time literacy coach at the high school before teaching for Boston College (BC) during her doctoral program; Barbara[2] the assistant headmaster and English department chair at Brighton High School (BHS), a Boston public school; and Saraha, graduate of BC's teacher education program and an English teacher leader at BHS. The three of them are discussing field placements for the 33 BC students who have been at the high school for university course meetings after school for two weeks to be introduced to their day-long, on-site course and field experience called Urban Immersion (UI). The university students have spent the last two Thursdays reading about, thinking about, and discussing the urban teaching context in preparation for this required experience of all secondary teacher candidates. Next Thursday, these prepracticum student teachers will catch an early train that runs a little more than a mile between BC and BHS to have a meet-and-greet of coffee and donuts with their cooperating teachers before the school day begins. Then, they will have the first part of their university course meeting, before venturing out with partners to work in at least two different teachers' classrooms with urban high school students and returning in the afternoon for the second part of their course meeting.

Most of their cooperating teachers have been hosting preservice teachers for years, long before the UI experience began in 2002, and most request that these novices work in their classrooms. The veterans enjoy discussing new pedagogical strategies that the student teachers are learning about in their courses, sharing their knowledge and experience, and improving their teacher-to-student ratio from 30–1 to 10–1. These mentor teachers purposefully plan hands-on activities and group work for Thursdays, and in a few weeks will allow their student teachers to plan and teach whole class lessons under their guidance. In addition to the authors, 12 of the cooperating teachers at the high school prepared to teach and/or earned advanced graduate degrees and/or taught courses at BC, serving as boundary spanners between the university and school communities.

The school and university partners are committed to making BHS a school in which "school-based and university-based individuals come together for the simultaneous renewal of both schooling and the education of educators" (Goodlad, 1993, p. 25). In this chapter, co-authored by the two university-based faculty who conceptualized, designed, and implemented UI with school partners, we discuss how locating part of BC's secondary teacher education program in BHS has impacted preservice teachers. First, we share the conceptual framework from which we operate that prioritizes community strengths, then we describe how the partnership developed and the evidence of impact on preservice teachers, and finally we conclude with our personal reflections on the UI experience as faculty with an emic perspective on UI research and practice over the 10 years since we moved teacher education into an urban school and community.

Prioritizing Community Strengths

Two theoretical frameworks ground the UI experience and our research on it: the situative perspective on learning, and cultural competence.

Situative Perspective on Learning

The situative perspective posits that learning cannot be separated from the context in which it occurs. Learning is dependent on social, cultural, historical, and institutional contexts, not solely on one's individual cognitive processes independent of context (Resnick, 1991). We agree with Putnam and Borko (2000) that "how a person learns a particular set of knowledge and skills, and the situation in which a person learns, become a fundamental part of what is learned" (p. 4). They suggest that close partnerships between schools and universities offer one possibility for designing teacher education experiences "that can be difficult to accomplish in either setting alone" (p. 7). Furthermore, contextualizing preservice teacher learning in supportive "intersecting" experiences can potentially help novice teachers negotiate the dissonance of practice shock and cultural mismatch in a way that encourages teacher and student growth. This practice shock and cultural mismatch are critical factors that contribute to urban teacher attrition (Friedman, 2012).

The situative perspective draws on sociocultural learning theories that emphasize the influence of culture (broadly defined) on learning, as well as the social nature of learning (Tracey & Morrow, 2006). Feiman-Nemser (2008) notes the usefulness of sociocultural theories in research on teacher learning:

> Socio-cultural theories are particularly useful in longitudinal studies of learning to teach because they focus on how the various settings in which

teachers learn—university courses, student teaching, schools and classrooms, mentoring relationships—enable and constrain their adoption and
use of new knowledge and practices and their ongoing learning. (p. 700)

The situative perspective prioritizes community strengths as it puts community at the heart of teacher learning. There can be no learning independent of
the context and community in which learners are situated. Donnell and Stairs
(2010) assert that "urban teacher learning is not represented by discrete pieces of
knowledge but by teachers' grappling with professional decisions that take into
account their knowledge, skills, commitments, and dispositions while situated
within their social context" (p. 192). Similarly, Samaras and Gismondi (1998)
argue that "through situated engagement and negotiation with practitioners and
peers in a teaching community, preservice teachers come to define for themselves what it means to be a teacher" (p. 715). As faculty members intricately
involved with UI, it has been critical that we keep the urban school community
at the center of how we design learning opportunities for BC preservice teachers. Any impact that we discerned from our research on UI was directly related
to the learning opportunities provided in the urban high school context viewed
through the situative lens.

Cultural Competence

Over the past decade, a consistent focus in UI is the development of cultural
competence. Cultural competence demands a complex set of dispositions, sensi-
tivities, pedagogies, and knowledge that results in effective cross-cultural teaching
(Diller & Moule, 2005, p. 5). It incorporates "the cultural knowledge, experiences,
frames of reference, and performance styles of ethnically diverse students to make
learning more relevant and effective" (Gay, 2000, p. 29). Culturally competent
practitioners value, affirm, and validate the cultural identity of students. Garmon
(2004) identifies "dispositional factors" (p. 204) of openness, self-awareness or
self-reflectiveness, and a strong sense of social justice and "experiential factors"
(p. 207), which address intercultural and educational group experiences as variables that predict a teacher's ability to develop cultural competence. In addition
to course work, UI works to develop these dispositional and experiential factors
through journaling, self- and instructor probing, exploring in depth the social and
cultural context of pupils, interviewing pupils, and challenging preservice teacher
biases and assumptions.

Understanding the relationship between and among language, culture, and
identity can prevent miscommunication that often occurs within classrooms
(Wolfram, Adger, & Christian, 1999). For diverse students to succeed, teachers
must be cognizant of and attuned to the interplay of language, culture, and identity (Brisk, 2008; Cummins, 2000; Menyuk & Brisk, 2005). Gallavan (2007) as-
serts that novice "teacher efficacy that values cultural diversity advances when

synchronized with three factors: (1) building funds of knowledge, (2) developing cultural competence, and (3) realizing the significance of social reproduction or generational perpetuation of practice" (p. 10). Thus, it is critical that teacher educators and prospective teachers understand the "ideological dimensions" of their practice, asserting that pedagogy must emerge from a genuine sense of humanity that "nurtures hope, innovation, and successful intervention" (Bartolomé, 2008, p. 22). Clearly, cultural competence prioritizes community strengths.

Developing the School–University Partnership

UI is a teacher preparation experience for secondary teacher candidates at BC, a large, northeastern research university offered in collaboration with BHS, a local Boston public school. BC has a long-standing relationship with BHS. Prior to 2002, BHS served as the field experience site for the small number of prepracticum and practicum student teachers who began their undergraduate or graduate teacher preparation program with an interest in urban education each year. University professors, including the second author of this chapter, had provided professional development opportunities for BHS faculty, served on school-site committees, and prepared BHS students for college through a College Bound program, while BHS teachers and administrators served as cooperating teachers, enrolled in university courses, and even co-taught courses with university faculty. In contrast to the ethnically diverse high school student population represented in Table 3.1, the demographics of BC preservice teachers have remained consistent across the past decade: 96% White and 85% female.

UI arose at the high school's request for a stronger relationship with the university and its student teachers. A meeting was called by the high school's administrators asking for further classroom-level support from their university partner. To address this need, the collaborators determined that all secondary teacher candidates would complete course work and fieldwork one day per week at BHS. The dramatic increase in numbers of preservice teachers in the building would support teachers and students operating in overcrowded classrooms, and the experience would provide the mostly White, privileged preservice teachers an opportunity to become part of an urban school culture and community, with which few were familiar.

TABLE 3.1 Demographics of Students at Brighton High School[a]

Year	African American/ Caribbean	Latino/a	Asian	White	Other	Male	Female	% Free or reduced lunch
2002	47%	35%	7%	9%	2%	48%	52%	69%
2012	38%	52%	4%	5%	1%	54%	46%	79%

[a]Approximately 50% of students were nonnative English speakers in 2002 and 2012, though reported English language learner numbers were lower, due to underreporting on home language surveys and in assessments of limited English proficiency.

The school and university partners believe that there is specialized knowledge that new teachers to the urban context must develop to successfully teach urban students, including identifying the resources and challenges urban teachers face. They determined that through course work and experiences in classrooms, participants should develop their knowledge of content and pedagogy, but more importantly, develop their knowledge of the urban context and how to balance the multiple demands so that all students might learn and improve their life chances. This is in keeping with the five themes of the teacher education department at the university, which include promoting social justice, constructing knowledge, inquiring into practice, accommodating diversity, and collaborating with others. These themes are based on the assumption that educators have a responsibility to challenge the status quo and effect social change as America's public schools grow increasingly diverse and inequitable.

Urban teachers who choose to leave the field often cite student factors (motivation, discipline) as their reason for leaving teaching (Ingersoll, 2001). Urban retention scholars have noted that "given this link between deficit conceptions and urban teacher attrition, we suggest conversely that nondeficit conceptions may be a crucial factor in retaining good urban teachers" (Quartz & TEP Research Group, 2003, p. 106). We believe that forming positive conceptions about urban teaching at the very beginning of the teacher education program is a significant purpose of UI.

Key Features of Urban Immersion

There are several key features of the UI innovation that distinguish it from traditional teacher preparation experiences at the university:

1. A cohort model: Rather than placing a few prepracticum students in many schools across the city, 20–35 preservice teachers comprise a cohort that spends every Thursday at one school from 8:00 to 3:30 each semester.
2. Site-based course work: Course work in secondary curriculum and instruction (3 credits) and inquiry (1 credit) are completed in the morning and afternoon as "bookends" to the prepracticum field experience (1 credit). The bookend design allows for exploration of theory in the morning before fieldwork and afternoon inquiries into the intersections of theory and practice. (See Table 3.2 for more information about a typical Thursday schedule.)
3. A collaborating instructor: The course work is co-taught by a BC instructor and a BHS teacher. The exemplary high school teacher is relied on heavily to facilitate afternoon course sessions and brings a context-specific classroom teacher's perspective from the school community to each class meeting.
4. Partnered field experience: Preservice teachers are placed in classrooms with a partner and typically work in two different teachers' classrooms each Thursday. Prepracticum field experience supervisors also spend the day at BHS, allowing students immediate access to support from their supervisors.

TABLE 3.2 Typical Schedule for an Urban Immersion Preservice Teacher

Time period	Activities
8:00–9:30 AM	University course work led by instructor; brief meetings with field experience supervisors (high schools' Block A)
9:30–10:25 AM	Work in classrooms, Block B (shortened block for participants due to university course meeting)
10:30–11:50 AM	Work in classrooms, Block C
11:55–12:20 PM	Lunch with instructor, field experience supervisors, and/or cooperating teachers
12:25–1:45 PM	Work in classrooms, Block D
1:45–2:15 PM	Meet with cooperating teachers and/or field experience supervisors
2:15–3:30 PM	University course work led by instructor and collaborating instructor (high school teacher)

These key features have remained constant since the inception of UI 10 years ago, though each set of instructors, cooperating teachers, and field experience supervisors place their own imprint on each semester.

Impact of Urban Immersion

We systematically studied the impact of UI on preservice teachers over five years, focusing primarily on six cohorts of BC students' learning to teach at BHS over three years' time. In this chapter, we will summarize findings from the qualitative research we conducted that has been previously disseminated. We will also report on survey data we collected over the three years that has not been previously analyzed and published. The findings we share here illustrate the transformative possibilities of locating preservice teacher education experiences in local communities.

Findings From Qualitative Studies

The qualitative research we conducted on UI focused primarily on preservice teachers' learning. We aimed to understand what preservice teachers learned in the integrated course and field experience, how their learning informed their practice with urban pupils, and how the context and conditions of the UI experience influenced their learning and practice. Major findings are highlighted here.

The Complexity of Urban Teaching

First, one of the most salient themes that emerged from our research was that participants in UI learned about the complexity of urban teaching (Stairs, 2008). Data collected at the beginning of each semester compared with data collected at the end showed that most students were initially uninformed about the realities of urban teaching. When describing what makes urban teaching different from teaching in other contexts, "most responses located the differences of urban teaching with differences in students and families, all of which were negative and revealed a deficit view of these 'others'" (p. 100). However, by the end, most participants cited a change in their initial assumptions and described multiple factors that influence urban teaching, from limited resources to bureaucracy to school policies that interfere with the teaching and learning process. This was an important change captured in the research that revealed how participants came to understand the complexity of urban teaching.

Translating Theory Into Practice

A second theme that emerged from our research is that these novice student teachers struggled to enact culturally responsive pedagogy (CRP) during the semester-long experience (Stairs, 2010b). Data suggested that though most students could explain the importance of CRP in urban teaching, they struggled to connect theory with practice. Few lessons applied CRP consistently for an entire lesson; some lessons showed evidence of aspects of CRP, and some did not apply aspects of CRP at all. We argue, "It may be that certain aspects of CRP are more easily enacted by new teachers, such as developing relationships with students and sharing personal stories during class versus drawing on students' cultures as part of the regular curriculum, or some new teachers may simply be more developmentally ready to enact new learning" (p. 34).

Understanding the complexity of urban teaching and the importance of CRP in the urban context are meaningful outcomes, despite evidence that participants struggled to translate theory into practice in their lessons. This is, after all, their first field experience, and it is a very unfamiliar school context for nearly all participants.

Participants who were longitudinally tracked did enact CRP and believed in their roles as urban teachers. In addition to the 3-year qualitative study, we followed four English teachers over five years from the UI experience through their student teaching at BHS and into their first teaching positions in urban high schools (Stairs, 2010a). This qualitative, collective case study provided a view of teacher learning over time not typical in the research literature. Using Feiman-Nemser's (2001) framework of learning to teach on a continuum, we found that participants analyzed beliefs and formed new visions of themselves as teachers during the preservice phase of their learning, and showed evidence of designing responsive curriculum and instruction during the induction phase. Participants identified themselves less as "English" teachers and more as "urban" teachers, revealing a strong commitment to their students' learning and development as human beings, as well as a commitment to teaching for social justice. We argue that "if teacher preparation is designed for urban PDSs [professional development schools] with inquiry-oriented, learning-focused conditions, graduates may be more likely to enact their beliefs and learning in practice even several years after graduation" (p. 57).

Findings From Survey Research

The purpose of giving a selected-response survey was to determine participants' perceptions of the UI program, program elements, and individual participant outcomes. For the first three years of the program, a survey with five selected-response questions was provided at the time course evaluations were administered, allowing for anonymous collection of data. An 89% response rate was achieved (146/164 participants over six semesters). Survey questions included the following:

1. This integrated on-site course/prepracticum experience was valuable.
2. I would be interested in having another course on-site in conjunction with a field experience.
3. I found it valuable to attend high school classes with other prepracticum students.
4. I would be interested in working in an urban school as a result of this experience.
5. On an average day at BHS, what percentage of time do you spend in classrooms working directly with students? (a) 0%–25% (b) 26%–50% (c) 51%–75% (d) 76%–100%

A Likert-type scale was used, where 1 = Strongly agree, 3 = Unsure, and 5 = Strongly disagree for the first four questions; the last question asked them to select the amount of time they were interacting directly with students. We first present the data that revealed participants' perceptions of the program in general and program elements, and we finish by sharing their interest in urban teaching.

The Value of an Integrated On-site Course and Prepracticum

Over three years and six cohorts, 91% of UI participants strongly agreed or agreed that the integrated on-site course/prepracticum experience was valuable (see Table 3.3). This was meaningful information as we considered whether the university would continue investing resources for a faculty member, three prepracticum supervisors, and a collaborating high school instructor to coordinate,

TABLE 3.3 The Value of an Integrated On-site Course and Prepracticum

Semester	Responses to question 1					n	M
	1	2	3	4	5		
Fall 02	22	7	1	0	0	30	1.30
Spring 03	13	4	3	0	0	30	1.50
Fall 03	20	3	0	0	0	23	1.13
Spring 04	15	8	2	0	0	25	1.48
Fall 04	16	9	3	2	2	32	1.91
Spring 05	13	3	0	0	0	16	1.19

TABLE 3.4 The Value of a Partnered Field Experience

Semester	Responses to question 3					n	M
	1	2	3	4	5		
Fall 02	22	7	0	1	0	30	1.33
Spring 03	11	5	2	0	1	18	1.68
Fall 03	19	3	0	0	0	22	1.14
Spring 04	17	4	2	1	1	25	1.60
Fall 04	22	6	1	2	1	32	1.56
Spring 05	12	3	1	0	0	16	1.31

teach, and supervise the experience. Additionally, cooperating teachers who hosted partnered BC students earned a three-credit graduate course voucher for every five prepracticum students they hosted in their classrooms. Knowing that participants highly valued the experience overall has been powerful in continuing UI to this day (10 years from inception).

The Value of a Partnered Field Experience

Working with a partner all day in a field experience placement earned high marks by nearly all participants; 91% strongly agreed or agreed that it was valuable to attend high school classes with other prepracticum students (see Table 3.4). Partnered placements were made by the course instructor at the beginning of the semester based solely on content area interests, not on student requests or interest in working with particular classmates, yet these fairly random assignments worked well for most participants.

Interest in Another On-site Course and Field Experience

Though 91% found the experience and partnered student teaching valuable, slightly fewer than that (75%) reported they would be interested in having another course on-site in conjunction with a field experience (see Table 3.5). In a collaborative research study, which aimed to understand more about UI's partnered field experience, five former UI participants and co-researchers described the isolation they experienced in their next prepracticum field experience as they were placed singly in classrooms with only four total BC prepracticum students in the high school (Stairs et al., 2009). They ended up creating their own community of learners, commuting to the site together, observing one another teach, and eating lunch together. The co-researchers argued that "the critical reflection and peer communication encouraged by the UI experience at BHS continued to manifest itself in later teaching environments, thereby establishing healthy and dynamic career habits for BC's future teachers" (p. 84). Though collaborations to the scale of UI have not yet been developed, the second author is working closely

TABLE 3.5 Interest in Another On-site Course and Field Experience

	Responses to question 2						
Semester	1	2	3	4	5	n	M
Fall 02	14	8	5	3	0	30	1.90
Spring 03	11	4	4	1	0	20	1.75
Fall 03	19	2	2	0	0	23	1.26
Spring 04	15	3	4	3	0	25	1.80
Fall 04	12	5	5	8	2	32	1.47
Spring 05	9	7	0	0	0	16	1.44

with the Office of Practicum Experiences and Teacher Induction to develop a second prepracticum, cohort experience on-site in an urban Catholic context for Secondary Education/English majors, who comprise more than 40% of undergraduate secondary teacher candidates.

Percentage of Time Working With Students

Of the six cohorts of participants, 58% spent more than half of their time working with students, while 42% spent less than half (see Table 3.6). Would more time working directly with students rather than observing impact participants positively or negatively? This question remains to be answered. What is clear is that the amount of time spent working with students did not have an adverse impact on the participants' perceptions about the value of the experience overall or their classroom placements with their partners. We have reiterated to our prepracticum student teachers and their cooperating teachers that we expect them to collaboratively determine what constitutes appropriate and meaningful involvement of BC students from classroom to classroom. Our hope is always that they have as many hands-on opportunities to work with high school students as possible.

TABLE 3.6 Percentage of Time Working With Students

	Responses to question 5					
Semester	1	2	3	4	n	M
Fall 02	5	4	17	7	33	2.79
Spring 03	5	6	7	7	16	2.64
Fall 03	6	4	9	4	23	2.48
Spring 04	5	9	6	4	24	2.25
Fall 04	4	6	15	7	32	2.78
Spring 05	3	5	6	2	16	2.44

Interest in Urban Teaching

Survey responses to question 4 about whether participants would be interested in working in an urban school as a result of this experience revealed that 62% strongly agreed or agreed, 28% were uncertain, and 10% disagreed or strongly disagreed (see Table 3.7). This outcome is encouraging, as only one to two students each semester (about 5%) expressed interest in urban teaching when they began the UI experience; 62% shows a dramatic increase in interest in urban teaching by the end of the semester. In addition, it is also encouraging that just over a quarter (28%) of the participants viewed urban teaching as a possibility and had not decided to rule it out (as did 10% of participants), meaning 90% of participants may teach in an urban school on graduating. In the next section of the chapter, we will share evidence that reveals UI participants do in fact choose to teach in urban schools, further supporting the impact of UI on graduates initially revealed by these data.

Urban Immersion: 10 Years Later

Since its inception, UI has evolved to address the numerous academic, linguistic, cultural, contextual, and leadership changes that have occurred not only at BHS but also statewide and nationally. As with any school–university partnership, we at the university must respect and collaborate with those stakeholders who have so graciously invited us into their "house." In this section, we will share how UI has developed since the initial research was conducted, as well as promising recent research and unintended outcomes of the preservice teacher education collaboration.

The Cohort Model: Elaborated

Currently, a university faculty member, the collaborating instructor, and three preservice teacher supervisors work together to provide instruction, supervision, and mentoring to a group of 15–30 secondary education majors each semester.

TABLE 3.7 Interest in Urban Teaching

	Responses to question 4						
Semester	1	2	3	4	5	n	M
Fall 02	9	9	10	2	0	30	2.17
Spring 03	8	5	4	2	0	19	2.00
Fall 03	12	5	5	1	0	23	1.78
Spring 04	7	10	7	1	0	25	2.08
Fall 04	8	6	9	7	2	32	2.66
Spring 05	4	7	5	0	0	16	2.06

Due to changes in the school's block schedule, the day now begins 30 min. earlier, at 7:30 AM, following the "bookend" format, where morning course meetings focus on planning effective instruction following a "working backward" design, reading and critiquing research that addresses cultural competence, investigating in detail BHS's school culture, and learning about theories that inform effective teaching and learning.

At 9:15, students move in pairs to classrooms assigned according to subject matter area and compatibility with cooperating teachers, in efforts to provide pre-service teachers with the most rewarding and simultaneously challenging experience. Students co-teach and/or individually teach three required lessons in two different classes in their subject area, and a third class in a bilingual, special needs, or another content area classroom. Approximately 60% of students choose to teach in a bilingual or special needs classroom. Additionally, students now spend at least 80% of their classroom time teaching and working with students.

From 1:55 to 2:20 PM, students meet with cooperating teachers and supervisors to debrief, plan instruction, and address paperwork. Per students' requests to become more cognizant of policy and national and international trends, the last hour features speakers, such as BC Professor Marilyn Cochran-Smith who presented on current major trends in teacher education; documentaries such as *Waiting for Superman* and *Race to Nowhere* followed by critical discussion including BHS teachers; BHS student panels who share experiences and ideas about improving education for themselves and others; and teacher panels on charter schools, Education Maintenance Organizations (EMOs), and topics such as cyber bullying, abuse, gay, lesbian, bisexual, transgender (GLBT) issues, legal responsibilities, classroom management, union issues, and so on.

Ongoing Development of Cultural Competence

In response to increasing numbers of English language learners and students who are bilingual and multilingual in BHS's and the nation's classrooms, the cohort participates intensively throughout the semester in required workshops that develop their understanding and application of academic language objectives. Based on BC professor Maria Brisk's research and her Title III TALCA grant (Teaching Academic Language in Content Areas), students learn how to integrate and address specific academic language objectives into instruction. Alongside course instructors, cooperating teachers, and researchers, preservice teachers develop and implement academic language instruction in their classrooms, assuring a more genuine mediation of theory and practice, and instantiating teaching and learning as process across the professional lifespan. Students also interview several English language learners from their classrooms, which encourages them to interrogate misconceptions and beliefs about second language learners and learning.

In addition, UI participants are required to describe in detail the school, neighborhood, and community culture of BHS and its students, faculty, and staff and to compare these contexts to those in which they were educated with specific attention to privileges and opportunities afforded to them. All of these current activities and experiences are intended to further develop students' cultural competence.

Increased Commitment to Urban Teaching

As a result of UI, an increasing number of secondary education majors have gone on to teach in urban schools, not only in Boston but also in other metropolitan districts. Out of the original cohort, one graduate is teaching at BHS and working on a Ph in Administration and Leadership. Two members of the second cohort are also teaching at BHS. Still another has moved on to administration in an urban middle school, and one who has taught in an urban high school for seven years has just been accepted into our Ph program in Curriculum and Instruction.

In 2006, and as a result of the Teachers for a New Era Initiative, the Lynch School began collecting specific data about its graduates via Entrance and Exit Surveys to revise our teacher education programs, based on evidence. Now graduates complete a yearly survey throughout their professional careers. Table 3.8 presents the number of undergraduates who participated in UI and are still teaching in urban contexts. From 2006 to 2010, the number of undergraduate teacher candidates entering secondary education has decreased, yielding a five-year average of 27 students. Given this average, the percentage of graduates going into and remaining in urban education after graduation is impressively high.

From 2006 to 2010, approximately 135 students participated in UI, yielding an average of 27 students each year. In 2002, only 9% of all secondary education majors (~4 students) accepted positions in urban settings. By 2005, this percentage had increased to 33%. The average percentage of UI students entering and

TABLE 3.8 Number of Urban Immersion Participants in Urban Teaching

Subject matter area	Graduation year					
	2006	*2007*	*2008*	*2009*	*2010*	*Total*
English	3	4	9	5	1	22
Environmental science					1	1
French			3			3
History		6	4	2	1	13
Mathematics	2	4	6	6		18
Spanish		3		1	1	5
Hispanic perspectives				1		1
Totals	5	17	22	15	4	63
Percentage based on average of 27 students/year	37%	62%	81%	56%	15%	47%

remaining in urban contexts since 2006 is 47%. This percentage is impressive, and participation in UI may indeed be contributing to this increase, but more evidence is needed. Although 2008 was a banner year, figures show a significant decline in 2009 and especially 2010. According to other data gathered from Exit Surveys, ~42% of graduating 2010 seniors went on to graduate school, which may account for the recent drop. Pursuing graduate study makes sense, considering increased school closings, hiring freezes, and layoffs throughout many urban and suburban districts; state takeover of low-performing schools, which are predominantly urban; and emergence of for-profit and charter schools. Nevertheless, we believe UI is making a difference by recruiting BC students into urban teaching, based on data over time.

Unexpected Outcomes From Urban Immersion

The school–university partnership has resulted in two important and unexpected outcomes, which are detailed in this section.

National Board Certification

The partnership with BHS has created a relationship of mutual respect, trust, and collaborative learning. As a result, cooperating teachers requested support in preparing for and acquiring National Board Certification. Over the past four years, 13 BHS teachers who have consistently served as cooperating teachers for UI students have received National Board Certification. Five are BC graduates, three of whom were once UI students.

Sustainability

During the inception of UI in 2002, BHS administrators were truly instrumental in developing and supporting this partnership. Despite administrative turnover, UI continues to have a powerful presence at BHS. This is due to the truly collaborative nature of the partnership, the enthusiasm each exiting cohort shares with the incoming cohort, the investment teachers have made not only in BC students but also the program, and these teachers' profound sense of professionalism. We are grateful for the sustainability of the UI program, as it is making a marked difference in how BC teachers are prepared for urban teaching contexts.

Conclusion

UI continues to provide an effective and productive venue for all stakeholders. Teaching and learning alongside classroom teachers grounds faculty in the increasingly difficult dilemmas of practice, trenchant infrastructural variables consistent with the urban context, and deprofessionalization that urban classroom teachers experience each day. Although research can provide qualitative and quantitative data that describe the urban teaching context, it cannot replace the knowledge and understanding derived from living the experience, which reemphasizes the daily challenges urban teachers face in the current context of often oppressive educational reform. And while our own research may develop promising practices for effective instruction, classroom teacher knowledge apprises us of strategies, assignments, and methodologies that actually work: strategies and methods that enhance our personal practice, making us more "real" as educators of those who will educate others.

Preservice teachers experience firsthand the social context of one urban school, replete with limited human and material resources, pupils' struggles with self-esteem, racism, alienation, poverty, and discrimination, tragedy, dreams, aspirations, and successes, poignantly reminding them of their own privilege and the power it brings, but also providing rich opportunities to develop relationships with the interested, interesting, engaged, and engaging cultural "other." Although variables of accountability and course requirements certainly influence teacher candidates to be more culturally sensitive, competent, and exploratory, when novice teachers' experiences are debriefed and critically interrogated, they challenge preconceived biases and catalyze changes in beliefs and personal epistemologies (Sleeter, 2009). Furthermore, these predominantly White, upper-middle-class students co-construct cultural understanding as they respond to students' academic needs and talents and develop critical knowledge about the multifaceted "other" through authentic interaction.

Classroom teachers serve as teacher leaders, sharing local knowledge, pedagogy, and pedagogical content knowledge. That they are willing to collaborate with university faculty and invite our students, supervisors, and us into classrooms is a testament to their commitment to teaching and learning across the professional lifespan, and their willingness to lay vulnerable to outsiders. Facing the pressures of accountability, which include producing proficient student scores on the state's standardized assessment and making adequate yearly progress in a societal environment of constant critique and deprofessionalization (Friedman & Daniello, 2009; Friedman, Galligan, Albano, & O'Connor, 2009), these teachers take the high road, realizing that instruction that privileges cultural identity development, process learning, and social construction of learning over teaching to the test and scripted pedagogy, leads to more authentic student learning. For these professionals, teaching is "burned in" (Friedman & Reynolds, 2011).

As educators, ongoing and dynamic enhancement of cultural understanding is essential not only to developing our cultural competence and critical pedagogy, but also to refining our "ideological clarity" and deeper awareness of "the sociopolitical, [emotional], and economic realities that shape [pupils'] lives and their capacity to transform them" (Bartolomé, 2008, p. 167). This consciousness must inform how *all* educators define and redefine the contexts in which they work and the pedagogy they implement. UI provides all of us a context for deepening personal ideological clarity and professional epistemology that truly prioritizes community strengths.

Notes

1 Portions of this chapter were previously published by the first author in *Teacher Education Quarterly, 37*(3), 2010, and are reproduced with permission.
2 Pseudonyms have been used when referring to school-based partners.

References

Bartolomé, L. (2008). *Ideologies of education: Unmasking the trap of teacher neutrality.* New York: Peter Lang.

Brisk, M. E. (2008). *Language, culture and community in teacher education.* Mahwah, NJ: Erlbaum.

Cummins, J. (2000). *Language, power, and pedagogy: Bilingual children in the crossfire.* Aberystwyth, UK: Cambrian.

Diller, J. V., & Moule, J. (2005). *Cultural competence: A primer for educators.* Toronto, CA: Thomson Wadsworth.

Donnell, K. A., & Stairs, A. J. (2010). Conclusion: Developing synergy between learning and context. In A. J. Stairs & K. A. Donnell (Eds.), *Research on urban teacher learning: Examining contextual factors over time* (pp. 191–197). Charlotte, NC: Information Age.

Feiman-Nemser, S. (2001). From preparation to practice: Designing a continuum to strengthen and sustain teaching. *Teachers College Records, 103*(6), 1013–1055.

Feiman-Nemser, S. (2008). Teacher learning: How do teachers learn to teach? In M. Cochran-Smith, S. Feiman-Nemser, D. J. McIntyre, & K. E. Demers (Eds.), *Handbook of research on teacher education* (3rd ed., pp. 697–705). New York: Routledge.

Friedman, A. A. (under review). *Cultural competence and cultural identity: Synergy and dysergy.* Manuscript submitted for publication.

Friedman, A. A., & Daniello, F. (2009). Professionalism > Politics + Policy + Pedagogy: The power of professionalism. In A. J. Stairs & K. A. Donnell (Eds.), *Research on urban teacher learning: The role of contextual factors across the professional continuum* (pp. 169–189). Charlotte, NC: Information Age.

Friedman, A. A., Galligan, H. T., Albano, C. M., & O'Connor, K. (2009). Teacher subcultures of democratic practice despite the oppression of educational reform. *Journal of Educational Change, 10*(4), 249–276. doi:10.1007/s10833-008-9090-x

Friedman, A. A., & Reynolds, L. (Eds.). (2011). *Burned in: Fueling the fire to teach.* New York: Teachers College Press.

Gallavan, N. P. (2007). Seven perceptions influencing novice teachers' efficacy and cultural competence. *Journal of Praxis in Multicultural Education, 2*(1), 6–22.

Garmon, M. A. (2004). Changing pre-service teachers' attitudes/beliefs about diversity: What are the critical factors? *Journal of Teacher Education, 55*(3), 201–213.

Gay, G. (2000). *Culturally responsive teaching.* New York: Teachers College Press.

Goodlad, J. (1993). School–university partnerships and partner schools. *Educational Policy, 7*(1), 24–39.

Ingersoll, R. M. (2001). Teacher turnover and teacher shortages: An organizational analysis. *American Educational Research Journal, 38*(3), 499–534.

Menyuk, P., & Brisk, M. E. (2005). *Language development and education: Children with varying language experiences.* New York: Palgrave Macmillan.

Putnam, R. T., & Borko, H. (2000). What do new views of knowledge and thinking have to say about research on teacher learning? *Educational Researcher, 29*(1), 4–15.

Quartz, K. H., & TEP Research Group. (2003). "Too angry to leave": Supporting new teachers' commitment to transform urban schools. *Journal of Teacher Education, 54*(2), 99–111.

Resnick, L. (1991). Shared cognition: Thinking as social practice. In L. Resnick, J. M. Levine, & S. D. Teasley (Eds.), *Perspectives on socially shared cognition* (pp. 1–20). Washington, DC: American Psychological Association.

Samaras, A., & Gismondi, S. (1998). Scaffolds in the field: Vygotskian interpretation in a teacher education program. *Teaching and Teacher Education, 14*(7), 715–733.

Sleeter, C. E. (2009). Developing teacher epistemological sophistication about multicultural curriculum: A case study. *Action in Teacher Education, 31*(1), 3–13.

Stairs, A. J. (2008). Preservice teacher learning in an urban school–university partnership: Understanding the complexity of urban teaching. *Journal of Urban Learning, Teaching, and Research, 4,* 96–108.

Stairs, A. J. (2010a). Becoming an urban teacher in a professional development school: A view from preparation to practice. In A. J. Stairs & K. A. Donnell (Eds.), *Research on urban teacher learning: Examining contextual factors over time* (pp. 41–60). Charlotte, NC: Information Age.

Stairs, A. J. (2010b). The learning and practice of preservice teachers in an urban school–university partnership: The struggle to enact culturally responsive pedagogy. In *2010 online yearbook of urban learning, teaching, and research.* Retrieved from http://www.eric.ed.gov/PDFS/EJ912044.pdf

Stairs, A. J., Corrieri, C., Fyer, L., Genovese, E., Panaro, R., & Sohn, C. (2009). Inquiry into partnered student teaching in an urban school–university partnership. *School–University Partnerships, 3*(1), 75–89.

Tracey, D. H., & Morrow, L. M. (2006). *Lenses on reading: An introduction to theories and models.* New York: Guilford Press.

Wolfram, W., Adger, C. T., & Christian, D. (1999). *Dialects in schools and communities.* Mahwah, NJ: Erlbaum.

4

BEYOND THE IVORY TOWER

The Role of Contextually Based Course Redesign in a Community-Embedded Urban Teacher Preparation Model

Robert E. Lee, Brent D. Showalter, and Lucille L. T. Eckrich

> *While I feel extremely confident in my abilities to connect with people of different cultural backgrounds and have always had an open mind, this experience opened my eyes to how much I still needed to learn and how many misconceptions I had in the beginning. (CDG Enrollee, Fall 2008)*
>
> *Being engaged in the community has had a significant impact on me as well—I feel if I do not take the steps to understand the community I am a part of, then I'm doing a disservice to myself and my students, limiting what can be achieved. (CDG Enrollee, Spring 2009)*
>
> *The more involved I am, the more people I will meet, the more connections I can make, and the broader realm of knowledge I can bring to my classroom . . . Now, I am so excited for the opportunities that lie ahead and I can't wait to get started. (CDG Enrollee, Fall 2007)*

A teacher's knowledge of how culture is formed and sustained comprises a vital component of effective student learning, particularly in classrooms where the teacher's background and culture are very different from those of the students (Loadman, Freeman, & Brookhart, 1999). Understanding the influence of culture on education has become increasingly important in recent years, and the relevance that cultural mapping has for learning is now recognized (Murrell, 2007; Vygotsky, 1962). "Cultural mapping is the method by which to uncover the ideologies and meaning systems that play a significant role in shaping cultural practices and how young people [and teachers] position themselves in relation to those practices" (Murrell, 2007, p. 21; for the relevance of this concept for teachers, see pp. 39–41 and chapter 7). An individual's cultural map is shaped through experience; one relates all new experiences to the previously learned map, thereby interpreting the new in terms of the old and possibly also changing the map. It is through this map that perceivers—including teachers and students—identify cultural behaviors in others that are relevant to their own respective culture.

Teachers—both preservice and in-service—who are put into radically new and different situations generally attempt to transplant their own cultural map onto the new environment, which can lead to misinterpretation of cultural behavior, dissatisfaction and/or alienation on behalf of the teacher and/or students, and a lowered learning threshold for the students (Wolffe, 1996). Gibson (2004) states, "In many pre-service education programs, there is still minimal understanding of race and ethnicity and yet a high incidence of ethnocentric power-struggles between pre-service teachers and their diverse students" (¶15). She contends that "despite the evidence of increased diversity and cultural segregation of many public schools in the United States, mainstream pre-service teachers consistently show lack of needed competencies in teaching students who are different from themselves" (¶32). Furthermore, without addressing the assumptions and beliefs that individuals have at the outset, classroom field experiences have the potential to actually increase prospective teachers' stereotypes of diverse students, compromising their effectiveness as urban educators and inhibiting future learning (Gomez, 1996; Haberman & Post, 1992).

Within the context of teacher education programming, university students are generally involved in a process that includes a series of learning changes. That is, learning is rarely static; each aspect of course work and experience is explicitly linked and interdependent. However, it is not merely the presence of these things that shape reality, but the meaning that is attached to them. It is the interpretation of the meaning of perceived reality that is important in establishing how students will ultimately view their world.

Collaborative university and school-based teacher education programs can address this situation by engaging preservice teachers in diverse, community-based field experiences combined with guided discourse about the beliefs, assumptions, dispositions, and concerns that they bring with them. Programs should "provide substantial field experience during teacher preparation that places prospective teachers in the kinds of hard-to-staff settings in which they will be teaching" (Allen, Palaich, & Anthes, 1999). As a result of course-embedded exposure and preparation within the urban classroom setting, awareness and cultural understanding can increase, and cultural differences can be treated as learning opportunities rather than as deviations from academic or mainstream norms (Gibson, 2004).

But do these suppositions bear out in practice? After reviewing the literature on urban teacher preparation, this chapter presents findings from the second and third years of one large Midwestern university's work to infuse existing teacher education courses with new content, guided discourse, and embedded diverse field experiences that juxtapose the redesigned course content to the context of high-density, urban communities that work in partnership in an urban teacher preparation (UTP) initiative.

The Context for Urban Teacher Preparation

In 1997, the National Center for Education Statistics (NCES) stated that over the next 10 years the United States would need to recruit 2.2 million teachers to fill our nation's classrooms. A decade later, actual figures were higher and continuing to rise. In addition to the need for new teachers due to our increasing population, accelerating retirements of baby boom teachers are exacerbating the teacher shortage. However, what is not often cited is that, when focusing on the economic principle of supply and demand, there actually exists an overall numerical surplus of qualified candidates to positions available. The shortage only exists when focusing on the distribution of these teachers—in particular, those willing to teach in high-poverty urban schools, and those who teach subjects that are in high demand: mathematics, science, bilingual education, and special education (Darling-Hammond & Sykes, 2003; Ingersoll, 2003). Higher levels of teacher dissatisfaction and attrition, as well as underqualified teachers, are also concentrated in high-need schools, making them even more underserved and harder to staff.

Given this demand for high-quality teachers in urban schools, recruitment of teachers has been aggressive and competitive (Kantrowitz & Wingert, 2000). However, such recruitment efforts often overlook the benefit of deliberate learning experiences in urban-focused course work and clinical experiences within those settings for preservice teachers who are preparing for these hard-to-staff urban schools (Lee, Creasey, Showalter, & D'Santiago, 2010). Instead of developing such partnerships between universities and school districts, several institutions of higher education and local educational agencies in cooperation with city/state boards of education have aligned to create what amounts to a quick reactionary solution to move individuals into classrooms who have met only limited requirements—such as a bachelor's degree in any subject, often with no formal teacher preparation.

While fast-track certifications often compromise quality with limited preparation, colleges of education have historically also been ill-suited to develop a systematic way to induct preservice teachers into actual classrooms, especially in ways that substantially improve the conditions of teaching and learning in those schools (Haberman, 1987; Lee & Radner, 2006). Many of the largest teacher education programs are not located in large cities (Lin & Gardner, 2006), posing challenges for forging meaningful and affordable partnerships with urban schools. Additionally, classroom-based instruction delivered in traditional university-based teacher education programs bears little resemblance to the realities of PK–12 classrooms, especially urban ones. Schools of education today do gradually increase preservice teachers' real-world exposure by placing them in classrooms for observations and practice teaching. However, the partnerships between universities that prepare future teachers and the urban high-need schools that will hire them are recent and as yet still weak. Bridging this gap between universities and urban classrooms and schools can be an integral component in preservice teachers' development (Haberman, 2000; Lee, Creasey, Showalter, & D'Santiago, 2010;

Lee, Eckrich, Lackey, & Showalter, 2010; Lee & Radner, 2006; Murrell, 2007; Thompson & Smith, 2005). Context-based exposure through these partnerships assists in the development of teacher skills, which can be best learned by observing, reflecting on, interpreting, and implementing practices appropriate and sensitive to the needs of children from diverse backgrounds.

A tenable theoretical basis for this approach to UTP is situated cognition theory (Lave, 1988), which posits learning as an essentially social phenomenon rooted in context and helps to transform learners' identities. Influenced by the works of both Dewey and Vygotsky, situated cognition theorists consider activities and cultural tools to be primary forces in human learning. Further, social interactions are vital components of cognitive development and the higher order functions—language, concept formation, mapping, knowledge acquisition, and its relative implementation—originating as relationships among individuals and within cultural communities. Through these lived practices within culturally bound situations, "communities of practice" are rooted in context for sharing through mutual engagements (Lave & Wenger, 1990). As the learning process and environment are inextricably linked, the learner's cultural map adapts and grows. Situated in part within the context of urban classrooms, UTP allows prospective teachers an opportunity to practice their teaching skills and become socialized into the role of teacher, connect theory with practice, and work with students they are likely to serve.

Because of the demands in urban environments, new urban teachers who have had limited prior exposure to—and, thus, have developed inadequate cultural maps for—low-income and Black and/or Latino/a classrooms may develop negative perceptions of the children they are serving, which undermines both their ability to teach effectively and the children's opportunity to learn (Aaronsohn, Carter, & Howell, 1995). Evidence from traditional teacher education paradigms suggests that separating learner from environment and knowing from doing can lead to detrimental effects on the beginning teacher's relative development and subsequent effectiveness in urban schools. Further, many traditional approaches toward teacher education use various degrees of abstract instruction that are not directly applicable to clinical situations, thus making learning an arduous process that is unrelated to the demands of an urban reality. In such environments, where learning occurs outside real-world settings, knowledge gained without the ability to relate and reflect within contextual domains remains inert and ultimately vitiates the relevance of practice in meaningful situations. Instead, preservice teachers benefit greatly from the identity and sense-making work they can do conjointly with children and cooperating teachers when situated in multicultural settings (Murrell, 2007; Quartz, Olsen, & Duncan-Andrade, 2008).

Clearly, more opportunities for preservice teachers to challenge and inform their cultural maps through community-based urban school experiences are needed if the shortage of well-prepared, culturally competent, and critically minded urban teachers is to be addressed. While the work described below continues to establish conditions that inculcate what Murrell (2007) calls "cultural mapping by doing cultural practices inquiry" (p. 22) among teacher education faculty and students, it has already helped to establish a broad and long-term commitment to stay this UTP course at this institution.

Research Context

The following studies examine the influence of urban education course work and field experiences on preservice teachers' intentions, perceptions, and attitudes toward urban teaching. Spearheaded by a large Midwestern public university located in a suburban city, this partnership brings a large urban school district, community-based organizations, businesses, not-for-profit educational organizations, and the university together in a collaborative project based in two neighborhoods—one Mexican American, one African American—in that large urban district. One component of this UTP initiative offered university faculty a summer grant opportunity to redesign a course they have regularly taught and/ or will teach so that it better prepares teacher candidates for urban and high-need settings. It emphasized the need for grantees to help preservice teachers:

- View public schools and their inhabitants as situated within and related through a nexus of social, cultural, historical, economic, political, and geographic contexts
- Have rich and sustained firsthand experiences in urban schools and neighborhoods preceded, succeeded, and accompanied by theoretical discussions with peers and experienced educators and community members
- Examine how identities shape understandings of and experiences in school
- Understand, critique, and, as possible, participate in overcoming the systemic sources of racial and economic inequity in our society and schools
- Experience and facilitate authentic student-centered learning and assessment
- Practice principles of universal design that benefit all students, and without which some students are unable to succeed

Grantees participated together in a 4-day, community-embedded, residency field experience similar to the kind of urban field experience they were expected to integrate into their redesigned courses. This research examines student data from the second and third years of this UTP Course Development Grant (CDG) program.

Methodology

Study 1

This study sought to reveal the impact of redesigned UTP courses and their course-embedded urban field experiences during 2007–2008 on preservice teachers' perceptions of urban education, their attitudes toward diversity and multiculturalism, and their intentions to teach in an urban setting. Three hypotheses framed this study:

H1: Preservice teachers' intentions to teach in an urban setting will increase significantly during the semester in which they take a redesigned course.

H2: Preservice teachers' intentions to teach in an urban setting will be positively related to their urban education perceptions, attitudes toward multiculturalism in schools, and personal level of exposure to such a setting.

H3: Among redesign enrollees, students who participated in an urban field experience will demonstrate significantly higher postcourse scores on (a) intentions to teach in an urban setting, (b) urban education perceptions, and (c) attitudes toward diversity and multiculturalism in schools, compared to those students who did not participate in the urban field experience.

Study 2

To assess the continuing impact of the CDG program, the procedure implemented in Study 1 was replicated in the next academic year (2008–2009). Because the CDG program seeks a cumulative effect on preservice participants' perceptions and attitudes regarding urban education, a number of hypotheses were proposed:

H1: Current CDG course enrollees with urban experience from other previously taken redesigned courses will demonstrate significantly higher precourse scores on (a) urban teaching intentions, (b) urban education perceptions, and (c) attitudes toward multiculturalism in schools.

H2: Growth in and levels of preservice teachers' attitudes, perceptions, and intentions will be more sizable than those observed in the previous year. This is hypothesized due to refinements in the CDG training, more established relationships with urban schools and community partners, and ongoing growth of the broader UTP initiative at the university.

Research Participants

Study 1

During the fall 2007 and spring 2008 semesters, students participating in 10 courses, which had been redesigned to focus on urban education topics with an urban-based field experience, were targeted for this study. A total of 491 students enrolled in the redesigned courses, 424 of whom participated in the research. Due to significant missing data and anonymous responses, 271 cases were omitted from analyses. Full sets of data suitable for analysis (including both pre- and postcourse surveys) were collected for 153 participants, constituting a response rate of 31%.

The mean age of the respondents was 21.5 ($SD = 3.3$) years. The sample included 87 women (57%). There were 24 freshmen (15.7%), 20 sophomores (13.1%),

26 juniors (17%), and 79 seniors (51.6%); 4 respondents (2.6%) did not specify. One hundred thirty-seven participants identified as White (89.5%), 5 as Black (3.3%), 6 as Latino/a (3.9%), and 5 respondents (3.3%) did not identify their race/ethnicity. The majority (63.4%) attended high school in a suburban area. One hundred-forty-three students (94%) declared a major in education and 132 (86%) respondents expressed that they planned to begin working as a teacher on graduation. At the beginning of the study, 103 respondents (67%) indicated having little or no experience in an urban school setting. As a central component of the CDG project, 89 students (58%) participated in the clinical urban experience and 64 (42%) did not go on an experiential trip.

Study 2

Students from eight newly redesigned courses offered during the fall 2008 and spring 2009 semesters were included in Study 2. Although 445 students enrolled in these courses, 205 complete cases from participants were suitable for analysis, comprising a response rate of 46%. The average age of participants was 21.33 ($SD = 3.72$), and the sample was mostly women (77.1%). Two freshmen (1%), 4 sophomores (2%), 126 juniors (61.5%), 72 seniors (35.1%), and 1 graduate student (0.5%) participated. One hundred-eighty-seven participants (92.2%) identified as White, 5 (2.4%) as Black, 5 (2.4%) as Latino/a, 3 (1.5%) as Asian, and 5 (2.4%) did not identify race. Most were graduates of suburban high schools (71.2%), with intentions to begin working as a teacher after college (94.1%). Thus, participants in both studies were quite similar, though students in Study 2 had higher percentages of female and junior participants than did Study 1.

Instruments

To evaluate the effects of the redesigned courses on students' attitudes and perceptions, the studies were conducted in a pre- and postcourse survey design. In Study 1, students in 10 newly redesigned courses were asked to complete a survey during the first weeks of the fall 2007 and spring 2008 semesters, and then again at the end of each respective semester. Two prior administrations of the pre/post-survey design were conducted with redesigned courses in fall 2006 and spring 2007 to pilot the measures. In Study 2, students enrolled in eight newly redesigned courses completed surveys at the start and end of fall 2008 and spring 2009. The survey instrument comprised four measures: Urban Teaching Intentions (UTI), Urban Education Perceptions (UEP), the Teacher Multicultural Attitudes Scale (TMAS), and the Teacher Sense of Efficacy Scale (TSES).

The UTI and UEP measures were specifically designed for this research and were composed of six and nine items, respectively. The UTI scale measured students' intentions to teach in an urban setting once they graduate; higher scores indicated greater intention to teach in an urban school. The UEP scale measured participants' endorsement of stereotypical beliefs about urban schools and was scored so that higher scores indicated more positive attitudes toward urban education. The first pilot administrations of the UTI scale yielded adequate reliabilities alphas of 0.87 and 0.88, respectively. The UEP scale also demonstrated adequate reliabilities during the pilot administrations, yielding alphas of 0.74 and 0.77. Using the current samples, the UTI scale demonstrated adequate internal consistency alphas, ranging from 0.79 to 0.82, over the course of the four survey administrations. The UEP scale was also reliable, demonstrating alphas ranging from 0.63 to 0.72.

The TMAS is a 20-item survey instrument designed to measure multicultural awareness of teachers working in kindergarten through Grade 12 (Ponterotto, Baluch, Greig, & Rivera, 1998). The wording of some items was adapted for administration to preservice teachers. Previous work has demonstrated the reliability and validity of the scale (Ponterotto et al., 1998), and higher scores indicated more favorable attitudes toward multiculturalism in the classroom. Employing the current samples, the observed alphas for this scale ranged from 0.87 to 0.90.

The TSES has a long form (24 items) and a short form (12 items), each of which measures a respondent's sense of efficacy as a teacher or preservice teacher, which is "a judgment of his or her capabilities to bring about desired outcomes of student engagement and learning, even among those students who may be difficult or unmotivated" (Tschannen-Moran & Woolfolk Hoy, 2001, p. 783). The short form was utilized for these studies and six items relevant to urban education were added to the scale—yielding an 18-item measure. Higher scores indicated greater self-efficacy in the classroom. During the pilot administrations, the observed alphas for the scale were 0.83 and 0.91. Reliability remained high with the current samples, with alphas ranging from 0.91 to 0.94.

Results

Major Analyses

Study 1

The data supported hypothesis 1. A paired-samples t-test was conducted to determine if there was a significant increase in UTI from the precourse survey (Time 1) to the postcourse survey (Time 2). A statistically significant increase over time in UTI was observed, $t(151) = -3.01, p = 0.003$. Participants' UTI scores went from 3.03 ($SD = 0.79$) to 3.20 ($SD = 0.77$), on a scale of 1 to 5. Respondents participating in the clinical experience demonstrated slightly higher UTI scores ($M = 3.26$) than those who did not ($M = 3.11$) at Time 2, although not significantly.

Using data at Time 1 and Time 2, hierarchical multiple regressions were conducted to test hypothesis 2. The demographic variables of race/ethnicity and high school setting were entered in the first step as control variables. The variables of self-rated experience in an urban school (per their respective high school setting), UEP, and multicultural attitudes (TMAS) were entered in the second step as hypothesized main predictors. Table 4.1 displays the results of these analyses.

Entered as a control, participants' respective high school setting emerged as a significant predictor of urban teaching intentions at Time 1. This finding indicates that those students from urban high schools exhibited significantly more intent to teach in an urban setting. All of the main predictors exhibited a significant relationship with UTI at either Time 1 and/or Time 2. Self-rated urban experience emerged as a significant predictor of urban teaching intentions at Time 1. That is, students who started with more extensive urban school experiences voiced stronger intentions to become urban teachers. The most robust predictor, urban education perceptions, exhibited a positive relationship with UTI at both Time 1 and Time 2. At Time 2, multicultural attitudes were positively related to the UTI scale. These findings indicate that those students who had or developed more positive perceptions of urban education and multiculturalism/diversity exhibited more intent to teach in an urban setting.

As detailed, the data supported hypothesis 2. Preservice teachers' intentions to teach in an urban setting were positively related to their urban education perceptions, attitudes toward multiculturalism in schools, and personal level of exposure to such a setting. These results suggest that participants' previous experiences,

TABLE 4.1 Hierarchical Multiple Regression of Urban Teaching Intentions Onto Demographic, Experiential, and Attitudinal Predictors at Time 1 and Time 2

	Time 1		Time 2	
	ΔR^2	β	ΔR^2	β
Step 1: Control variables	0.091★★[a]		0.023[c]	
Race/ethnicity		−0.120		−0.070
HS setting		−0.252★★		−0.121
Step 2: Main variables	0.250★★[b]		0.165★★[d]	
Urban experience		0.221★★		0.162
UEP		0.387★★		0.271★★
TMAS		0.138		0.187★
Total R^2	0.341		0.188	

Note: Race/ethnicity (coded 0 for non-Whites and 1 for Whites); HS setting (coded 0 for urban HS and 1 for nonurban HS); urban experience was on a continuum ranging from 1 (*no experience at all*) to 5 (*extensive experience*).

[a] F change $(2, 146) = 7.29, p = .001$.
[b] F change $(5, 143) = 14.82, p = .000$.
[c] F change $(2, 146) = 1.72, p = .183$.
[d] F change $(5, 143) = 6.60, p = .000$.
*$p < .05$, ★★$p < .01$.

perceptual understanding and attitudes are important predictors of their intention to teach in an urban setting. In sum, all five predictor variables combined to explain 34% of the variance in UTI scores at Time 1 and 19% at Time 2.

Hypothesis 3 received no significant support. Analyses of variance (ANOVAs) were run to test the effect at Time 2 of having attended an experiential trip. Trip participants demonstrated higher scores on the UTI scale (M = 3.26) than did students not participating in a trip (M = 3.11). Respondents completing a trip also scored higher on the UEP (M = 3.16) and TMAS (M = 3.95) scales, compared to their nontrip counterparts with a mean score of 3.03 on UEP and 3.79 on TMAS. Although these mean levels were higher for trip participants, no statistically significant differences were found on UTI, UEP, or TMAS at Time 2.

Post Hoc Analyses on Study 1

In addition to assessing the hypotheses, a number of supplemental post hoc analyses were run to investigate other potentially significant relationships.

Additional t-tests were conducted to determine if there was a significant change in participants' levels on the other study variables (i.e., UEP, TMAS, and TSES). Participants' UEP scores increased significantly from Time 1 to Time 2, $t(152) = -3.23, p = 0.002$. Participants' TMAS scores also increased, although not significantly, 3.82 (SD = 0.48) at Time 1 to 3.88 (SD = 0.54) at Time 2. TSES scores rose significantly over time, $t(146) = -2.87, p = 0.005$. Again, all scores are on a scale from 1 to 5. Table 4.2 depicts the means and correlations for the four scales.

Study 2

To test hypothesis 1, students were asked to provide the number of redesigned courses and urban experiences they had taken before enrolling in the current course. This was coded numerically and used as the independent variable in a series of linear regressions for urban teaching intentions, urban education perceptions, and attitudes toward multiculturalism in the classroom. Data partially supported hypothesis 1. CDG urban experience was found to be a significant predictor of urban teaching intentions, $b = 0.16, t(203) = 2.24, p = 0.022$, and accounted for 2.4% of the variance in urban teaching intentions, $F(1, 203) = 5.02$, $p = 0.026$. Previous CDG experience also significantly predicted scores on the multicultural attitudes scale, $b = 0.14, t(203) = 2.04, p = 0.043$. This experience explained a significant portion of variance in the multicultural attitudes scale, $R^2 = 0.02, F(1, 203) = 4.14, p = 0.043$. Therefore, as hypothesized, previous experience with CDG courses and urban trips was significantly predictive of higher urban teaching intentions and more positive attitudes toward multiculturalism and diversity in the classroom.

TABLE 4.2 Intercorrelations Between Variables

Variable	M (SD)	1	2	3	4	5	6	7	8
1. UTI (Time 1)	3.03 (0.79)	–							
2. UTI (Time 2)	3.20 (0.77)	0.63**	–						
3. UEP (Time 1)	2.96 (0.49)	0.40**	0.31**	–					
4. UEP (Time 2)	3.10 (0.52)	0.29**	0.32**	0.45**	–				
5. TMAS (Time 1)	3.82 (0.48)	0.25**	0.27**	0.07	0.26**	–			
6. TMAS (Time 2)	3.88 (0.54)	0.21**	0.28**	0.05	0.20*	0.75**	–		
7. TSES (Time 1)	3.95 (0.50)	0.41**	0.34**	0.34**	0.28**	0.18*	0.19*	–	
8. TSES (Time 2)	4.05 (0.55)	0.30**	0.30**	0.27**	0.38**	0.20*	0.33**	0.60**	–

*p < .05. **p < .01.

Echoing the findings in Study 1, participants in Study 2 demonstrated similar growth patterns on the four scales over time. In fact, significant increases were observed in urban teaching intentions, $t(204) = -3.81, p = 0.000$, urban education perceptions, $t(204) = -9.27, p = 0.000$, and teaching sense of efficacy $t(202) = -4.23$, $p = 0.000$. Table 4.3 depicts the means and change scores for each scale for both Study 1 and Study 2. To test hypothesis 2, a series of ANOVAs were run to test for differences between the two samples (Study 1 and Study 2) on the change scores for each of the four scales. Although larger growth was observed among the UI, UEP, and TSES scales, only urban education perceptions demonstrated a significant difference between the two groups, $F(1, 356) = 12.25, p = 0.001$. The average change score of the Study 1 sample ($M = 0.14, SD = 0.52$) was significantly different than that of the Study 2 sample ($M = 0.33, SD = 0.50$). Therefore, hypothesis 2 was partially supported.

As evidenced, larger growth between Time 1 and Time 2 was observed on three of the scales in Study 2, in comparison to Study 1. However, the difference was significant only for urban education perceptions.

Post Hoc Analyses on Study 2

As the elements of the UTP program (which includes but is not limited to the CDG courses) are designed to be cumulative, it was also expected that students enrolled in Study 2 (a year after Study 1) would likely begin with higher baseline scores on each instrument. A series of ANOVAs were run to test for differences in scores at Time 1 for each scale between the two samples. Only TMAS (multicultural attitudes) emerged with a significant difference, $F(1, 355) = 4.42$, $p = 0.036$. Specifically, Time 1 scores on the TMAS scale in Study 1 ($M = 3.28$, $SD = 0.48$) were significantly lower than those of the Study 2 sample ($M = 3.92$, $SD = 0.42$).

TABLE 4.3 Means, Standard Deviations, and Change Scores of UTI, UEP, TMAS, and TSES for Study 1 and Study 2

	Study 1 (N = 151)			Study 2 (N = 205)		
	Time 1	Time 2	Δ	Time 1	Time 2	Δ
UTI	3.03 (0.79)	3.20 (0.77)	0.17**	3.01 (0.76)	3.19 (0.76)	0.18**
UEP	2.96 (0.49)	3.10 (0.52)	0.14**	2.92 (0.45)	3.25 (0.50)	0.33**
TMAS	3.82 (0.48)	3.88 (0.54)	0.06	3.92 (0.42)	3.93 (0.45)	0.01
TSES	3.95 (0.50)	4.05 (0.55)	0.10**	3.85 (0.48)	3.98 (0.46)	0.13**

$*p < .05. **p < .01.$

Discussion

Research has established that separating learner from environment can have detrimental effects on the learning process, introducing unique and specific barriers in the development of urban teachers who study in the Ivory Tower. As these traditional teacher education approaches are often abstract, preservice teachers fail to see practical importance and applicability to clinical situations. We conclude that traditional teacher education outside of contextual classrooms is weak, making it difficult to develop skills relevant to specific communities. In response, the UTP CDG program reported in this chapter constitutes just one of the interconnected fronts of an initiative to fundamentally redesign how urban teachers are trained at our institution.

Students participating in redesigned courses and related clinical actions amid the situated environment are inextricably entwined in the production of knowledge. That is, course knowledge is contextually situated and is fundamentally influenced by, and inseparable from, the activity, context, and culture in which it is situated. "The activity in which knowledge is developed and deployed . . . is not separable from nor is it ancillary to learning and cognition" (Brown, Collins, & Duguid, 1989, p. 32). Moreover, as knowledge is dependent on the community to negotiate its full meaning and construct understanding, it is seen as a product of activity, rather than a set of mental abstractions to acquire first and then apply in practice later.

Within our studies, participation in a course redesigned to focus on urban education increased and enhanced participating preservice teachers' intentions to teach in an urban setting, their perceptions of urban education, their attitudes toward diversity and multiculturalism, and their developing sense of self-efficacy toward urban teaching. Furthermore, the course-embedded urban field experience seemed to reinforce and augment the positive effects of participation in the redesigned UTP courses, although not as significantly as anecdotal evidence suggests. Finally, study subjects' intentions to teach in an urban setting were positively related with more open and informed urban education perceptions, positive attitudes toward diversity and multiculturalism, and more personal exposure to urban settings.

As the UTP initiative gains momentum, we have discovered that the exposure to the practices, language, and rituals of an urban community through a singular clinical experience is not enough (as was the case in Study 1). Repeated, follow-up experiences whereby students continue their community-based, facilitated acculturation allow those in the community of practice to support a mutually negotiated goal that helps to define the enterprises in which students are engaged, consequently creating a feeling of mutuality among participants.

As reported in Study 2, previous experience with CDG courses and urban trips was significantly predictive of higher urban teaching intentions and more positive attitudes toward multiculturalism and diversity in the classroom. As this

program is designed to have a cumulative effect on changing attitudes and interests of preservice teachers, it was encouraging that baseline levels of multicultural
attitudes were significantly higher in the Study 2 (one year later) in comparison
to the levels reported in Study 1. This finding would seem to support the ground-
swell effort of the initiative to alter fundamental attitudes about urban education
and diverse classrooms among the institution's preservice teachers. We believe that
by further expanding the UTP CDG program's reach into increasing numbers of
undergraduate courses, students' exposure to urban schools and communities will
break down stereotypes and subtle racism. As we continually enhance and refine
the preservice teacher preparation experience, we hope that many of these highly
qualified educators will identify themselves with the students who need them the
most, especially as they reconceptualize their cultural maps through physical and
cultural interactions and contextualize each new experience by relating it to history specific to that particular community.

Conclusion

Research and experience from this university indicate that hands-on, community-
based, immersive activities, combined with structured opportunities for critical
reflection, provide students with powerful tools for examining and possibly rethinking or redrawing their cultural maps of underserved urban areas and in vari-
ously diverse classrooms. Being immersed in an environment that approximates
the context in which their new knowledge and behavior would be applied was
related to intentions to teach in urban high-need schools.

As preservice teachers who are enrolled in redesigned courses gain meaning
from each new experience, it becomes part of their cultural map, which is governed by historical facts and their unique personal histories. By participating in
the lived community with its complex framework of language, rituals, symbolism,
and culture, guided as Brown et al. (1989) wrote to aid in the socialization toward
situated norms and adept performance, preservice teachers trained in situ are able
to take learning to the intersection of meaning, practice, community, and professional identity development.

Actualizing such a premise under a university-, school-, and community-based
partnership model of urban teacher education has the potential to afford learners opportunities to generate problems, test hypotheses, reflect on experiences,
and assume multiple roles, all the while accessing, through guided acculturation,
the resources that a site-based contextualized community provides. This crucial knowledge, embedded within, cannot be fully understood or taught wholly
within the confines of the university or within a school alone, isolated from the
community it is intended to serve. Rather, only in collaborative partnership—
actualized within the work setting in which learners will soon be a part—can
full-participatory learning and acculturation occur and generate well-prepared
effective teachers.

Through active site-based participation, preservice teachers begin to acquire the skills necessary for proficiency in their profession as they transition from student teacher to teacher professional with a growing panoply of real-world experiences that have been reflected through metacognition and guided discourse. Equally relevant is that the individual learner has partaken in the mysteries, practices, and rituals to be deemed part of the culture. Essentially, it is not enough to perform within a culture; one must also know what the performance means. While individual trajectories remain unique, preservice teachers who are willing to move beyond the Ivory Tower and learn within contextualized urban communities develop the propensity to be guided by others who are advocates for social justice through transformative school progress.

References

Aaronsohn, E., Carter, C. J., & Howell, M. (1995). Preparing monocultural teachers for a multicultural world: Attitudes toward inner-city schools. *Equity and Excellence in Education, 28*(1), 5–9. (ERIC Document Reproduction Service No. ED378135)

Allen, M., Palaich, R., & Anthes, C. (1999). *Teacher recruitment, preparation and retention for hard-to-staff schools.* Retrieved from http://www.ecs.org/initiatives/geringer/chicago%20hard-to-staff%20meeting%20report.htm

Brown, J., Collins, A., & Duguid, P. (1989). Situated cognition and the culture of learning. *Educational Researcher, 18*(1), 32–42.

Darling-Hammond, L., & Sykes, G. (2003). Wanted: A national teacher supply policy for education: The right way to meet the "Highly Qualified Teacher" challenge. *Education Policy Analysis Archives, 11*(33). Retrieved from http://epaa.asu.edu/epaa/v11n33/

Gibson, C. (2004). Multicultural pre-service education: Promising multicultural pre-service teacher education initiatives. *Radical Pedagogy, 6*(1). Retrieved from http://radicalpedagogy.icaap.org/content/issue6_1/gibson.html

Gomez, M. L. (1996). Prospective teachers' perspectives on teaching "other people's children." In K. Zeichner, S. Melnick, & M. L. Gomez (Eds.), *Currents of reform in preservice teacher education* (pp. 109–132). New York: Teachers College Press.

Haberman, M. (1987). *Recruiting and selecting teachers for urban schools.* Retrieved from http://www.eric.ed.gov/ERICDocs/data/ericdocs2sql/content_storage_01/0000019b/80/1c/8b/e5.pdf

Haberman, M. (2000). *What makes a teacher education program relevant preparation for teaching diverse students in urban poverty schools? (The Milwaukee Teacher Education Center model).* Milwaukee: University of Wisconsin–Milwaukee. (ERIC Document Reproduction Service No. ED442745)

Haberman, M., & Post, L. (1992). Does direct experience change education students' perceptions of low-income minority children? *Midwestern Educational Researcher, 5*(2), 29–31.

Ingersoll, R. (2003). *Is there really a teacher shortage? Research report using data from the Schools and Staffing Survey and the Teacher Followup Survey conducted by the National Center for Education Statistics.* Seattle, WA: Center for the Study of Teaching and Policy. Retrieved from http://repository.upenn.edu/gse_pubs/133/

Kantrowitz, B., & Wingert, P. (2000, October 2). Teachers wanted [Electronic version]. *Newsweek,* pp. 36–41.

Lave, J. (1988). *Cognition in practice: Mind, mathematics, and culture in everyday life.* Cambridge: Cambridge University Press.

Lave, J., & Wenger, E. (1990). *Situated learning: Legitimate peripheral participation.* Cambridge: Cambridge University Press.

Lee, R. E., Creasey, G., Showalter, B. D., & D'Santiago, V. (2010). Cognitive development of social justice through re-designed courses and community-based partnerships: An initial investigation. *Perspectives on Urban Education, 8*(1), 29–34.

Lee, R. E., Eckrich, L.L.T., Lackey, C., & Showalter, B. D. (2010). Pre-service teacher pathways to urban teaching: A partnership model for nurturing community-based urban teacher preparation. *Teacher Education Quarterly, 37*(3), 101–122.

Lee, R. E., & Radner, B. (2006). It takes a school to raise a teacher. *Success in High-Need Schools, 2*(2). Retrieved from http://www.sucessinhighneedschools.org/journal/issue/2/2/888

Lin, Z., & Gardner, D. (2006). Benchmarking teacher education: A comparative assessment of the top ten teacher-producing universities' contributions to the teacher workforce. *Planning and Changing, 37*(1–2), 258–282.

Loadman, W. E., Freeman, D. J., & Brookhart, S. M. (1999). Development of a national survey of teacher education program graduates. *Journal of Educational Research, 93*(2), 76–89.

Murrell, P. C., Jr. (2007). *Race, culture, and schooling: Identities of achievement in multicultural urban schools.* New York: Routledge.

Ponterotto, J. G., Baluch, S., Greig, T., & Rivera, L. (1998). Development and initial score validation of the Teacher Multicultural Attitude Survey. *Educational and Psychological Measurement, 58*(6), 1002–1016.

Quartz, K. H., Olsen, B., & Duncan-Andrade, J. (2008). The fragility of urban teaching: A longitudinal study of career development and activism. In F. P. Peterman (Ed.), *Partnering to prepare urban teachers* (pp. 225–247). New York: Peter Lang.

Thompson, S., & Smith, D. (2005). Creating highly qualified teachers for urban schools. *Professional Educator, 27*(1–2), 73–88.

Tschannen-Moran, M., & Woolfolk Hoy, A. (2001). Teacher efficacy: Capturing an elusive construct. *Teaching and Teacher Education, 17*(7), 783–805.

Vygotsky, L. (1962). *Thought and language* (E. Hanfmann & Gertrude Vakar, Eds. & Trans.). Cambridge, MA: MIT Press.

Wolffe, R. (1996). Reducing preservice teachers' negative expectations of urban students through field experience. *Teacher Education Quarterly, 23*(1), 99–106.

PART III
Focus on Children

5

THE POETRY OF VOICE

Susan Catapano and Candace M. Thompson

> *Behind their fearful silence, our students want to find their voices, speak their voices, have their voices heard. A good teacher is one who can listen to those voices even before they are spoken—so that someday they can speak with truth and confidence. (Palmer, 2007, p. 47)*

The bell sounds and with it comes the jostling and shouting of adolescent voices and bodies making their way through crowded hallways to the next class. Their youthful energy spills into the usually sedate calm of the school library. It's 1:15 on a Wednesday and the media center is buzzing with energetic poetry recitations, last minute rewrites, and call and response greetings between students and their young university collaborators as preparations for the sixth-grade Poetry Slam get underway. As it has been for the past two months, a self-selected group of 31 sixth graders at an urban middle school meet with their university mentors—beginning teacher education students from the local university. Together, they learn about and perform diverse genres of poetry using music, research, and spoken word performances.

For some of the sixth graders, the road was rocky—struggling readers with varying degrees of understanding, love and distaste for poetry; students who sometimes felt they had little of value to share; some fearful of failure or concerned about how "doing" poetry would be perceived by their peers. But every Wednesday, in the bright and open space of the Media Center, a diverse group of young people moved against their fears and misgivings to use their creative powers and living hopes to create and perform poetry. Adoria, one of the young poets, captured the essence of this experience: "We can read and write poetry and we do not have to be scared to express our feelings. It teaches us we can express ourselves and it is good to teach other people that it is okay" (2011). As Adoria and her peers prepared to perform their original poems on the theme "My Legacy" for the sixth-grade Poetry Slam celebration, it was clear that even once-reluctant students grasped the positive outcomes of learning to speak for themselves in creative ways. The young university students who have worked closely with the sixth graders are proud partners in the growth and confidence of their young poets. They are also benefactors of this university–school partnership—as beginning teacher education students this is their first experience in understanding the complex and wondrous poetry of student–teacher relationships. In engaging with adolescents working to express their world through poetry, they too are engaged in a process of developing their own voices as teachers and learners in relationship with students and each other. The creative learning journey of these young people began with a university–school partnership.

This chapter examines the evolving story of a university–school partnership in an urban middle school in a small city in southeastern North Carolina. Although the project is unique and develops communities of practice to support learning of state-mandated skills in language arts, the focus is on finding out what the learners think about having preservice teachers spend part of the day with them each week and what they believe about themselves as learners and authors of original poems and stories.

Background

In the fall of 2009, faculty at a university teacher education program sought to provide early preservice teachers with authentic experiences working in high-need schools. University–school partnerships are especially important in urban schools where many of the new teachers are not culturally prepared to meet the unique needs of the learners and families in this setting. Teacher education students are overwhelmingly White, middle class women who grew up attending economically and, in many cases, racially segregated suburban and rural K–12 systems (Bell, 2002; McIntyre, 1997; Sleeter, 2001). If their first job is in an urban school, this generally means working with low-income students who are living in high-poverty areas, and who are children of color. Nothing in the new teacher's prior experience prepares them to make sure their learners are performing well in the classroom and on high-stakes, standardized tests. Yet, the one factor that has been identified that can have a positive impact on student performance in urban schools, where poverty and other factors impact learning, is the teacher (Ediger, 2003; C. Thompson, 2008–2009; S. Thompson & Smith, 2005).

Faculty in this project taught two foundation courses in the teacher education program: social foundations of education and an educational psychology class. By scheduling their courses back to back, they were able to provide a three-hour block of time for students to work in schools without asking them to spend additional time outside of class for this experience. Faculty would also be present, supervising the experience and bringing lessons learned back into the university classroom. Faculty were specifically interested in low-performing schools located in high-poverty areas so preservice teachers would get experiences they never had in their own K–12 classrooms. Students at this highly selective university come from southern (83%), suburban, or rural areas where schools are predominantly racially and economically segregated. They are from affluent families and are in the top tier of their graduating class. As a result, they are not familiar with life from the perspective of low-income, low-performing students. The purpose of this field experience went beyond practice with children; it was a way to help preservice teachers recognize what it means to work with wide diversities in perspective, income, abilities, cultural backgrounds, and expectations.

Middle School

University faculty identified a low-performing middle school located in a high-poverty area of the city. The principal welcomed the influence of the university students, and provided open access to the sixth-grade language arts teachers who helped arrange for 20 struggling sixth graders in reading to come to the media center every Wednesday for 90 min. to work one-on-one with a university student.

Middle school is a place where a lack of proficient reading skills accelerates the chance of students dropping out of school (Rumberger & Lim, 2008). The focus of school curricula on achieving specific scores on state-mandated tests leaves little room for a consideration of student voices and their experiences of the impact of curricula, teaching, and school culture. Dewey urged teachers to listen to learners and respond by recognizing the learner's voice as a critical component of what to teach and how to teach it (Stefl-Mabry, Radlick, & Doane, 2010). A survey of middle and high school students about what they were learning (curriculum) and how they were learning (instruction) yielded an 80% response rate, with 91% of open-ended questions answered completely (Wiggins, 2011). What does this mean? As Palmer stated in the opening quote, learners want to be heard. What did they say? They said they wanted fewer lectures and more hands-on, meaningful activities that would allow them to learn while applying new and familiar skills. When given the chance to let their teacher know what they like and need in their language arts class, eighth graders made it clear to one teacher: Learning should be engaging and grounded in relationship, with positive and interesting activities that are meaningful to the learner, and lead to better reading and writing in preparation to succeed in high school and beyond (Hubbard, 2011).

The host middle school had low achievement scores on state-mandated standardized tests for the previous few years. In 2010–2011, 60% of sixth graders in this school were on grade level for reading, however, that dropped dramatically to 42% for seventh graders. More than 75% of the student population was children of color. Only 44% of African American and 50% of Hispanic students passed their end-of-grade tests in reading (North Carolina Department of Public Instruction, 2011).

As part of No Child Left Behind, student enrollment at the school was dwindling, as parents selected other middle schools for their children. In fall 2010, the county board of education undertook a major redistricting of middle schools to address issues of overcrowding in several schools and respond to growing calls from a powerful group of mostly White constituents to move toward a neighborhood school configuration. During this time, a new middle school opened and enrollment at this school dropped to half capacity. The school closed in June 2011 and students were sent to another urban middle school a few miles away.

The middle school where many of the students attended the next year had a similar profile, with 64% of sixth graders reading on grade level and dropping to 54% by seventh grade. Only 43% of African American and 47% of Hispanic students read on grade level in 2010–2011 (North Carolina Department of Public Instruction, 2011). This school had a population that was three times larger than the first school. As a result, the number of students identified to participate in the university–school partnership program rose to 50 for fall 2011, and each preservice teacher worked with two to three sixth graders.

University–School Partnership

University–school partnerships are established to provide a reciprocal relationship between the university teacher education program and the local school district. The desired outcome of these partnerships range from improved student performance to well-designed projects that result in reduced violence and school failure (Bosma et al., 2010; Teitel, 2008–2009). John Goodlad, through the National Network for Educational Renewal, determined the value of university–school partnerships as an opportunity for simultaneous renewal rather than mutual disappointment and blame. The most desirable model is where universities and schools work together toward a purpose of student achievement and teacher (both preservice and in-service) improvement, has a chance to lead to educational reform and renewal (Teitel, 2008–2009). The close proximity of the university to the school in this project allowed for the partnership to move along the continuum for university–school partnerships suggested by Teitel (2008–2009), that described growth from little or no connection to a transactional relationship heading to a transformational partnership. Transitionally, the faculty from the university and the staff from the school collaborated at the beginning and end of each semester to plan and review successes/failures.

Theoretical Framework

Communities of Practice

The university–school partnership for this project was established based on a framework of communities of practice (Murrell, 2001). Lave and Wenger (1991) noted that communities of practice is a concept that emphasizes the importance of developing strong ties between the individuals within a community and between the individuals and the community itself. Barab and Duffy (2000) note the importance of models of community-based support for learning that also support the development of self through participation in the community. They believed that the development of self in a community occurs through legitimate participation in the community. With the development of self being the main focus, more reflective dialogue will occur between varieties of people with varying levels of expertise, thus enforcing the communities of practice (Buysse, Sparkman, & Wesley, 2003).

Participation in communities of practice is not merely one of many experiences preservice teachers will log in their portfolio as a means to practice new knowledge. It is a reciprocal community, where learners at all levels collaborate to meet a shared goal (Catapano, Huisman, & Song, 2008). A spirit of reciprocity was evident in the storytelling and poetry project. The following comment by Keisha, a sixth-grade participant, showed that her work with one of the preservice students involved not only working on poetry, but also supporting and challenging each other as they learned. She stated, "I had a wonderful time with my mentor. We had fun and laughed and liked the same things. We helped each other and helped each other build confidence during our poetry breaks [performance of poetry]."

Unfortunately, too many times, field experiences for preservice teachers are conducted as if the classroom is a laboratory for the preservice teacher, without regard for the classroom teacher or the students. Wenger (1998) defined communities of practice, as groups of individuals who share interests, tasks, beliefs, and practices to accomplish a specific goal. The community is ever evolving, with novices learning the beliefs, norms, and practices of the group. Through a true model of communities of practice, preservice teachers can guide and support struggling learners to be successful and connected with school, as well as learn from their students how best to engage, support, and push them to achieve. This is critical for struggling middle school students, at a crucial point in their educational experience that too often leads to dropping out by high school.

Culturally Responsive Teaching

The important role teachers play in the nation's increasingly diverse classrooms, be they K–12 or higher education, demand that teachers be prepared for working with ethnically, culturally, racially, and linguistically diverse student body (Banks, 1997; Banks & Banks, 1999; Diller & Moule, 2005; Gay, 2000; Hefflin, 2002). Gay (2000) contends that an "important part of that preparation is becoming critically conscious of one's own knowledge, attitudes, and skills in multicultural education and the process of how these evolve" (p. xi). Efforts toward greater multicultural literacy in teacher education and teaching in K–12 schools draw from recent theoretical and pedagogical frameworks for cultural competency and cultural responsiveness.

Gay (2000) defines culturally responsive teaching (CRT) as an approach that draws on student's cultural knowledge and prior experiences a foundation for acknowledging and affirming students' cultural heritages, forging connections between home communities and school, and as building blocks for meaningful and effective instruction. In short, CRT uses "cultural referents to impart knowledge, skills, and attitudes" (Ladson–Billings, 1992, p. 382). In her work with successful teachers of African American students, Ladson–Billings (1995) posited three criteria of a culturally relevant pedagogy: "(a) students must experience academic success; (b) students must develop and/or maintain cultural competence; and (c) students must develop a critical consciousness through which they challenge the status quo of the social order" (p. 160). A CRT practice for critical consciousness seeks to prepare preservice teachers to actively engage in a process of critique of "the cultural norms, values, mores, and institutions that produce and maintain social inequities" (p. 162), and in doing so, develop their roles as agents in addressing the conditions that shape their lives as active and able learners and citizens engaged in what Ladson–Billings and critical theorists describe as a pedagogy of opposition.

Grounded in reciprocal relationship with others, CRT requires that teachers draw on students' voice in the broadest sense, to engage them in the learning process. Building on student experiences and the cultural home/community knowledge, teachers may gain insight into how, why, and what students think and make sense of what they are learning. A review of literature on student voice by Ruddick and Flutter (2000), found that this careful attention and inclusion of student voice in school positively impacts student leaning, "especially when student voice is linked to changing curriculum and instruction" (p. 289). A culturally responsive approach to teaching, then, engages student voice and experience to enhance their understanding of how they learn and affirm and nurture students' sense of their abilities as capable learners (Nicholls, 1995).

Language Arts Project

The purpose of the 10-week project with the sixth graders was to support the development of language arts skills in an authentic setting. Written, oral, and reading skills were supported by preservice teachers helping sixth graders to write original stories and poems. The first two semesters of the project focused on connecting high-quality multicultural children's literature, with settings in urban communities, with sixth graders writing about their own urban community. As in Galettta and Jones's (2010) study using participatory action research to develop inquiry and advocacy skills in middle school youth by developing films about their community, this project would unfold as the preservice teachers, assigned to a sixth grader, would develop activities and work with their student each week to feature their community in story and poetry. Preservice teachers were taught to see the assets in the community and help the student feature positive aspects of their everyday world.

By the end of the project, the student would present his or her original story to the group in a final celebration that included parents, the sixth-grade language arts teachers, and the preservice teachers. Students would receive a book of their choice from the set of children's literature used during the project. One student selected the book *Ron's Big Mission*, an inspiring story based on a childhood incident in the life of the late Dr. Ron McNair, an African American astronaut. When he was asked why he selected that book, his response was, "Because he [boy on the cover] looks like me."

By the third semester, faculty meeting with the language arts staff at the middle school looked for ways to more closely support the required curriculum for sixth grade. It was suggested that the project focus on poetry as a framework for developing original stories. The language arts staff was enthusiastic and noted that it was difficult to get the sixth graders, especially those struggling with reading skills, to be interested in the typical poetry unit. The intention was for the preservice teachers to plan a unit of instruction on poetry, teaching it one-to-one with the sixth graders, and then guide the students in writing and performing original poetry. A graduate student in the university's administration program and a former middle school language arts teacher assisted in preparing the unit of poetry. University faculty brought poetry, specifically written by diverse poets, to share with the sixth graders. Students read and performed poems from works by Nikki Giovanni, Gwendolyn Brooks, Langston Hughes, Shel Silverstein, Maya Angelou, Emily Dickenson, Claribel Alegria, and Pat Mora, as well as poetry collections by various Latino and Asian poets and poetry anthologies showcasing the original voices of middle and high school youth.

Preservice teachers were responsible for bringing activities each week to help the sixth graders develop their poetry skills. A highlight of the program was the "poetry break" that was announced several times during the work session. Students would stand on the tables (a practice supported by the media specialist) and read poetry they were working on—either original or readings from famous poets.

The Project Moves

The program moved in fall 2011 to a nearby middle school, under the same principal, and flourished with a larger student population. At this site, preservice teachers were assigned two to three sixth graders to work with. The media specialist would not allow "poetry breaks" to include standing on the tables, so a step stool was substituted. In addition to the poetry unit, preservice teachers and sixth graders had access to technology bags to enhance their work. The bags had iPads, cameras, and laptops, and students were encouraged to explore elements of poetry, including imagery, figurative language, mood, rhythm, and meaning, in creative ways. Preservice teachers used music early in the semester to engage the students. One preservice teacher led a lesson with three sixth graders by saying, "Listen for the figurative language in this song;" soon lyrics from a Beyoncé song were part of the discussion, "To the left, to the left." The sixth graders were busy taking notes and sharing what they knew about the story the lyrics told. The use of information and communications technology (ICT) as part of the process of learning is a natural merging of what learners do during their social and out-of-school time with securing key concepts they will need in language arts (Stefl-Mabry et al., 2010). Recognizing and using technology as a tool to engage learners is another way of promoting student voice.

In their work with preservice teachers, sixth-grade "poets" expressed this sense of affirmation of their emerging voices and abilities as learners. As inexperienced novices in unfamiliar territory, participating preservice teachers understood that the only way to engage their learner was through uncovering who they were and what they thought, and then thoughtfully planning activities that tapped into the rich fount of their learner's personal knowledge. Many were successful in this endeavor, prompting this nod of gratitude from a student shortly after performing in the culminating Poetry Slam: "She was really nice and I would like to thank her because she helped me do things I never thought I could do." This reciprocity of understanding and the inclusion of student voice in directing and framing the learning process becomes a vital part of the relationship between teacher and learner and perhaps a first taste of the possibilities inherent in a culturally responsive approach.

When asked if the work with preservice teachers was important, Danielle said, "Ms. Rachel was nice, I liked her. She had a good personality and helped me. Some people [teachers] don't do nothing to help you; they expect you to do everything on your own. She helped me find poems. Then she helped me write them. I missed a few times and felt bad. I missed going to the elementary school and that was just terrible." Jasmine noted, "The teacher [preservice] made it fun because we used iPads to tape ourselves. She had us make up a poem with other people on Halloween. That was a lot of fun. Ms. Shelly never got upset; she encouraged us and made us feel better if we got stuck or didn't do ours good. She went with me on stage to read my poem during the Slam. That helped me not be afraid. I liked listening to her iPod. She brought her favorite music to share with us." As middle school students and preservice teachers formed meaningful relationships, the project included sharing stories and poems with elementary students.

Service Learning

The service-learning portion of this project was a two-level approach. It included preservice teachers providing a needed service at the middle school that supported students learning in small groups and one-to-one tutoring in language arts concepts and skills. It also involved putting the middle school students in a position of service learner when they shared picture books, poetry, and their original writing with a nearby elementary school, also a low-performing, urban school.

Studies indicate that "school-based service-learning programs with young adolescents have been shown to improve students' health and educational outcomes" (Bosma et al., 2010). The first step was for the middle school students to select a picture book to practice and read aloud to a small group of elementary students. Studies indicate that the use of picture books with older students is an effective way to engage struggling readers (Roser, Martinez, & Fowler-Amato, 2011).

When they went to the elementary school to read, nametags were made for the middle school students that identified them as "Poet," "Reader," and "Author." This activity served to build self-esteem in the middle school students by placing them in the position as role models for the elementary students. The teachers and the students in the elementary school were excited to host the middle school students, and each student's confidence in their ability to write a story or poem and read and perform it in front of an audience grew after this experience. For one, sixth-grade author Rico, the visit to the elementary school proved to be an important experience in building his confidence as both a learner and a "teacher." When asked how it felt to create and share his book with the younger students, he declared simply, "Yes. It made me feel smart." For LaShawn, a sixth grader who participated in the poetry project, the visit to the elementary school sparked her understanding of what and how she was learning, as well as providing her with the opportunity to act as teacher as she shared her burgeoning poetry knowledge. She stated, "My favorite part was when we went to elementary schools and showed the little kids all the fun things you could do with poetry and teaching them what we learned and how we learned it and why we learned it." Another young man, who was reluctant at times to work seriously on his project, was all business when he read aloud to the kindergarteners, asking them open-ended questions and pointing out key points of the story through the illustrations. When asked how he learned his book-sharing skills, he stated, "That is how my granny read to me and I liked it. It helps the little kids learn to read better."

One student, Dante, had difficulty focusing on the process of writing his story. His teachers identified him as a struggling reader. Dante was on the school football team and towered over his classmates and his university student mentor. He scoffed at reading picture books and for the first four weeks was disinclined to participate in the project. After the visit to the elementary school, the light came on for Dante. He began arriving in the media center with some of his writing ideas ready to implement. When complimented on his renewed focus, he replied, "Reading to the little kids was fun, man. They looked up to me. I want to get my book finished so I can show people."

The success of this project rested on meeting several key criteria for service-learning projects that required learners to engage in critical thinking, active participation, and reflective thinking. Both levels of the service-learning include all three criteria (Szente, 2008–2009). Reflective journals were required for both undergraduate and middle school students. Each session ended with an opportunity to write about what was accomplished during the session. At times, preservice teachers and middle school students used this time to make decisions as they planned for the next session. As co-teachers and co-learners together, preservice teachers and middle school students engaged in a dialogue of reciprocity in which they come to know each other through this mutual process of learning.

Reflective writings from the fourth meeting between sixth graders and preservice teachers yielded information to inform both university faculty and preservice teachers. Thirty-two students responded to two essential questions during a reflective writing activity: "So far, working on poetry is . . . and I want my teacher [pre-service] teacher to know . . . Twenty-six students mentioned terms like fun (14), awesome (4), cool (4), and good (2) to the first question (So far, working on poetry is . . .)." The comments for question two (I want my teacher [preservice] to know . . . was more varied. Many of the students wrote compliments like, "They are awesome," or "I like doing this." However, a few students wrote some statements that were more reflective, such as, "I can do things in life," "Get to know me," "That I am real and I am a good child and I can sing," and finally, "Thanks [for] not getting upset." A young man in a wheelchair, who had been discouraged from participating by his special education teacher, wrote the final comment. The week following this reflection, he read his original poetry aloud to the entire group. One of the classroom teachers commented, "He never says a word to anyone."

In contrast to the intensive group work that takes place in this program, it was rare that the classroom teachers at the middle school would use group work, because of discipline issues. The young poets and authors eagerly rose to the challenge of working in groups with relative ease. Because they were seen as valued partners in the process, and given the informal nature of the program, students were less inhibited in leading and suggesting reading, writing, and performance activities with new and unfamiliar classmates and preservice "mentors" as they worked and learned. Moreover, a space was provided for the middle school students to have a say in their learning as they engaged as scholars of their own experiences who, through opportunities for written and spoken expression and performance, rejected deficit labels and resisted the silence imposed by a tyranny of teaching. A culturally responsive approach offers rich possibilities for teacher education faculty, university–school partners, preservice teachers, and K–12 students to meaningfully respond to, and engage diversity at multiple sites through a humanizing pedagogy that places student's realities, histories and perspectives at the center of the educational practice and process (Bartolome, 1994).

Finding Their Voice

Each semester, this project continues to evolve as new members enter the communities of practice. School board members, the district superintendent, and other community leaders come to the school and read their favorite poems to the students. Each member is responsible and has a voice within this network of people who enjoy poetry and sharing it with others. This provides the voice that students need to express their thoughts and ideas, know that someone finds it valuable, and there are people within their community who want to hear what they have to say.

At the end of the each semester, faculty collect feedback from the language arts instructors, the preservice teachers, and the middle school students to inform the project for the next semester. They also collect samples of the experience that include copies of students' poems and stories, their weekly reflections, film of their performance at the end of the project, and anecdotal comments. Graduate students interview the students about their experience in the project and transcribe the interview tapes. Faculty review the tapes and field notes to identify emerging themes to inform ways to improve the project for the next semester.

At the end of one semester, one of the language arts teachers noted that one of the male students who was not a strong reader had given his classmates detailed descriptions of his work with the elementary school students and the importance of the story he was crafting to share with them in the future. The student said, "Yeah, I'm an author and we have to go read to the little kids so they learn to read better. I have to write a book for them."

The language arts teachers also explained that the students who were part of the project were typically the ones who were not given much voice in the classroom. As they struggled with reading and writing, many of the other students would ignore them or resist working with them on any project. Many times, the students did not complete or submit homework and fell further behind. Now, they were the ones selected for a special project with university students. It was important for the students to not seem foolish or lacking in any way in front of their university mentor. One of the language arts teachers noted, "They want to seem smart to the university students. They aren't going to do anything to jeopardize participating in the program during the week and they aren't going to do anything during their time with the university student so they can't come back. It is important to them to have this time with the university students—it is very special to them. They talk about their university teacher in class all the time." One of the students made this comment during a postproject interview, "It was fun working with people at my school and kids that go to [the university] and making books and seeing what I can do when I get older. " The data illuminated the many ways the middle school students were able to speak back to teachers and speak up for themselves and each other when given a challenging task, support for success, and an affirmation of their experiences and perspectives; in essence—the stage.

Conclusion

The communities of practice established between university faculty, preservice teachers, classroom teachers, and middle school students continues to evolve and move toward a transformational partnership, one of simultaneous renewal. At the heart of the work is the voice of students as they tell their stories, engage with university students who hope to be teachers, community members, and their classroom teachers who note the depth of the work they do within this project. Preservice teachers learn about their sixth-grade students through a framework based on culturally relevant teaching. They must discover what music their students like and how they live their lives, finding value as a catalyst to turn their students' experiences into stories and poems that can be illustrated, written down, and shared with each other, as well as with elementary students. The student voices that emerge from this project give credibility and power to that which is possible but never seems to come forth in the typical middle school classroom. Too many tests, a structured curriculum, and no opportunity to get to know each other drive the typical day in the classroom.

As this communities of practice grows within a culturally relevant teaching framework, university faculty and classroom teachers need to work to share information, regardless of the project at hand and blend projects initiated by the university with learning in the sixth-grade curriculum. The long-term goal is to move this project beyond the isolated space where sixth graders and university students come together once a week. As classroom teachers have the opportunity to hear their students' voices through their stories and poems, the opportunity to move this from unique project to institutionalized curriculum becomes a possibility.

Making room for student voice is essential if the project is to have relevance for the students beyond the chance to spend time with college students. In working with language arts teachers and co-developing writing themes with middle school students that encourage students to examine the realties of their lives, their school, and their communities, students can teach preservice teachers about the cultural strengths they bring to their learning. As preservice teachers build relationships with these scholars of their own experience, they develop authentic and culturally responsive ways of using these cultural funds of knowledge to build meaningful learning experiences grounded in the lives of their students, and in so doing, challenge preconceived deficit notions of students who may be culturally different from their teachers. Weaving a community of diverse learners and preservice teachers together with poetry, multicultural literature, picture books, and learning through service is essential to developing a layered experience that centers student voices. Ongoing engagement in developing communities of practice, such as the language arts project discussed here, "requires that, as teachers/ learners, we each give ourselves to the process of transformation through our own personal means and in dialogue with others" (Freire, 1998, p. 126). As the middle school students test their voices as learners, emerging scholars of their own experiences, and partners in a learning journey, so too do preservice teachers learn the value of their critical voices, through asking questions and in dialogue with their classmates and their students. It is within this rich community of difference that the evolving dialogues between and among the powerful bright voices of 20 fledgling poets and their emerging young teachers that transformation becomes more than just a notion. It becomes poetry.

References

Banks, J. A. (1997). *Teaching strategies for ethnic studies* (6th ed.). Needham Heights, MA: Allyn and Bacon.

Banks, J. A., & Banks, C. A. (1999). *Multicultural education: Issues and perspectives* (3rd ed.). New York: John Wiley.

Barab, S. A., & Duffy, T. M. (2000). From practice fields to communities of practice. In D. Jonassen & S. Land (Eds.), *Theoretical foundations of learning environments* (pp. 25–55). Mahwah, NJ: Erlbaum.

Bartolome, L. (1994). Beyond the methods fetish: Toward a humanizing pedagogy. *Harvard Educational Review, 64,* 173–194.

Bell, L. A. (2002). Sincere fictions: The pedagogical challenges of preparing White teachers for multicultural classrooms. *Equity & Excellence in Education, 35*(3), 236–244.

Bosma, L. M., Sieving, R. M., Ericson, A., Russ, P., Cavender, L., & Bonnie, M. (2010). Elements for successful collaboration between K–8 school, community, and university partners: The Lead Peace partnership. *Journal of School Health, 80*(10), 501–507.

Buysse, V., Sparkman, K. L, & Wesley, P. W. (2003). Communities of practice: Connecting what we know with what we do. *Exceptional Children, 69*(3), 263–277.

Catapano, S., Huisman, S., & Song, K. H. (2008, March). Are we there yet? Perspectives from partners in a community of practice. *Learning Communities: International Journal of Learning in Social Contexts, 1,* 2–20.

Diller, J. V., & Moule, J. (2005). *Cultural competence: A primer for educators.* Belmont, CA: Thomas Wadsworth.

Ediger, M. (2003). The psychology of improving teacher quality. *Education, 124*(2), 321–328.

Freire, P. (1998). *Pedagogy of freedom: Ethics, democracy, and civic courage.* Lanham, MD: Rowman and Littlefield.

Galetta, A., & Jones, V. (2010). "Why are you doing this?" Questions on purpose, structure, and outcomes in participatory action research engaging youth and teacher candidates. *Educational Studies, 46*(3), 337–357.

Gay, G. (2000). *Culturally responsive teaching: Theory, research and practice.* New York: Teachers College Press.

Hefflin, B. R. (2002). Learning to develop culturally relevant pedagogy: A lesson about cornrowed lives. *Urban Review, 33*(2), 131–149.

Hubbard, J. (2011, March). Three student perspectives: An introduction. *Voices From the Middle, 18*(3), 37–48.

Ladson-Billings, G. (1992). Reading between the lines and beyond the pages: A culturally relevant approach to literacy teaching. *Theory Into Practice, 31*(4), 312–320.

Ladson-Billings, G. (1995). But that's just good teaching! The case for culturally relevant pedagogy. *Theory Into Practice, 34*(3), 159–165.

Lave, J., & Wenger, E. (1991). *Situated learning: Legitimate peripheral participation.* New York: Cambridge University Press.

McIntyre, A. (1997). *Making meaning of whiteness: Exploring racial identity with white teachers.* Albany: State University of New York Press.

Murrell, P. C., Jr. (2001). *The community teacher: A new framework for effective urban teaching.* New York: Teachers College Press.

Nicholls, J. G. (1995, March). *What knowledge is of most worth? Student perspectives.* Paper presented at the Biennial Meeting of the Society for Research in Child Development, New Orleans, LA.

North Carolina Department of Public Instruction. (2011). *North Carolina school report cards.* Retrieved from http://www.ncreportcards.org/src/

Palmer, P. J. (2007). *The courage to teach: Exploring the inner landscape of a teacher's life.* New York: John Wiley & Sons.

Roser, N., Martinez, M., & Fowler-Amato, M. (2011). The power of picturebooks: Resources that support language and learning in middle grade classrooms. *Voices From the Middle, 19*(1), 24–31.

Ruddick, J., & Flutter, J. (2000). Pupil participation and perspective: "Carving a new order of experience." *Cambridge Journal of Education, 30*(1), 75–89.

Rumberger, R., & Lim, S. A. (2008, October). *Why students drop out of school: A review of 25 years of research* (Policy Brief No. 15). Santa Barbara: University of California–Santa Barbara.

Sleeter, C. (2001). Preparing teachers for culturally diverse schools research and the over-whelming presence of whiteness. *Journal of Teacher Education, 52*(2), 94–106.

Stefl-Mabry, J., Radlick, M., & Doane, W. (2010). Can you hear me now? Student voice: High school and middle school students' perceptions of teachers, ICT and learning. *International Journal of Education and Development Using Information and Communication Technology, 6*(4), 64–82.

Szente, J. (2008–2009). Academic enrichment programs for culturally and linguistically diverse children: A service-learning experience. *Childhood Education, 85*(2), 113–117.

Teitel, L. (2008–2009). School/community collaboration: The power of transformative relationships. *Childhood Education, 85*(2), 75–80.

Thompson, C. (2008–2009). Infusing multicultural principles in urban teacher preparation programs. *Childhood Education, 85*(2), 86–90.

Thompson, S., & Smith, D. (2005). Creating highly qualified teachers for urban schools. *The Professional Educator, 27*(1), 73–88.

Wenger, E. (1998). *Communities of practice: Learning, meaning, and identity.* Cambridge, MA: Cambridge University Press.

Wiggins, G. (2011, Spring). Giving students a voice: The power of feedback to improve teaching. *Educational Horizons, 89*(3), 23–26.

6
LISTENING TO K–12 STUDENTS' ADVICE

Barbara Morgan-Fleming

Finding and using the strengths of urban schools and communities is vital if we want to achieve our goal of educating all students for the future. One such strength that I discuss in this chapter is the voice of K–12 students. To hear this voice, those of us in university committees need to establish the on-going partnerships that will make K–12 students and teachers comfortable talking with us.

The partnership between Best Elementary (pseudonym) and Texas Tech's College of Education has been in place over 15 years. During this time, field-based methods classes have been taught at Best, graduate and undergraduate students have been involved in tutoring programs, and activities such as field trips have been conducted in partnership between the two schools. Best Elementary is a Title I school with a student population that is primarily minority and economically disadvantaged. It is also high achieving, receiving excellent rankings on a variety of state tests.

I began teaching Language Arts methods at Best over 10 years ago. In the first year, I partnered with a teacher who had been at the school more than five years. He was experienced at teaching field-based methods courses, and had close relationships with the school principal, as well as with teachers and students. Walking down the hall with him, I saw students wave and greet him, and I watched him interact with Best teachers to educate the college and elementary students. After his retirement, I began teaching a post-bac Language Arts methods course at Best, and have continued to the present time.

At times, we in academia argue that there is a conflict between service, teaching, and research. Field-based partnerships allow these areas to overlap in a meaningful way. Tutoring elementary students and participating in activities such as judging poetry contests or supervising field trips allows me to contribute to the success of Best students, while keeping me involved with contexts and skills necessary to be a successful teacher, thus informing my teaching in higher education. Working as tutors and classroom helpers at Best benefits my students, and also helps the students and teachers at Best by providing more opportunities for individual instruction. My long-term relationship with students at Best Elementary helps make them comfortable sharing their ideas and wisdom with me. It is then my pleasure to pass those ideas on to the public.

I frequently tell preservice teachers in my field placed methods class that the students they teach are the only ones who watch current teaching all day every day, and while the public and national conversation about teaching may focus on averages, the insights of individual students are helpful in breaking down stereotypes and helping teachers understand that teaching is a complex phenomenon. K–12 students' voices also remind us that, while it might be comforting to invent simple, universal solutions to "educate everyone," to be successful, an educator must be able to view the world through a variety of lenses. Talking with individual students is vital if we want to succeed. As I tell my preservice students, "every child can learn, but not in the same way."

I first learned the importance of students' voices when I had the dual roles of graduate student and elementary school teacher. I published several articles (Morgan-Fleming, 1999, 2000; Morgan-Fleming & Doyle, 1997), attempting to show the alliances and contradictions between the two roles. While the two roles provided different perspectives, I also found both viewpoints important in helping myself and my students learn. As practitioners, it is sometimes tempting to reject the "ivory tower," just as academics may reject the insights of individual teachers and students. I often point out to my graduate students that every-day questions such as, "What knowledge has value? Why? and Who decides?" have been discussed by philosophers for some time, and that, while the language may be different than educators use on a daily basis, teachers' answers to these questions are important to include in the conversation (see Morgan-Fleming, 2010).

In this chapter, I draw on previous work that I have done at Best Elementary. Working in a school with a population that is predominately African American, 93% free and reduced lunch, and high achieving is extremely important in breaking down stereotypes my preservice students (who are predominately white, middle class) may bring to class.

The principal has been at the school for 18 years, and has an exceptional talent for finding creative teachers who can make sure students pass tests (important in Texas), but can also creatively apply their knowledge in a variety of situations. Several other faculty members from Texas Tech also tutor at the school, and one, Doug Simpson, has found funding to pay for all the fifth graders to visit Albuquerque or Dallas. My preservice students help plan activities and accompany the students on the trip, which includes visits to zoos, museums, and universities.

In this chapter, I try to include the voice of K–12 students in our educational conversations, hoping that these voices can potentially change the thinking of administrators, policy makers, researchers, and the public at large. We need to understand that everyone has something to teach, and something to learn, and that including multiple voices in the conversation benefits us all.

Theoretical Framework

As Apple (1979) reminds us,

> any serious appraisal of the role of education and curriculum in a complex society must have as a major part of its analysis at least three elements. It needs to situate the knowledge, the school and the educator him- or herself within the real social conditions that "determine" these elements. (p. 40)

This points to the importance of multiple partnerships with schools. Partnerships are important for future educators, but also for citizens who have a great effect on public schools. Teaching is a complex phenomenon, and it is therefore important that we offer multiple representations of teaching. As Cornell (1993) states, "what we need may be more stories not fewer, braided tales woven from multiple points of view rather than the illusionary objectivity of the supposedly omniscient narrator" (p. 332).

This goal is especially important with reference to African American students. Tucker et al. (2000) point to the importance of including this group in discussions about education:

> The views of African-American students, whom are, perhaps, the real experts regarding problems that occur among themselves, are often excluded from this theorizing and intervention planning. Several benefits may arise from requesting the opinions of African-American students. For example, students may generate novel insights and interventions for boosting school success that have been overlooked by education experts and researchers. Additionally, students may participate more fully in policies and intervention programs that included their input. (p. 206)

Understanding the importance of shared power in relationships is important here, too. We must understand that those who usually dominate the conversation about education (adults with economic and professional power) do not have all the necessary information to improve education. As Nicholls (1992) states:

> if students were seen as active theorists, their theories might be given more attention in school. Rather than attempting to manipulate students' theories, teachers and researchers might treat them the way scientists

> should treat other scientists with divergent theories: by engaging in dialogue where it is uncertain whether one perspective will prevail or a new one will emerge. . .young children are capable of spirited discussion of the nature and point of what they learn in school and can see such discussion as a valuable way of figuring out what matters in school and how to learn. (p. 280)

Hegel (as cited in Jackson, 2011) also offers insight into the importance of dissent and dialogue:

> Identity is merely the determination of the simple immediate, of dead being; but contradiction is the root of all movement and vitality; it is only in so far as something has a contradiction within it that it moves, has an urge and activity. (p. 5)

The importance of hearing individual voices in particular settings is something that has been addressed by philosophers since ancient times. Engaging diverse voices in conversations about education can also help teacher educators and researchers refine and adapt our methods and practices. When I was in the dual roles of fifth-grade teacher and graduate student in a philosophy of education course, I published an article (Morgan, 1993) that offered the following conclusion:

> The tension which exists between the rigorous philosophical form of practical argument and the day-to-day practice of teaching is a useful one. The demands of teaching are complex, and teachers must be able to manage competing and at times mutually exclusive goals. That very complexity, however, can cause one to lose one's sense of meaning and reason. The use of a rigorous analytical model to reflect on teaching action then serves as a way to maintain some elevation and perspective, but no analytical framework can completely encompass the complexity of teaching performed. The ill fit between teaching practice and formal models of teaching can be mutually beneficial, pushing the teacher to make explicit certain reasoning about actions in order that such reasoning can become vulnerable to change, and challenging formal models to deal with the practice of day-to-day teaching. (p. 124)

Voices From Best Elementary

This section offers an opportunity to view the advice of students from Best Elementary published previously (Morgan-Fleming, Kendrick-Mercer, Myers, & Anderson, 2008; Morgan-Fleming, Marbley, & White, 2005). The original writing

is provided so that student voices are heard, not synthesized. Pseudonyms are used throughout.

In a previous book chapter (Morgan-Fleming et al., 2005), I worked with a Best teacher and Texas Tech colleagues to gain insights from my "grandstudents." This term emerged when I told a fifth grader that his teacher was good because she had been my student. He said, "That makes you our grandteacher." I had not thought of myself as a grandteacher, but it is a role I now cherish. Best students were asked to write letters to preservice teachers, advising them on what they needed to learn and do to be good teachers. Following are their letters and pictures (reproduced with the kind permission of Emerald Group Publishing) illustrating their ideas about what makes teaching work.

Don't be so strict.
Have a game day once a week.
Don't be so nice.
Have a tutoring class (AST) (After School Tutoring)
Have a snack time between 9 and 10 o'clock.
Don't be so scared on your first time teaching at school.
Nikendra (letter 1)

You should always help children to see what they are learning and you should always be nice to your students, and when you leave and then come back they will have a welcoming sign or something because they missed you! Also, you must be patient. You have to be patient because you have to know that not everybody learns fast.

Joletha (letter 2)

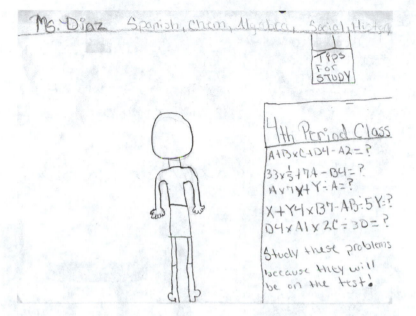

Ms. Diaz   Spanish, Chem, Algebra, Social, History

Tips For STUDY

4th Period Class

$A+B \times C+D4-A2=?$
$33 \times \frac{1}{3} + 74 - B4 = ?$
$A \vee 7 \times Y + Y \div A = ?$
$X + Y4 \times B7 - AB \div 5Y = ?$
$D4 \times A1 \times 2C \div 3D = ?$

Study these problems because they will be on the test!

Dear Future Teacher,

I just have a few recommendations on how I think of a good teacher. For one thing, don't start out being strict or very, very nice. What I mean by being very, very nice is by giving us candy and treating us like kindergarten. Now, being too strict will not gain a bond between students.

Being on time, now that's a good one. When students wait for the teacher to come (they) can start something. What can happen is that we might start talking real loud, and start playing games that are not appropriate for school. Now don't get me wrong, but I'm always late to school so I really don't know what happens in the mornings in the library.

To make kids feel like learning isn't boring, play games, give good examples and explanations. Now, learning doesn't seem so boring.

When your class gets ready for a break, you'll start talking and then you'll start to get off topic, in your classroom during learning. It's okay to get lost in a subject except in class. That's how to maintain your focus.

To help kids with work they didn't understand, find a technique to help them when they are at home doing homework. It could be helpful for one student, but not for all.

This is a great letter to help teachers.

Tamesha (letter 3)

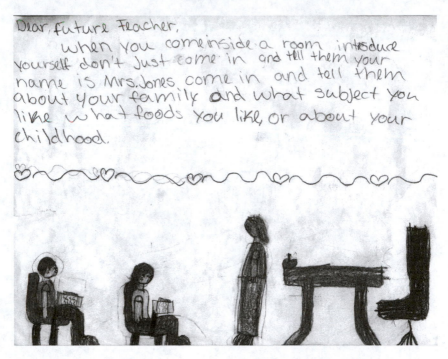

Dear Future Teacher,

When you come inside a room, introduce yourself. Don't just come in and tell them your name is Mrs. Jones. Come in and tell them about your family and what subject you like, what foods you like, or about your childhood.

Amimee (letter 4)

Dear Future Teacher,

If you are my future, I would prefer you to:
not be too strict or too nice
be on time
do what's right
stay on task
make kids happy
play games
get people's attention
give good explanations
work the problem with kids
keep control of yourself
participate in what some of the kids do
give kids something if the kids are doing good like M&Ms, Skittles, or Laffy
Taffy
have good expectations for
your kids

Donna (letter 5)

On another occasion, the students were given the following handout and asked to complete it (Morgan-Fleming et al., 2008):

Draw a good teacher
What's in her/his head?   What's in his/her heart?
How should teacher educators help people become good teachers?
Following are the students' answers to each of the four questions:

- Math, reading, algebra, social studies, science. (Bill)
- In her/his head they should think how should they make students learn but have fun. (Mary)
- Knowledge. What they need to know to be a teacher. (Debby)
- Not to be prejudiced to other people. To be kind to others. To be patient with others if they are doing it too long. (Peggy)
- How will I make this day as educated as possible? (Katy)
- "Education is a key." Smart role model. (Sarah)
- Teach children to love one another. Always have a smile. (Sam)
- She wants me to do what I can, wants me to achieve all that I can, and wants me to be a leader not a follower. She is behind me 100%. (John)
- I'm going to show my students what they got to learn to go on. (Doug)
- Brain, knowledge, what they need to know to be a good teacher (Kelly)

What's in his or her heart?

- Blood, ability to listen to kids. (Bill)
- In the teacher's heart they should love all the students. (Mary)
- They do not need to be prejudiced. They need to tell students they are doing well. (Debby)
- Not to be mad at others when they are mad at somebody else. To be responsible to work with others. To have faith in others. (Peggy)
- I love to teach these hard workers. (Katy)
- Attitude. (Sarah)
- Have fun and be willing to help others out and teach them to their full potential. (Sam)
- To never ever give up. Do not want to yell all the time at one person. Let the students have a little fun every blue moon? (John)
- Teacher educators can help teachers by giving them more education and passion. To teach a teacher to be patient you have to be patient with them. (Doug)
- A good person, an excellent teacher, a trustworthy person. (Kelly)

Because I wanted advice not only for preservice teachers but also for teacher educators, on the back of the handout students were asked, "How should teacher educators help people become good teachers?" This question was harder for the students, so I explained that it was my job as a teacher educator to help college students become good teachers. I found the students' advise relevant and inspiring.

How should teacher educators help people become good teachers?

- Show how to keep their cool and not get mad. Take time to listen. Respect their boss and show respect. (Bill)
- The teacher educators should let the student teacher learn before they start teaching, and to make them patient, you have to be a role model so they can be like you. (Mary)
- Teacher educators can help others by tuffing them up and teaching them the math, science, reading and social studies. We can also send them to other schools to see how to do that certain kind of thing. To teach a teacher to be patient, you got to be patient yourself. (Debby)
- Teach others not to judge people by the way they look or act by asking teachers that are nonprejudiced how not to be prejudiced. When you are mad before you come to work you should not take it out on others like your students. Not to tell others you do not want to work with them because they will feel bad. (Peggy)
- Learn more to teach more, and to be a strong and caring teacher so you can do and know more about the child and *NOT* be prejudiced. Smile and make them feel better. Help them with their anger against others. If you are talking to the child, ask if they dream of anything and if they are having problems. (Katy)
- I think they should experience college success, fun, knowledge, happy, victory, patience, responsible, smile, kindness, athletic, against prejudice, algebra, mathematics, understanding science, passion, calm attitude, available, dependable. (Sarah)
- To become a leader you have to be a follower. Lead them to education and success, because it is the key to victory. Teachers have to know how to spell. Kids need to know knowledge. Teachers cannot be prejudiced to one either. Maybe have some experience with the life they are going through. Try to have some friends and teach them with respect and with love not hatred. Show and tell about your life and how it got better. Have history of all the people we know. (Sam)
- Stay on them. Teach them not to be mean. Show them not to be prejudiced. Tell them it's okay to have fun. Teach them to do the right thing. Tell them why it is good to work with one another. Give them some homework. Teach them not to pick on one student because others are. To help, teach them how to be nice. (John)
- By teaching them not to be prejudiced, to be kind to students and treat others like you want to be treated. (Doug)
- You teach them. You tell them to stand up for myself. You do what you have to do. You have to model what they need to do to slow your rode with the students. (Kelly)

What We Can Learn From Fifth Graders

The students from Best Elementary provide advice that is useful for all partners in education, whether they be researchers, teacher educators, K–12 current or future teachers, policy makers or parents. While their individual voices and perspectives are important to maintain, there are also suggestions made by many that would improve education. What follows is a summary of those suggestions.

First, the students advise challenging prejudice in ourselves as well as in others. I often tell students in my methods class that everyone has lenses and blind spots, and diverse conversations are often the only way to realize what our blind spots are. While we as teacher educators may frequently speak of the importance of overcoming prejudice, hearing these statements from fifth-grade students helps our students understand the importance of challenging the assumptions they may bring into classrooms.

Best students also advise that we work with, and have faith in others, and focus on instruction. Both of these ideas are important to new teachers. They need to understand that schools are a community, and that to be successful they must create opportunities for real dialogue with other teachers, parents, and administrators. It is also important to work hard on creating lessons that effectively teach the curriculum to every student in the room. Best students also offer excellent advise about management, advising future teachers not to be too strict, but also not to be too nice. This helps future teachers understand the importance of balance in management—making sure that their classroom is a caring environment where every child can concentrate on learning.

Finally, these students talk about the importance of tenacity. Many of us assume that we don't have the power to change education. These students' voices help us realize, that small changes can have large effects for individual students, and are definitely worth the effort.

Conclusions

It is my hope that this chapter, and the other chapters in this book, will help us understand the importance of partnerships in education. Particular, diverse voices help us understand the complexity of education, and motivate us to creatively adjust to a changing world.

These conversations also help us remember why we became educators, and motivate us to generate and institutionalize high, pragmatic ideals. Let's listen to each other and do what's right.

References

Apple, M. W. (1979, Winter). On analyzing hegemony. *The Journal of Curriculum Theorizing*, *1*(1), 10–43.

Jackson, P. (2011, February 1). Speaking of thinking: A beginner's guide to Hegel's *Science of Logic, Part 1*. *Teachers College Record*, 1–11.

Morgan, B. A. (1993). Practical rationality: A self-investigation. *Journal of Curriculum Studies*, *25*(2), 115–124.

Morgan-Fleming, B. (1999, Fall). Teaching as performance: Connections between folklore and education. *Curriculum Inquiry, 29*(3), 273–292.

Morgan-Fleming, B. (2000, Fall). Characteristics of the teaching art and nature of competencies that insure learning. *Education, 121*(1), 159–168.

Morgan-Fleming, B. (2010). Dewey, Aristotle, and you. In D. Fehr & M. Fehr (Eds.), *Teach boldly* (pp. 57–66). New York: Peter Lang.

Morgan-Fleming, B., & Doyle, W. (1997, August). Children's interpretations of curriculum events. *Teaching and Teacher Education, 13*(5), 499–511.

Morgan-Fleming, B., Kendrick-Mercer, M., Myers, S., & Anderson, C. W. (2008). The wisdom of fifth graders: A voice in the renaissance. In C. J. Craig & L. F. Deretchin (Eds.), *Teacher education yearbook XVI: Imagining a renaissance in teacher education* (pp. 118–130). Lanham, MD: Rowan and Littlefield.

Morgan-Fleming, B., Marbley, A., & White, J. (2005). Letters from my grandstudents: Recommendations for future teachers. In J. Brophy & S. Pinnegar (Eds.), *Learning from research on teaching: Perspective, methodology, and representation* (pp. 75–93). New York: Elsevier.

Nicholls, J. G. (1992). Students as educational theorists. In D. H. Schunk & J. L. Meece (Eds.), *Student perceptions in the classroom* (pp. 267–286). Hillsdale, NJ: Erlbaum.

Tucker, C. M., Herman, K. C., Keith, C., Pedersen, T., Vogel, D., & Reinke, W. (2000). Student-generated solutions to enhance the academic success of African American youth. *Child Study Journal, 30*(3), 205–222.

Turner, V. (1986). Images and reflections: Ritual, drama, carnival, film, and spectacle in cultural performance. In *The anthropology of performance* (pp. 30–36). New York: PAJ.

PART IV

Focus on Practicing Teachers and Schools

7

TRANSFORMATIONS IN SITE-BASED TEACHER PREPARATION COURSES

The Benefits of Challenges

Jill V. Jeffery and Jody N. Polleck

If you ask a teacher whether she'd like to participate in a university-initiated program in her school, don't be surprised if her response is something like, "What's in it for us?" Though many teacher educators and researchers assume benefits of their involvement in K–12 contexts, such benefits may not be obvious to school-site stakeholders, who face increasing demands on their time in increasingly hostile political environments. School leaders might speak to you of the "burden" that outside involvement places on schools and their staff; and principals and teachers might view this burden as robbing students of vital educational resources. In the high-poverty urban school context we examine here, the burden of collaboration is perhaps even heftier, as such schools have greater needs and fewer resources to share.

To hone in on the issue of burden in university–school collaborations, we examined one school's perceptions regarding the challenges and benefits of implementing a partnership initiative. The partnership model we investigate here involves the co-instruction of a teacher preparation course situated in a neighboring school. The typical burdens shouldered by schools participating in the site-based, co-instructed course model are substantial: Schools provide classroom spaces in which university courses meet, and devote time and energy to managing logistical issues, such as scheduling classroom observations. Further, a co-instruction model places additional demands on school-site teachers, since they share equal responsibility with collaborating university professors. This means that, as co-instructors, host-school teachers face the added task of achieving with a partner an acceptable degree of consensus with respect to instructional goals, lessons plans, and assessment of student progress (Musanti & Pence, 2010).

How, then, might universities participate in the work of schools in ways that are, in the eyes of school stakeholders, transformational rather than burdensome?

To address this question, we investigated a school–university partnership model that was designed with the goal of achieving reciprocity. Through an analysis of emic perspectives regarding the challenges and benefits of implementing and sustaining a partnership initiative, we explore how school stakeholders viewed the burdens involved in working with a university.

Education scholars have long argued that universities and K–12 schools must work as partners in teacher education so as to narrow gaps between preservice preparation and in-service practice (e.g., Anagnostopoulos, Smith, & Basmadjian, 2007; Bullough & Draper, 2004; Darling-Hammond & Baratz-Snowden, 2007; Patterson, 1999). In theory, these school–university collaborations achieve "simultaneous renewal" wherein the members of each institution contribute to the building of a "mutually beneficial relationship" (Goodlad, 1993, p. 29). However, because partnerships are commonly initiated by universities, research on the outcomes of these efforts has typically focused on benefits and challenges for university, rather than host-school, stakeholders (e.g., Adams, Bondy, & Kuhel, 2005; Darling-Hammond & Baratz-Snowden, 2007). Partnership logic assumes that schools benefit because institutional collaboration contributes to the effective development of teachers' dispositions, knowledge, and skills. But do school stakeholders perceive these and other benefits? And if so, do they view benefits of collaboration as a fair trade for the work that it requires? Thus far, school staff perspectives have been underrepresented in scholarship around school–university partnerships. To address this gap, we examined the views of teachers and the principal from one urban high school regarding their collaboration with a university teacher preparation program.

Our inquiry is situated within the context of a partnership joining New York University (NYU) with New York City public secondary schools in the goal of preparing teachers to thrive in urban classrooms. With the support a grant-funded initiative in partnership with the New York City Department of Education, NYU began situating foundational teacher education courses in neighboring secondary schools, so that preservice teachers might benefit from direct contact with urban schools, with the expectation that this effect would be enhanced when the courses were co-instructed by host schoolteachers and university professors. Additionally, this partnership model was designed so that host schools might develop capacity alongside the aspiring teachers enrolled in site-based university courses.

To examine the extent to which school stakeholders perceived such effects, our inquiry addressed two questions: (a) What benefits and challenges are perceived by school stakeholders as being associated with a site-based co-instruction partnership model? (b) To what extent, if at all, do school stakeholders view collaboration with a university as a viable strategy for transforming their school? Throughout this chapter, we emphasize the potential for schools to be transformed through collaboration with universities. However, in doing so, we do not wish to lose sight of the mutually transformative possibilities for school–university partnerships. That is, in transforming schools, universities will, or should, likewise be transformed by developing understandings of what it means, and what it takes, to prepare teachers to thrive in culturally rich urban schools.

Partnership Theory of Action

Research suggests that graduates from site-based teacher education programs (e.g., professional development schools) are better prepared to teach than are graduates from conventional campus-based programs (Darling-Hammond & Baratz-Snowden, 2007). However, though universities and host schools, in theory, benefit reciprocally from partnerships (e.g., Shroyer, Yahnke, Bennett, & Dunn, 2007; Trachtman, 2007), researchers have repeatedly noted conflict between these institutions, citing issues of "distrust and wariness" by the K–12 teachers toward university faculty and students (Lewison & Holliday, 1997, p. 105). Lewison and Holliday (1997) discuss "unequal power" (p. 106) among participants, suggesting that imbalances can be leveled when site-school teachers enact greater authority and control in instruction and research conducted at their schools. White, Deegan, and Allexsaht-Snider (1997) propose that collaborating researchers and practitioners should critically examine how power shifts are occurring and evolving, looking at how roles and relationships are sustained to promote development and durability of collaborative structures.

Intercultural Competence

The urban context of our study is important in that central to the partnership's objectives is the preparation of teachers to work in urban schools, whose strengths, weaknesses, and institutional goals are often not experienced nor understood by university students who may look, sound, and behave very differently from the students they will eventually teach. Research regarding the need to prepare a predominantly White, middle-class teaching force to work in culturally diverse urban schools suggests that aspiring teachers need well-structured support for field-based work if they are to develop the sensitivity they need to teach effectively (Wiggins, Follo, & Eberly, 2007); failure to provide such support can lead to reinforcement of negative stereotypes regarding students in urban schools (Sleeter, 2001). Recent evidence suggests that carefully designed site-based teacher education programs may enhance aspiring teachers' engagement with urban communities (Shirley et al., 2006) and serve to develop their intercultural competence (Adams et al., 2005).

However, the success of partnership programs hinges on "the elaboration and enactment" of their inherent features" (Zeichner & Conklin, 2008, p. 285). The existence of programs aimed at bringing preservice teachers into deeper engagement with urban schools and surrounding communities does not guarantee they will develop the skills and dispositions they need to teach effectively in these environments. A goal of our project, then, was to explore aspects of the partnership model that urban schoolteachers view as facilitating preservice teachers' development of intercultural competence.

Teacher Professional Development

The partnership model we examine uses an underresearched teacher professional development model: that of enlisting schoolteachers to serve as teacher educators in university programs. Researchers have identified transformational effects of this model (Perry, Walton, & Conroy, 1998; Russell & Chapman, 2001), including improved mentoring skills, enhanced involvement in school leadership roles, and increased appreciation for the interdependence of theory and practice. However, though employing in-service teachers as university teacher educators has been identified in this research as a means of transforming teacher practice, we do not yet understand the particular program features that contributed to teacher transformations.

The dearth of opportunities for collaborative professional development and career growth, or the development of communities of practice within schools, has been identified as a reason that new teachers leave the classroom (Smith & Ingersoll, 2004). Research in teacher professional development (TPD) suggests that for teachers to transform their practice, they need opportunities to engage in activities that honor their professional experience, relate directly to their practices, offer intrinsic motivation, and enhance collaboration (Beavers, 2009; Hiemstra & Brockett, 1994; King, 2004; Musanti & Pence, 2010; Taylor, 2006). The role of collaboration is essential to effective TPD, because these experiences allow teachers to reflect critically on the relationships between their theories and practices by disrupting the status quo. University teacher education programs may be able to assist in this kind of development if they can establish egalitarian institutional relationships with schools. The partnership model examined in this study assumes that co-instruction will assist practicing teachers in developing their own knowledge and skills by facilitating collaborative and critical inquiry with university faculty and students. Because the partnership theory of action we have described was conceptualized by university rather than school-site stakeholders, we were curious as to the extent to which teachers at a host school perceived these and other intended benefits. What were the burdens of implementing and sustaining the model, and to what extent were these viewed by school staff as worthwhile? We investigated perceived challenges and benefits of the partnership by examining questionnaire, field observation, and interview data obtained from schoolteachers and administrators involved in this model.

Partnership Context

University Context

The context of this study is a partnership between NYU and 19 secondary schools in high-poverty, culturally diverse New York City neighborhoods. We narrow the scope of our inquiry to focus on the co-instruction of a foundational teacher education course, Inquiries, at one partner school, Creative Works High School (CWHS).[1] Aspiring elementary and secondary teachers at the university are required to take one semester of Inquiries, the purpose of which is to provide students with a foundational understanding of educational theories, along with a space in which to investigate how these theories are enacted in practice. Students explore such issues as how knowledge is constructed, what constitutes effective instruction, how the politics of education affect classroom practice, and what benefits are associated with enacting culturally responsive pedagogy. Meeting at partner schools allows much of the class time to be spent on classroom observations, which provide springboards for discussions where students can reconcile the pedagogical concepts they read about with the realities of urban schooling. Though Inquiries instructors are provided with a list of required core texts and a syllabus template, they are encouraged to experiment with innovative instructional approaches. Thus, the individual sections of the course vary depending on the instructors and the host schools in which classes are taught.

School-Site Context

For the 2008–2009 school year, CWHS served approximately 400 students, of whom 59% are Latino, 33% African American/Black, 4% Asian or Native Hawaiian/Other Pacific Islander, 3% White, and 1% Native American/Alaskan Native. Receiving Title I funds, the school has a 77% poverty rate. Of this population, 19% of CWHS students receive special education services, and 5% are English language learners with Individual Language Plans. A recent progress report (2007–2008) gave the school an "A rating" when compared to similar schools in the city, as it demonstrated Adequate Yearly Progress for English language arts and math. Specifically, 67% of CWHS students passed the state's English Exam and 77% passed the Math Exam.

Although CWHS is a high-poverty school, it is perhaps inaccurate to label the school as "underresourced," given its professional composition. The principal, Kyle, attributes the school's success to the hiring of well-trained professional teachers. Emphasizing a mission of college preparation, the teaching staff consists of seven administrators and other professionals and 38 teachers, of whom 100% are licensed, 37% have been teaching for more than five years, 84% have master's degrees, and 92% are designated as "highly qualified" by NCLB/SED criteria. We focus on CWHS because it has the longest history within the NYU partnership. The strength of the relationship between CWHS and the university may be due to the fact that several key individuals have long been in place at CWHS and the university. For example, the second author, Jody, obtained her doctoral degree from NYU and has worked at CWHS for nine years. Additionally, several university doctoral students have taught at the school, and many CWHS teachers are graduates of NYU's teacher preparation programs. Another factor in the strength of the collaboration is the disposition of the CWHS principal, whose support is based on his belief that the model will augment professional growth for university students and CWHS teachers. As a result of this long-standing relationship, multiple Inquiries courses have been held at the school over the past six years.

Researcher Perspectives

The first author, Jill, was responsible for coordinating and researching partnership initiatives from 2006–2010. In spring 2009, she co-instructed a course with a CWHS math teacher at a partner middle school, an experience through which she developed greater insight into the model's challenges and benefits. As of the writing of this chapter, Jody continues to teach a tenth-grade English Language Arts class at CWHS and also is an Assistant Professor at Hunter College. She has previously worked as the school's literacy coach and as an NYU–CWHS partnership liaison.

Data Sources

We examined a variety of data sources representing multiple perspectives: field notes from two Inquiries class observations; CWHS co-instructor electronic questionnaires; and an in-depth interview with the CWHS principal. Observation field notes include participants' verbatim speech when relevant to this study's research questions. Questionnaires were emailed to the five teachers at CWHS who co-taught at least one Inquiries course between 2006–2009 (Appendix A); all five returned complete responses. The interview with CWHS's principal was semistructured with a protocol (Appendix B).

Methods of Analysis

We used a combination of inductive and deductive procedures to generate code labels from our data sources (Miles & Huberman, 1994). We deductively analyzed field data according to descriptive categories derived from our research questions (e.g., challenges, benefits, processes); we next inductively analyzed data (Corbin & Strauss, 2008) to generate interpretive code labels reflective of more nuanced patterns. To gauge the coding reliability, each of us separately coded 20% of the data and then compared codes, producing 87% interrater agreement. Remaining discrepancies were reconciled through discussion. We then organized interpretive codes into matrices (Miles & Huberman, 1994) to examine interaction between descriptive codes and stakeholder categories (e.g., CWHS, University, CWHS faculty, University faculty, CWHS students, and University students).

Partnership Impact

Professionalism

Our results suggest that the partnership transformed the school by promoting professionalism among faculty and students. Teachers often discussed professionalism in terms of status, explaining that the site-based co-instruction model enhanced the school's identity. Ryan, for example, emphasized elevated status for the school when discussing benefits of the partnership:

> [The partnership] gives [CWHS] a nice rep. I also think that the idea that teachers are studying *us*,[2] and finding *our* experiences interesting and informative (by us I mean the whole [CWHS] community) gives the kids a sense of their own value and power. Future teachers choose to come here to learn about the school and teaching. I trust that that message results in a greater sense of mission and self worth for the institution, and for the individuals who make it up.

Participants invariably discussed the status associated with their participation in partnership initiatives as a benefit in that it contributed to a more positive impression of their urban school.

Another aspect of professionalism supported by the partnership was the development of communities of practice. This occurred within the context of two partnership activities that generated structures facilitative of professional collaboration: (a) CWHS teachers' and NYU professors' collaborative planning of Inquiries curricula, and (b) panel discussions in which CWHS staff visited Inquiries classes to discuss their practice after university students had observed their classes. Kyle, the principal, elaborated, "All of the sudden my teachers are becoming experts. It's that confidence building. To see my teachers serve on panels and articulate what they do and how they do things is just a benefit. It's also like professionalizing the business, which I don't think we get to do a lot." Ryan reiterated this benefit, explaining, "Having educated people who have a more nuanced understanding of teaching and high school helps all of us in this work create political space for what we do." Professionalism was additionally discussed in the area of needed reforms; Mark wished for more incentives for CWHS teachers to be involved in collaborative work, suggesting that "we need to reward [CWHS] teachers who participate by opening their doors to us in some very powerful way that honors them as professionals, practitioners actively involved in the education of pre-service teachers."

Teachers further reported that the partnership provided opportunities to reflect critically on their teaching, stating that collaboration helped them to make implicit practices explicit, articulate the rarely examined, and reexamine their teaching practices in light of new perspectives. When discussing this impact, Nancy explained how "in addition to reading texts I hadn't read before and holding them up against my own experience as a teacher, I was pushed to reflect on the field and my practices, in a way that I don't normally do. It made me more conscious of my assumptions and methods." Mark mirrored Nancy's statement, explaining, "It helped me reflect on my teaching more. Whenever you teach others learning to become teachers, you're forced to think about your own values." CWHS co-instructors discussed reflective practice as a benefit not only to themselves but also to their colleagues who were observed by university students. Nancy explained, "It might have made the teachers who allowed their classes to be observed and then agreed to talk with university students afterwards to be more reflective about their practices." Ryan concurred: "Answering questions [during panel discussions] helped [CWHS] teachers really clarify their own ideas and brought out into the open some of their assumptions and how they had changed." Participants identified this aspect of professionalism as beneficial to university students as well, in that they had access to models of collaborative critical reflection. Such reflections, transparently discussed with aspiring teachers, allowed for modeling of how teachers think about and adjust their own pedagogical practices based on new information.

Patterns in participants' responses also suggested that the site-based teacher education model held the potential to transform teachers' perceptions of the role of theory in teaching practice. Participants viewed this integration of theory and practice as a benefit to aspiring teachers enrolled in Inquiries courses and to CWHS co-instructors and their colleagues. Alan, for example, indicated that the model "provides the chance to square on-the-ground realities with theoretical ideals." Similarly, Serena asserted, "It was good for those grad students to be able to observe students in the high school setting and see school in action. It really makes the course not just about theory, but about practice as well." This reported benefit was seen in the observational field notes, when the university students, who were returning from observations, discussed their reactions to the practices they were observing. Responding to a student's comment that the "dynamic" of a class was radically altered when it "went from one to three teachers," Ryan segued, "That's a good link to today's reading on team-teaching." Such illustrations suggest the model's potential to, by physically situating course work in clinical contexts, support teacher educators' efforts to make educational concepts come alive. In fact, many CWHS teachers discussed how they redesigned Inquiries courses with this goal in mind. For example, some used protocols to structure classroom observations around a specific concept from the course readings, while others assigned field-based research projects. Mark explained how he and his co-instructor "insisted that students situate the theory in the practice they're observing and the burgeoning practice they enact in our class."

Sensation

Another potentially transformative impact of the partnership reported by CWHS staff was that of sensation, or the perception that the school setting affected aspiring teachers' understandings of what it "feels like" to teach in an urban school. For example, Mark explained, "What we hear in the hallways, see on the walls, notice in the faces of the students who bump into us as we navigate crowded hallways— reading about pedagogy is one thing. Using a high school bathroom . . . makes it all the more real." Similarly, Nancy proposed that the on-site class allowed aspiring teachers to be situated in the "reality" of public, urban schools rather than in a "vacuum," elaborating, "What is so wonderful about taking this course in an actual high school is that the students are surrounded by the chaotic and loud world of public school. . . . Being in the high school 'keeps it real.'" Furthermore, Ryan also explained how the on-site course is an opportunity to debunk the deficit models often associated with urban schools, explaining his goal is "to move to a more realistic and positive image of teaching and schools, particularly city schools with lots of students of color and poverty." Simultaneously, CWHS co-instructors reported that university students were often dismayed by what they perceived as "chaos" in the school environment. Yet while participants cited this a challenge, they also unanimously agreed that this challenge benefited university students in that it provided them with concrete, lived understandings of urban schools. Ryan discussed this phenomenon as creating dissonance that was necessary for challenging aspiring teachers' assumptions regarding urban students:

> I think that many of my students found the population of students quite jarring, some of the behaviors they observed, or skill levels they saw, were really upsetting to them. Some of them had a really hard time seeing past those to other issues, to what was the kid learning, what were their ideas, etc. This was, indeed a challenge, but also an incredible opportunity, and an essential set of assumptions and perceptions to work through. This challenge and struggle really helped them and all of us figure out what to look at when we were looking at teaching. It helped us meet head on some of the basic misconceptions people may have about teaching.

Ultimately, teachers' discussions of sensation suggested an overlap between perceived benefits and challenges involved in co-instructing courses on the school site, which we discuss further later.

Logistics

Challenge–benefit overlap was particularly pronounced in participants' discussions of logistics. Unsurprisingly, CWHS faculty and staff described logistics—time, space, and monetary factors that affected collaborative work—as a challenge to implementing and sustaining partnership initiatives. The principal, Kyle, discussed difficulties in finding empty classrooms and working around teachers' busy schedules. He explained that many panel presentations were canceled, as CWHS teachers could not be reimbursed for their time after school.[3] The logistical challenges involved in implementing the model were also evident in Jill's memo following an Inquiries observation when she spoke with the co-instructors about challenges that included multiple room changes, schedule restructuring wherein the courses met once rather than twice weekly, and agenda reengineering in which students went directly "from the train to their observations" rather than meeting as a class before engaging in assigned field work. Our findings suggest that it is precisely this ingenuity and flexibility that is truly needed to make site-based courses meaningful to all stakeholders involved.

In addition to space and scheduling issues, CWHS co-instructors discussed their lack of time and energy as logistical challenges. Both Ryan and Nancy reported feeling overwhelmed by teaching full-time at CWHS and teaching an NYU class. Mark explained, "I literally stop teaching teenagers at 2:20 and start teaching graduate students at 2:30. Diminished energies from teaching all day aside, it's intense to make that psychic shift into a calm, reflective, authoritative space that focuses on graduate study demands." Yet logistics were not always identified as a challenge that needed to be addressed through revisions to the model. Rather, as with sensation, challenge and benefit were integrally connected in participants' descriptions of their experiences with the partnership. For example, Ryan discussed logistical challenges as they related to the benefits of sensation, explaining how "some logistical stuff was difficult. I guess it was not totally comfortable sitting at desks, with noisy hallways, heat in the summer, and so on. However, that did not bother me, and I think that those things were actually helpful." When participants discussed logistics as both challenge and benefit, it was construed as a *necessary* challenge, one that was integral the model's effectiveness. As Serena put it, addressing logistical issues was "the only way high school teachers can actually be involved in co-teaching." Alan was similarly pragmatic in his response, explaining, "There's a ton of negotiation I must do to keep the classroom observations consistent. No big deal. It's what we do." Though the logistical issues participants discussed were substantial and persistent, they felt they had made great progress over time in negotiating these challenges, to the benefit of themselves and the aspiring teachers in their Inquiries classes. Furthermore, when discussing logistics, participants saw the existence of such challenges as unavoidable and, ultimately, integral to the task of preparing teachers to work in urban schools.

Integration

Finally, participants referred to systemic, long-term integration between the NYU and the CWHS as a needed reform, as teachers worried that the university's involvement with CWHS was a "one-off" collaboration. Participants described integration as their desire to move beyond day-to-day instantiations of collaboration and toward a more sustained, normalized, and mutually beneficial relationship with the university. This theme was particularly evident in Kyle's interview when he insisted that "universities really need to think about long-term relationships with schools and really developing those. I mean this stuff going on with NYU has been really nice but it could be so much stronger." He also felt that university students needed more time to interact within the school community, explaining:

So what? We have a 2-hour class and I'm going to spend 15 minutes with the same kid. I mean the complexity that's not happening is that they're not really getting to know kids on a deeper level. You know when you are a teacher you are dealing with families, culture, health, learning styles.

Kyle further indicated his belief that CWHS teachers could benefit from greater access to university resources. He wished CWHS teachers were invited to Inquiries classes, especially when guest lecturers were present, so as to enhance their own professional development. He felt having a "university professor on-site" could really make these efforts more integrated. Kyle also discussed integration as a benefit, reflecting on how "teachers have really built relationships with the NYU professors, teaching for several semesters in a row together." Though the CWHS instructors were less likely than Kyle to identify integration as an issue, several worried about the university's long-term commitment, with one teacher suggesting that it might amount to a "drive by." In such cases, integration overlapped with logistics when teachers expressed uncertainty as to whether the collaborative model they had worked so hard to develop could be sustained in the absence of financial support.

Discussion

Host-school stakeholders' perspectives on partnership reported here suggest that the site-based co-instruction model transformed their school in important ways, by providing structures that enhanced the professional atmosphere on their campus. Our findings regarding professionalism, which was discussed by all five teacher–participants as a benefit of partnership, suggest that the model can help schools develop the communities of practice that have been identified as facilitating teachers' professional development (Beavers, 2009; King, 2004; Musanti & Pence, 2010). However, while CWHS instructors perceived their school colleagues as benefitting from enhanced professionalism, we do not know the extent to which those teachers perceived such effects. And while we are unable to draw conclusions regarding the model's impact on teacher retention, given that the school's principal is the only participant who discussed this as a potential benefit, we are encouraged to find that participants' perceptions of their work as university professors were consistent with the partnership's goal of expanding teachers' career opportunities. We also wish to emphasize teachers' perceptions that their partnership work had elevated their school's status, a crucial benefit given the negative stereotypes that are often attached to urban schools.

These findings suggest that situating teacher education courses in urban schools can potentially help aspiring teachers develop the dispositions necessary to be effective working in such schools. One important medium through which CWHS teachers perceived aspiring teachers as developing cultural competence was the school's sensory impact—a product of the very logistical challenges they identified. The teachers at the school encouraged aspiring teachers to discuss their dismay at how, as one university student put it, student behavior and inter-action with adults at the school was "not what I'm used to." Co-instructors were able to quickly assist university students in processing their assumptions about urban schools by discussing how the school's philosophy was tailored to meet the needs of its student population; how students' backgrounds and experiences affected their educational interactions; and how DOE policies regarding, for ex-ample, the instruction of special education students, affected teaching practice. Such transparent conversations provided CWHS teachers with safe, structured opportunities to cultivate "the openness and compassion with which we want [preservice teachers] to approach the unfamiliar" (Adams et al., 2005, p. 59). However, we do not know the extent to which aspiring teachers themselves perceived this benefit.

The benefits that urban school stakeholders associated with the model—linking of theory to practice, professional community building, and thoughtful introductions of aspiring teachers to urban schools—reflect intended outcomes, as stated in the partnership goals. This study's results also point to an interde-pendence between challenges and benefits in partnership work. The finding that participants did not typically view the cultivation of professional communities within the partnership model in terms of conflict is unexpected, given that partnership literature suggests entrenched institutional conflicts present great obstacles to school–university partnership development (e.g., Lewison & Hol-liday, 1997; White et al., 1997). Instead of focusing on challenges identified in partnership literature regarding institutional culture clashes (Knight, Wiseman, & Smith, 1992; Miller & Hafner, 2008), our participants emphasized *logistical* challenges involved in interinstitutional partnership; yet, significantly, CWHS staff did not identify logistical challenges as obstacles. Rather, they viewed these challenges as providing precisely the mechanisms that were necessary for bring-ing about transformations.

Despite the perceived benefits to individual participants, however, our re-sults suggest that all stakeholders must continually work toward the goal of achieving simultaneous renewal at the institutional level. The relationships be-tween individuals at CWHS and the university appear to be well developed and authentically collaborative, and these collaborations were perceived by the participants in this study as being beneficial to themselves and aspiring teachers. We suspect that CWHS teachers did not discuss difficulties involved in work-ing across institutional boundaries partly due to the fact they had been working with their university co-instructors for as many as five semesters. Perhaps if we had conducted our study at earlier stages of these collaborations, participants would have discussed the need to reconcile competing institutional goals as a challenge.

Despite the fruitful development of interpersonal relationships, CWHS ed-ucators expressed a lack of confidence regarding the university's long-term commitment to institutional collaboration. Their suspicions suggest that school-site stakeholders perceived a fundamental imbalance in the collaboration in that the university defined the parameters of contact. True reciprocity in school–university partnerships, as discussed by Hamlin (1997), requires extraordinary perseverance on the part of both institutions. To be effective, school–university partnerships must begin with this understanding and proceed with patience and steadfastness. Thus, we join White et al. (1997) in urging researchers to "examine how changes in roles and relationships are maintained, sustained, and continue to interactively fuel curricular renewal and development," which includes considering durability and vulnerability of "old and new structures and processes over a longer time span" (p. 65). We would also advise educational reformers to be mindful of the need to construe partnership as an evolving relationship that requires long-term commitment to change. Otherwise, partnership initiatives run the risk of becoming "boutique" programs that are unlikely to achieve the goal of systemic reform.

Notes

Findings from this study were previously reported in J.V. Jeffery & J. Polleck, 2010, "Reciprocity through co-instructed site-based courses: Perceived challenge and benefit overlap in school–university partnerships," *Teacher Education Quarterly, 37*(3), 81–99.

1 A pseudonym, as are all of the participants' names.
2 Emphases in original, typed questionnaire response.
3 Despite this lack of funding, it should be noted that most CWHS teachers still came to the Inquiries classes for discussion of the university students' observations.

References

Adams, A., Bondy, E., & Kuhel, K. (2005). Preservice teacher learning in an unfamiliar setting. *Teacher Education Quarterly, 32*(2), 41–61.

Anagnostopoulos, D., Smith, E. R., & Basmadjian, K. G. (2007). Bridging the university–school divide: Horizontal expertise and the "two-worlds pitfall." *Journal of Teacher Education, 58*(2), 138–152.

Beavers, A. (2009). Teachers as learners: Implications of adult education for professional development. *Journal of College Teaching and Learning, 6*(7), 25–30.

Bullough, R. V., Jr., & Draper, R. J. (2004). Making sense of a failed triad: Mentors, university supervisors, and positioning theory. *Journal of Teacher Education, 55*(5), 407–420.

Corbin, S., & Strauss, A. (2008). *Basics of qualitative research* (3rd ed.). Los Angeles, CA: Sage.

Darling-Hammond, L., & Baratz-Snowden, J. (2007). A good teacher in every classroom: Preparing the highly qualified teachers our children deserve. *Educational Horizons, 85*(2), 122–132.

Goodlad, J. I. (1993). School–university partnerships and partner schools. *Educational Policy, 7*(1), 24–39.

Hamlin, K. (1997). Partnerships that support the professional growth of supervising teachers. *Teacher Education Quarterly, 24*(1), 77–88.

Hiemstra, R., & Brockett, R. G. (Eds.). (1994). *Overcoming resistance to self-direction in adult learning*. San Francisco: Jossey-Bass.

King, K. P. (2004). Both sides now: Examining transformative learning and professional development of educators. *Innovative Higher Education, 29*(2), 155–174.

Knight, S. L., Wiseman, D., & Smith, C. W. (1992). The reflectivity–activity dilemma in school–university partnerships. *Journal of Teacher Education, 43*(4), 269–277.

Lewison, M., & Holliday, S. (1997). Control, trust, and rethinking traditional roles: Critical elements in creating a mutually beneficial university-school partnership. *Teacher Education Quarterly, 24*(1), 105–126.

Miles, M. B., & Huberman, A. M. (1994). *Qualitative data analysis* (2nd ed.). London: Sage.

Miller, P. M., & Hafner, M. M. (2008). Moving toward dialogical collaboration: A critical examination of a university–school–community partnership. *Educational Administration Quarterly, 44*(1), 66–110.

Musanti, S. I., & Pence, L. (2010). Collaboration and teacher development: Unpacking resistance, constructing knowledge, and navigating identities. *Teacher Education Quarterly, 37*(1), 73–89.

Patterson, G. (1999). The learning university. *The Learning Organization, 6*(1), 9–17.

Perry, B., Walton, G., & Conroy, J. (1998). Visiting teaching lecturers—an experiment in collaboration between university and schools. *Asia-Pacific Journal of Teacher Education, 26*(2), 151–160.

Russell, B., & Chapman, J. (2001). Working as partners: School teachers' experiences as university-based teacher educators. *Asia-Pacific Journal of Teacher Education, 29*(3), 235–248.

Shirley, D., Hersi, A., MacDonald, E., Sanchez, M. T., Scandone, C., Skidmore, C., et al. (2006). Bringing the community back in: Change, accommodation, and contestation in a school and university partnership. *Equity and Excellence in Education, 39,* 27–36.

Shroyer, G., Yahnke, S., Bennett, A., & Dunn, C. (2007). Simultaneous renewal through professional development school partnerships. *Journal of Educational Research, 100*(4), 211–224.

Sleeter, C. E. (2001). Preparing teachers for culturally diverse schools: Research and the overwhelming presence of whiteness. *Journal of Teacher Education, 52*(2), 94–106.

Smith, T. M., & Ingersoll, R. M. (2004). What are the effects of induction and mentoring on beginning teacher turnover? *American Educational Research Journal, 41*(3), 681–714.

Taylor, K. S. (2006). *Teachers' perceptions regarding professional development activities and their level of use.* Unpublished doctoral dissertation, Wilmington College, Wilmington, OH.

Trachtman, R. (2007). Inquiry and accountability in professional development schools. *Journal of Educational Research, 100*(4), 197–203.

White, C. S., Deegan, J. G., & Allexsaht-Snider, M. (1997). Changes in roles and relationships in a school–university partnership. *Teacher Education Quarterly, 24*(1), 53–66.

Wiggins, R. A., Follo, E. J., & Eberly, M. B. (2007). The impact of a field immersion program on pre-service teachers' attitudes toward teaching in culturally diverse classrooms. *Teaching and Teacher Education: An International Journal of Research and Studies, 23*(5), 653–663.

Zeichner, K., & Conklin, H. G. (2008). Teacher education programs as sites for teacher preparation. In M. Cochran-Smith, S. Feiman-Nemser, D. McIntyre, & K. E. Demers (Eds.), *Handbook of research on teacher education* (3rd ed., pp. 269–289). New York: Routledge.

Appendix A

CWHS Co-Instructor Electronic Questionnaire

1. How (if at all) did the experience of co-teaching Inquiries help you develop professionally?
2. What challenges were involved in co-teaching the Inquiries course?
3. What kinds of modifications did you and your co-teacher make to the Inquiries course?
4. In working with your co-teacher, how did you reach consensus and/or common understandings of what students should know?
5. How (if at all) do you think this course helped [Creative Works High School]?
6. When compared to a traditional university course, how did the unique setting of teaching at the high school make the course more effective?
7. When compared to a traditional university course, how (if at all) did the unique setting of teaching at the high school make the course more challenging to teach?
8. How was the unique setting of teaching at the high school beneficial (if at all) to your students?
9. How was the unique setting of teaching at the high school detrimental/challenging (if at all) for your students?
10. Do you have any other comments/concerns you would like to add about teaching the Inquiries course?

Appendix B

Semistructured Principal Interview Protocol

1. What is your vision for the school's professional development?
2. What is the history of the [University] partnership?
3. What do you notice about your teachers who co-instructed [University] courses?
4. How do make the decisions about recommending [CWHS] teachers to co-instruct the course?
5. What were some of the challenges that you've had in partnering with [the University]?
6. What has been your role in the partnership?
7. Why are we no longer doing the Inquiries panels?
8. What do you think [CWHS] gets out of this, if anything at all?
9. Describe the engagement you have had with [University] student teachers.
10. What (if any) changes are needed to make the partnership more beneficial?
11. Is there anything else you would like to discuss about the Inquiries course/University partnership?

8

CREATING INTENTIONAL PARTNERSHIPS IN URBAN SPACES

Schools, Communities, and Teacher Preparation Programs

Eleni Katsarou, Bree Picower, and David Stovall

> *The partnership with UIC and its urban teacher program has afforded our school the opportunity to support and help cultivate agents of change. UIC teacher candidates work with us the entire academic year becoming part of our school culture. Their presence represents an investment not only in our school, but the community in which we serve. As teacher candidates hone in on developing their craft, the school as a whole benefits from their socio-critical perspective, passion, and eagerness to help children. Students look to them as role models, a responsibility that is not only embraced but, nurtured through an ongoing effort in developing positive teacher/student relationships. It is because of these important attributes that I have continued to hire UIC teacher candidates to be a part of our faculty. (Lance School Principal, CPS)*

In many instances, teacher education programs have been positioned as apolitical entities with the task of preparing teachers to perform the duties and responsibilities of the profession. Instead, the position of the authors is that because teaching is a deeply political endeavor that requires expert knowledge of issues beyond the classroom, teacher education programs must embrace the responsibility of prioritizing community strengths. We agree with Cochran-Smith that teacher education is an endeavor that requires "an intentional blurring of the roles of teacher education practitioner, teacher education researcher, and critic/analyst of the policies, political agendas, and popular and professional discourses that directly or indirectly influence teacher education" (Cochran-Smith, 2004, p. 4). In so doing, we recognize that "political" in this sense is not referencing electoral partisan politics. Instead, it is in reference to the overt and nuanced power relationships between the state (both local and federal), public policy, and its residents.

By taking the position that teaching for social justice is an act of necessity and solidarity, this chapter seeks to highlight two examples of teacher education initiatives that prioritize community strengths. To open, David Stovall contextualizes the way in which local policy in both Chicago and New York create environments that marginalize community voices in educational reform. In the next section, Eleni Katsarou explains an attempt by a university College of Education to reconfigure its teacher education program toward developing justice-minded teachers teachers. Following Katsarou, Bree Picower offers her insights on a dual teacher certification program in New York City that developed explicit partnerships with a community school. Both are intentional with the ways in which teacher educators should consider their engagement with communities.

Toward a Working Definition of Social Justice Education

For educators at the classroom, community and university level, it becomes important to provide "working" definitions for several reasons. For the purposes of this work, we use social justice education to speak to *the day-to-day processes and actions utilized in classrooms and communities centered in critical analysis, action, and reflection (praxis) amongst all educational stakeholders (students, families, teachers, administrators, community organizations, community members) with the goal of creating tangible change in their communities, cities, states, nation, and the larger world.* Referenced as conscientization, or praxis, Freire referred to the concept as action and reflection in the world to change it (Freire, 1993). With the current attack on public education by government and corporate entities, authentic family/community engagement has been substituted with neoliberal ideology, test prep and models of competition (Lipman, 2011). Resisting these realities, social justice education connects the concerns of the aforementioned groups to the larger constructs of oppression in the form of racism, classism, gender subjugation, homophobia, ageism, and ableism. In this instance teachers are engaged in a struggle to learn and provide tangible examples of what justice looks like in a classroom and the community at large. Both are sites to engage solidarity, political clarity, and knowledge of one's self (Duncan-Andrade & Morrell, 2007; Ayers, Quinn, & Lyon, 2000; Camangian, 2009; Darder, 2002; Greene, 1988; Gutstein, 2005; Verma, 2010). Because the larger justice project in education is largely a lived and experienced phenomenon, the remaining chapter is an attempt to demonstrate tangible examples of said project via the transformation of theory to action.

Linking the Realities of Chicago and New York City

The politics of educational reform are pivotal in developing critical analysis in new teachers. Where this chapter only provides examples from two cities, they become important in the national dialogue on the preparation of urban teachers. Because practices and personnel (i.e., Arne Duncan, former CEO of Chicago Public Schools and current Secretary of Education, and Joel Klein, former chancellor of New York City Public Schools) from both cities are used as exemplary models, Chicago and New York City provide relevant examples for teachers and teacher educators in the current climate.

The city of Chicago has engaged a number of reforms that are used as models for urban school districts across the country. Simultaneously, said reforms have resulted in the deprioritizing of community strengths in favor of corporate interests. Predating the policy No Child Left Behind, Chicago Public Schools' (CPS) policy brief "Every Child, Every School" spoke for the need for change in the district. New York City's Department of Education (DOE), have observed these spaces and have made significant strides to replicate Chicago's efforts. Both cities currently share mayoral control (elimination of an elected school board while relinquishing the majority appointment of the school board to the mayor's office), benchmark high-stakes testing, mandated curriculum for low-performing schools, and massive school closings. The mayor's office in both cities are staunch supporters of initiatives to dispel the negative reputation of the district by introducing charter schools, magnet schools, and privatization—all supposedly to give parents more options for their children. Rarely mentioned, however, is the fact that the vast majority of charters have not outperformed traditional public schools. With the growth of privatization of public schools, communities that have historically had the least are getting even less.

Furthermore, mayoral control of the school board has centralized decision-making power when it comes to the allocation of funds to implement policy. The most recent example of this power came with the unveiling of Renaissance 2010. CPS, in conjunction with the Civic Committee of The Commercial Club of Chicago produced Renaissance 2010, an overarching policy proposing to close 70 existing underperforming schools and reopen them as 100 new schools under the rubric of charter, contract, or performance school. It is clear that such restructuring efforts are closely aligned with the goals of business elites as well as the certification and hiring of new teachers that are hastily prepared in nontraditional, alternative programs (Fleming, Greenlee, Gutstein, Lipman, & Smith, 2009; Kumashiro, 2010). In New York City, philanthropic and management organizations have teamed with the DOE to create privately managed public schools that undermine localized public educational options.

For teacher education, the political contexts of Chicago and New York City provide insight as to how the role of teachers and teacher educators are positioned within the national and local discourse around education privatization. As families supposedly "choose" their educational options under current reform strategies, missing from the equation is the fact that many are unable to select said opportunities. In both cities, due to the lack of affordable housing, the community concerns of poor and working class families of color are dismissed as they are unable to afford rents within the city limits, limiting their access to the newly presented "options." "Choice" in this sense is often a false one, because it is only afforded to the few community members that are able to navigate the complex terrain of educational "options."

Simultaneously, the loaded rhetoric of "accountability" and "responsibility" serve as coded proxies, marking tests scores as the de facto marker of academic achievement (Lipman, as cited in Koval et al., 2007, p. 480). Taking into account these realities, the following two case studies serve as examples of what teacher education programs can do in schools with preservice and new teachers to develop community-centered teaching. At the same time, we hope to encourage other teacher educators to explore the connections between their experiences, ultimately speaking to the collective significance of multiple perspectives on authentic community engagement.

Eleni Katsarou: Chicago—The Making of Critical Urban Teachers

The ensuing comments seek to identify a university College of Education's effort to redefine and reconceptualize its approach to teacher education with specific focus on site selection, mentor relationships, and assessments. Given the current climate of teacher preparation in which there is both an unprecedented barrage of criticisms on schools of education as well as the increasing opportunities for CPS to hire in its ranks from alternative routes (read Teach for America and the Chicago equivalent in the Chicago Teaching Fellows Program), several researchers have called for such recalibration (e.g., Darling-Hammond, 2006; Murrell, 2001). Notably, Zeichner (2006; see also Zeichner, 2010) finds essential that, among other considerations, as teacher educators we must "change the center of gravity of teacher education programs so that the connections between universities, schools, and communities in the preparation of teachers are stronger and less hierarchical" (p. 330), and offers the distinct notion of "hybrid" or "third" spaces that link teacher preparation programs with schools and communities in more egalitarian and collaborative partnerships. From this perspective, the Chicago case sketched here offers an example of a hybrid space, in which as the teacher educator, I concern myself with building and sustaining a more dialectical relationship with my colleagues in the schools and communities—spaces that are central in the development of the preservice teachers as critical, caring and ethical urban teachers. Additionally, in this endeavor, *teaching for social justice* acquires specificity by providing teacher candidates especially, with the sociopolitical knowledge and particular fieldwork opportunities in which to practice and prioritize community needs.

The UIC College of Education: Collective and Individual Visions in Working With Underserved Communities as Praxis

The overall ethos of the UIC College of Education is concentrated on *developing urban* educators who are informed in their course work about how culture, language, and poverty shape and influence students' lives; and, who have a deep understanding of how to use cultural and linguistic diversity as assets in the classroom. The development of committed urban teachers must presuppose that teacher candidates be situated in spaces—that is, *schools*—where the significant adults—that is, *mentor teachers, school leaders*—possess the clarity about what they need to be doing within their particular context—that is, the severe *constraints and politics* of the larger space/district—so that children stand to benefit. The current rendering suggests a possible means for such a complex and multifaceted aim to impact teaching and learning in urban schools by pointing to, first, how *relationships* among school folks in urban settings and university instructors are formed, and how these are sustained to better serve and thoughtfully prepare teacher candidates. Second, the notion of *community* as it is usually reported—that is, in the documentation and existence of "professional learning communities" and "teacher practice"—is shifting to include other topics of discussion and concern. To this end, the main topic of discussion among this *community* is the education of preservice teachers in terms of their dispositions and habits of mind during their student teaching field experience and subsequent induction into the same school sites and communities.

In concert with the college's Conceptual Framework, strategic plan, and mission that explicitly states a commitment to many of the underserved schools and communities of Chicago, as faculty, we have been making numerous recruitment and admission efforts as well as some very deliberate programmatic decisions. While programmatic and curricular changes in our teacher preparation programs are examined in detail elsewhere (e.g., Katsarou, 2009), the focus here is on the centrality of relationship building between the university and the schools in which teacher candidates are placed to conduct fieldwork. This enables the community of teacher educators to engage in the preparation of urban teachers. Such teachers are better positioned to prioritize community needs, because they are best suited to develop an acute sense of the sociocritical, cultural, and political considerations of the contested spaces in which they work.

The Importance of Selecting Mentor Teachers in Teacher Education: An Instantiation of Teaching for Social Justice

The process of selecting mentor teachers is critical, because this is the place where student teacher assumptions about students in urban spaces are either reified or challenged. For the past 15 years, I have chosen particular sites and teachers that would mentor my students for a variety of internships during their preservice training. This means that sites chosen are neighborhood public schools that have no entrance requirements or lottery systems, and are not part of the recent partnerships that have resulted in the closure of neighborhood schools. Given the de facto segregation of CPS, schools that serve all-Latino or all–African American students are historically underserved and underresourced. In light of this situation, the college has made a commitment to work in solidarity with schools in said communities by placing preservice teachers at these respective sites.

The teachers that serve as mentors to my students are typically teachers with whom I have some kind of connection: In the best-case scenario, these teachers may have graduated from our programs at UIC and are now selected to be included in what I have called elsewhere members of the *intergenerational/ interinstitutional community of teacher educators* (e.g., Katsarou, 2010). As the name suggests, this core group of mentor teachers is comprised of former students that are now mentoring teacher candidates. The next best-case scenario is that the selected teachers are folks with whom I have had ample conversations on the subject of urban teaching, or who have observed or witnessed their own enactments of social justice within the CPS curricular constraints. No match between a teacher candidate and a mentor teacher is ever made without the explicit and direct knowledge of a mentor's political and pedagogical stance on the teaching of urban youngsters.

Nonetheless, the selection of this group of mentors that I consider my collaborators in urban teacher preparation is mostly dependent on three important considerations: our joint commitment to caring and liberatory teaching for urban students; our common beliefs as to what constitutes good teaching practice in urban sites; and our understanding that field instruction for teacher candidates is manifested primarily via our very collaboration and mutual respect for one another and the work that we do with the teacher candidates. This means that as teacher educators, we—both the selected mentors and I—nurture teacher candidates' knowledge and attitudes about the communities in which they are conducting their fieldwork practice. Most often, this can only be accomplished by our explicit debunking of myths about students of color; and, changing or redefining the teacher candidates' imagined, unhistorical, and racialized formations of families and communities that may be different from their own. This is no simple task. These partners in teacher preparation are not only well aware of what it is that the college teacher preparation program needs for teacher candidates to understand about teaching and learning, but are equally committed to the notion of bringing the families and the larger community into the curriculum in significant ways. Indeed, teacher candidates are encouraged to embrace and become what Murrell (2001) aptly named, *community teachers*. The following section, by providing an example of authentic university–community partnerships, speaks to the necessity of developing community teachers by way of an intentional process.

The Lance School–UIC, College of Education Partnership: A Real Community Endeavor

Lance School houses nearly one thousand predominantly African American students. The vast majority of the students are from the neighborhood, which has historical significance as a port of entry for African American residents to Chicago in the 1950s. Under years of disinvestment, the community has been subject to blight and isolation. At the reporting of this work, the Lance School community partnership consists of the teachers, the principal, myself as the field instructor and main college liaison, two groups of teacher candidates, and four newly hired teachers that were my former students.

One benefit of this critical mass of university- and school-based teacher educators is the multiple opportunity to have "courageous conversations," as coined by Glenn Singleton, necessary exchanges about the role of race in education (e.g., Singleton & Linton, 2006). Working for many years with a teacher whom I followed to Lance from another school, Mr. Warren, has provided opportunities to have such conversations with candidates of varying abilities and dispositions. Some of these discussions were hurried, and some long and sustained, but, always, they were about what constitutes good teaching in an urban setting, the role of race in the education, the mind-numbing effects of the debilitating assessment and curricular constraints of the CPS system, and the role of a White school leader in lending support to teachers of color in an all–Black school. When Mr. Warren reached out to join Lance School, he interviewed Dr. Johnson as much he was interviewed for a Grade 6 position. Following our conversation regarding his interview, it was no surprise that he had found the school he had been looking for: Austin area neighborhood school, great new leader who did not shy away from addressing "race" with his teachers, and home to some great teachers, to boot. At present, even though my perspective of Lance has shifted somewhat, my sense is that it is essentially a place that can only develop in ways that I cannot predict.

The way in which the first group of teachers was matched with the five candidates in year one of the collaboration was a strategic plan. Four of the mentors were Lance teachers, with an average teaching experience of 30 years in CPS; the fifth teacher was Mr. Warren. The five candidates were matched by paying close attention to areas of concentration, as well as to perceived dispositional alignment. These matches proved to have been made in fieldwork-placement heaven. In one instance, the science K–4 teacher who had followed Dr. Johnson to Lance was matched with a Latino male candidate who currently holds his mentor's science position: She convinced the principal that the candidate, Joel, was "made for this position" and she has subsequently moved to a self-contained Grade 2 classroom. Between the two of them, they initiated the growth of a vegetable and flower garden that received district and media attention. Besides the children that were the main beneficiaries of the garden, parents and grandparents also participated in unprecedented ways and vied to take charge of and sustain it over the school breaks and summer. In another instance, an iconic Lance School teacher of 30 years, Ms. Ruhl, found her match in the spirit of an equally vibrant and bright woman, Cora, who catapulted the Grade 6 youngsters and Ms. Ruhl into a deep historical study of the neighborhood, its inhabitants—complete with interviewing the elders of the community, and its many places of worship and cultural significance. All this was concurrent to the national campaign and election of the new president, Barack Obama. Cora, single-handedly—though she acknowledges the president having played a role, as well—has paved the way for Ms. Ruhl to see what a new generation of Black teachers can provide for the students she has loved. Cora was also hired as a new teacher on graduation and remains Ms. Ruhl's protégé.

The Design of an Assessment Tool: A Community Effort in Determining Who's Got the Goods to Become an Urban Teacher

What follows is a second, albeit abbreviated, example of the Chicago case and the ways in which there was a deliberate choice in further actualizing the Murrell (2001) notion of *community teacher*. The backdrop of this story begins with how all of us, as teacher educators, deal with the perennial dilemma in assessing our candidates at numerous points during our programs. At UIC, such dilemmas reflect both our steadfast resolve that we do not let unwilling and unreflective candidates slide through, but, at the same time, make explicit and transparent for our students what it is that we expect them to be able to sense and do as urban teachers. In such an effort to explore what candidates' dispositional knowledge could be and how to develop ways to make that apparent to them, a few years ago, I turned to my partners—a group of mentoring teachers. I was interested in finding out what we could jointly design, that would allow for *conversations* in the mentor/candidate dyad and that would have a sharp focus on how this knowledge/stance can be nurtured. The intent of this work with the first group of seven teachers—that came from one CPS site with ample experience in mentoring teacher candidates, was to recount their particular conversations with their teacher candidates and how they pointed them to good, solid practice.

By bringing this group of teachers together, we jointly designed a tool called *The Development of Ethical and Caring Actions in Urban Teaching (DECA-UT)*. As it now stands, the tool was refined and rearticulated by a second group of mentoring teachers, all of whom share the *intergenerational* quality alluded to earlier. The DECA-UT is currently being used in our programs and it assesses candidates' dispositions, sensibilities, and deliberate actions in urban teaching.

This work, that is examined fully elsewhere (Katsarou, 2010), was a deliberate effort to include *mentoring teacher knowledge* within a teacher preparation program and its assessment of teacher candidates.

Working Within CPS Without Compromising

Placing teacher candidates within labyrinthine and sclerotic schools systems such as that of Chicago need not be devoid of caring, effective, critical urban learning and teaching; indeed, and to paraphrase Freire, *invading* such contested spaces may be the only approach for all concerned within teacher preparation to become deeply cognizant of the communities in which we are working with kids, and families and, thus, become truly enmeshed in the local realities and challenges.

I am also convinced that the relationships that exist between colleges of education and those urban schools/spaces, that are intentional about the work they do with underserved students and communities, are central in our developing teacher candidates that will engage in deeply caring, ethical, and socially and politically relevant teaching. The school folks and we—both teachers/instructors and teacher candidates—are in a relationship that is reliant, first, on our common and deep caring for urban youngsters in our public schools and, second, on our numerous political conversations that have revealed to us that we have very similar understandings of what constitutes praxis in education. Both of these common visions on education are, of course, the very *reasons for* our relationship. More interestingly, these common visions on education have given us permission to muster our strength and attempt to understand our own struggle in making explicit to aspiring teachers what it is that they need to know and understand about urban students and teaching; our trust that some of them will succeed eventually, while others do not have what it takes; our insistence that deep and caring urban teaching begins with deep and caring relationships with and *in* urban sites that face all the sclerotic and insensitive systems of schooling and learning. I find that in recognizing and acknowledging the systemic recalcitrance, teacher educators and school folks can build unshakable alliances and trust in one another. As this mutual respect and trust are considered, it is important to examine how these impact teacher education and fieldwork placements. It is clear that unless we view the relationship between teacher educators and urban school faculty as critically important and decisive, our candidates' development will remain partial and decontextualized.

Bree Picower: New York City—Prioritizing Community Needs Through Teacher Education Assignments

The following section examines how a dual certification program in New York City attempted to prioritize local community needs through their on-site work at a local public elementary school. This section of the chapter provides concrete examples of efforts of teacher education to recognize and prioritize community needs by challenging deficit thinking, rethinking "expertise," developing social justice curriculum and providing ongoing support.

Many teachers, particularly those who come from communities different from the ones in which they teach (with particular regards to race and class), hold deficit views of their students and neighborhoods (Weiner, 2006) that makes prioritizing community needs impossible. Deficit thinking can only be interrupted when brought to the teaching candidates' attention, as the candidates are often unaware that they are judging children through stereotypes and assumptions.

As the teacher educator who supervised student teachers at a New York Public School, a strategy I used to attempt to help move teacher candidates away from deficit thinking toward becoming advocates was a Child Connection Assignment. In this assignment, the teacher candidate begins by identifying a student with whom she struggles to connect. The candidate writes an observation of this child as well as an "empathy journal" in which she writes from the child's perspective to imagine how the child is experiencing the classroom. Before turning this in, the class examines a write-up from a former teacher candidate that is riddled with deficit descriptions of a student who is presented as nothing but a list of problems. The current candidates identify examples of "deficit" thinking, a term that is introduced in seminar. They return to their own observation, identifying their own deficit thinking, and reframe these sentences to present their students in less-judgmental terms. For example, candidates may reframe "Darnell is uninterested in learning" to "During read-aloud, when most students are looking at the teacher, Darnell is playing with his shoelaces." By focusing on the behavior rather than labeling the student, the teacher candidates begin to move away from making sweeping assumptions about their students. After reflecting on what they notice about themselves and how they observe children, the candidates work on developing a personal connection with their assignment student. Finally, they write letters to the student's future teacher, advocating for the student and identifying strategies that could help this student in their future classroom.

This assignment has a strong impact on how teachers see their students by helping them reframe deficit thinking. When the teacher educator asks the candidates to move from seeing only deficits to recognizing the whole child and their strengths, candidates are in a better position to be able to develop solidarity with their students' communities. Teacher educators must hold up a mirror to the candidates we prepare, helping them to recognize the potentially dangerous conceptualizations they may hold about their students and explicitly helping them to reframe their stance to that of solidarity and advocacy.

Rethinking "Expertise" for Solidarity and Empathy

Traditional teacher education is often designed on the banking model (Freire, 1993); train the teachers on discrete skills so they can replicate them in the classroom. This model sets up a paradigm in which teachers internalize that only "experts"—professors, curricular program vendors, and the like—have valuable knowledge. By disregarding other educators, parents, and students as potential "teachers," candidates are cut off from a knowledge base that can prepare them to prioritize the needs of the students they will teach.

To shift this paradigm, education programs need to rethink who is in a position to educate teachers. By bringing in recent graduates who are new teachers, parents, and children to campus to lead classes, candidates are able to set up a pattern of tapping into alternative bases of expertise. It also helps to shatter the myths of what social justice topics teachers can address and how students respond to such material. For one such project, I invited my recent graduates back to lead a class on campus. They taught the current candidates about how to integrate social justice curriculum, specifically a book called *Leon's Story* (Tillage, 1997), about a sharecropper in the south, into the mandated curriculum. Hearing that this was possible in first-year teachers' classrooms transformed the candidates concerns that they would have to wait until they were tenured to begin this kind of teaching:

> Since the beginning of class, I have questioned the possibility of including books such as *Leon's Story* in a curriculum and have always been afraid to "go against the tide" of the general curriculum. Because some of my classmates knew you [the current teachers] and knew that you were in our positions only a few months ago, it helps us believe that we can do it too. *It is possible to start this work as soon as I start teaching!*

First-year teachers, typically thought of as having little experience or knowledge, actually bring a great deal to the table as teacher educators of people about to enter the classroom.

Later in the semester, these teachers returned to campus, this time with their fifth-grade students, who lead a panel discussion on race and racism. Positioned as experts, the fifth graders spoke about complex issues of historical and current racism. This prompted the teacher candidates to quickly rethink their assumptions about what kind of content younger students can handle. As one candidate expressed to the first-year teachers, "hearing your students talk with such confidence and comfort about the topic of racism shows that you guys have built a very strong foundation and a safe environment for them to discuss such a serious and heavy topic." In more recent years, parents have also presented on the panel, sharing their thoughts on their students learning about such topics. One parent explained that racism is a part of their life, and so they are glad to see teachers address it in school, dispelling the candidates' fears that parents would be angered by addressing social issues.

By being exposed to nontraditional "experts" within their traditional teacher education program, teacher candidates tap into knowledge that they may have not learned from. This has a strong impact on how they are positioned to prioritize community needs, because they can begin to see other educators, students, and parents as people from whom they need to learn. By interrupting the "missionary" orientation many candidates enter with, they can no longer see themselves as saviors when they recognize the strength, wisdom, and contributions of those around them. Without this mindset, teachers developing solidarity with urban communities is highly unlikely.

Developing Empathy and Solidarity and Their Role in Social Change to Recognize and Act on Community Concerns

To prioritize community needs, teacher candidates must recognize issues and concerns that affect their students and the communities in which they teach. They must have the mindset that by working in solidarity with communities, they can do something about it. The school in which I supervised student teachers is located in a community of color that is experiencing rampant gentrification. In fact, the mayor recently revealed a major redevelopment effort for the local waterfront that is currently a community-used space. Traditional teacher education would not address this community concern in preparing teachers to teach there, but rather would focus solely on the mechanics of teaching. To help candidates recognize this community concern, I used this issue to shape their student teaching experience.

The first step in this process was to help the candidates become aware of the issue and familiar with grassroots efforts to have community input in the redevelopment issue. I invited two local community organizers to the school during our on-site seminar to inform the candidates and their cooperating teachers of the first- and third-grade classrooms about their campaign to bring community voice into the redevelopment efforts. We then created an integrated unit on gentrification of the waterfront and developed projects that allowed the children to participate in the organizations' ongoing campaign. The project culminated with a publishing party in which the students read their persuasive essays to the Economic Development Corporation in charge of the redevelopment to their families, who were then invited by the organizers to participate in a community rally that week. During this semester-long project, which impacted all stakeholders, the teacher candidates became aware of this issue facing the community, collaborated with organizers to become aware of how change happens, and developed academically rigorous lessons to introduce their students to gentrification and activism. By shifting the focus of the on-site teacher education class, a collaborative partnership emerged that raised the awareness of the candidates to community concerns and their role in creating change with their students and families.

Developing Communities of Support to Grow and Sustain Social Justice Teaching

To sustain their commitment as they enter the field, graduates need to participate in ongoing communities of support. Teachers who enter the field specifically with the hope of working toward social change are often the first quickly to leave the profession, as they find themselves alienated and alone while trying to navigate highly political terrain (Miech & Elder, 1996). Preparing educators to prioritize community needs is not enough. If teacher education wants to truly honor its commitment of providing educators who can teach in solidarity with their communities, we must continue to support our graduates as they struggle through the difficulties of induction. New teachers need protection from hostile environments, practice developing curriculum, and a community of like-minded people who are going through what they are going through (Picower, in press).

An example of such a group is the Social Justice Critical Inquiry Group. The group, open to alumni from the undergraduate childhood program, met on a biweekly basis to discuss issues they faced in the classroom and to develop social justice curriculum. The participants were able to develop a safe space where they could push, support and learn from one another as role models. The group reminds the members of why they went into teaching and keeps them true to their ideals. As one member shared what would have happened had she not participated:

> I'd have quit teaching . . . [CIP] inspires me to keep being a teacher, because I know that you've got to start somewhere . . . I just see now that being a teacher is not about teaching this, this and this. It's is about preparing our kids for being knowledgeable human beings that understand the way of the world, and to understand not just their cause and their situation, but all causes . . . It keeps me going, it definitely keeps me going.

With over 50% of new teachers leaving within the first five years, CIP had a significant impact in helping members put their vision of preparing human beings who understand the way of the world into practice. The satisfaction they gain by teaching with a purpose and being able to improve their craft in a community of peers kept them going.

Conclusion: Embracing Justice, Solidarity, and Teaching as a Political Act

To truly prioritize community needs and to teach in solidarity with schools and communities requires of teachers both specific mindsets and skill sets. Teachers need to develop empathy and see the strengths and assets of the students and communities in which they teach. Their classrooms must be in and of the community, blurring the boundaries between who teaches and who learns, and the borders between schools and neighborhoods. It is critical that they are able to recognize the structural forces that impact their students' lives, and have the sense that they are in a position to act on them. However, this approach to teaching and understanding of the role of the teacher is not enough; educators must also develop specific skill sets designed to help them use their classrooms as spaces in which to address community concerns. Given the neoliberal context of urban schools, in which almost every minute of the academic day is geared toward preparation for tests or spent on a standardized program, teachers must integrate social justice teaching into the mandated curriculum. Teachers should involve parents and community members as partners in these projects. Finally, it's essential that social justice educators find like-minded communities of support to sustain and deepen their efforts. If these are some of the mindsets and skill sets required to teach for social justice, we owe ourselves to develop ways in which teacher education programs can develop these qualities in their teacher candidates.

References

Ayers, W., Quinn, T., & Lyon, G. (2000). *Teaching for social justice*. New York: Teachers College.

Camangian, P. (2009). *Teaching like our lives depend on it: Critical pedagogy and classroom research*. Unpublished doctoral dissertation, University of California, Los Angeles.

Cochran-Smith, M. (2004). *Walking the road: Race, diversity, and social justice in teacher education*. New York: Teachers College.

Darder, A. (2002). *Reinventing Paulo Freire: A pedagogy of love*. New York: Westview.

Darling-Hammond, L. (2006). Constructing 21st-century teacher education. *Journal of Teacher Education, 57*(3), 300–314.

Duncan-Andrade, J. M. R., & Morrell, E. (2007). *The art of critical pedagogy: Possibilities for moving from theory to practice in urban schools*. New York: Peter Lang.

Fleming, J., Greenlee, A., Gutstein, E., Lipman, P., & Smith, J. (2009). *Examining CPS' plan to close, phase out, consolidate, turn-around 22 schools*. Chicago: Collaborative for Equity and Justice in Education, University of Illinois.

Freire, P. (1993). *Pedagogy of the oppressed*. New York: Continuum.

Greene, M. (1988). *The dialectic of freedom*. New York: Teachers College.

Gutstein, R. (2005). *Reading and writing the world with mathematics: Toward a pedagogy of social justice*. New York: Routledge.

Katsarou, E. (2009). Reading African-American literature to understand the world: Critical race praxis in teacher preparation. *Race, Ethnicity, and Education, 12*(2), 253–266.

Katsarou, E. (2010). Developing teacher candidates' dispositions, sensibilities, and practice in urban teaching: A teacher-designed formative assessment tool in teacher preparation. In P. C. Murrell Jr., S. Feiman-Nemser, M. E. Diez, & D. L. Schussler (Eds.), *Teaching as a moral practice: Defining, developing, and assessing professional dispositions in teacher education* (pp. 163–176). Cambridge, MA: Harvard Education Press.

Koval, J., Bennett, L., Bennett, M., Demissie, F., Garner, R., & Kim, K. (Eds.). (2007). *The new Chicago: A social and cultural analysis*. Philadelphia: Temple University Press.

Kumashiro, K. K. (2010). Seeing the bigger picture: Troubling movements to end teacher education. *Journal of Teacher Education, 61*(1–2), 56–65.

Lipman, P. (2011). *The new political economy of urban education*. New York: Routledge.

Miech, R. A., & Elder, G. H. (1996). The service ethic and teaching. *Sociology of Education, 69*(3), 237–253.

Murrell, P. (2001). *The community teacher: A new framework for effective urban teaching*. New York: Teachers College.

Picower, B. (2011). Resisting compliance: Learning to teach for social justice in a neoliberal context. *Teachers College Record, 113*(5), 1105–1134.

Singleton, G. E., & Linton, C. (2006). *Courageous conversations about race*. Thousand Oaks, CA: Corwin Press.

Tillage, W. (1997). *Leon's story*. New York: Farrar, Straus, and Giroux.

Verma, R. (Ed.). (2010). *Be the change: Teacher, activist, global citizen*. New York: Peter Lang.

Weiner, L. (2006). Challenging deficit thinking. *Educational Leadership, 64*(1), 42–45.

Zeichner, K. (2006). Reflections of a university-based teacher educator on the future of college- and university-based teacher education. *Journal of Teacher Education, 57*(3), 326–340.

Zeichner, K. (2010). Rethinking the connections between campus courses and field experiences in college- and university-based teacher education. *Journal of Teacher Education, 61*(1–2), 89–99.

PART V

Focus on Community Partners

9

PARTNERING IN A COMMUNITY'S EFFORTS TO TRANSFORM URBAN EDUCATION

Jana Noel

> *After 3 years of being at the school and working in the community, the matriarch took my hand and said, "You are welcome in our neighborhood anytime." (from my journal as Coordinator of the Urban Teacher Education Center)*

Urban Teacher Education Center

Responding to the calls for teacher education to develop stronger connections with their local schools and communities, the Sacramento State Urban Teacher Education Center (UTEC) was created, operating from 2004 to 2009, with ongoing collaborations today. UTEC was a teacher preparation program designed to prepare future teachers to work in low-income, culturally and linguistically diverse urban schools and communities. UTEC moved teacher preparation off of the university campus and into Broadway Circle School (pseudonym), a very low-income, very diverse elementary school in Sacramento. While UTEC's partner was originally intended to be the school, it turned out that the strongest and most meaningful partnership was with the neighborhood's resident-developed nonprofit tutoring and mentoring organization.

Broadway Circle School is a very low-income, culturally and linguistically diverse elementary school in Sacramento that serves children from two neighborhood public housing projects. Every family in the projects receives some form of federal assistance, and 99% of students in the school receive free or reduced lunch, a federal measurement of poverty. The school's student demographics are 55% African American and 97% children of color. English Language Learners make up 23% of the school's population, with the main home languages being Spanish, Vietnamese, Cantonese, Marshallese, and Mien.

UTEC's level of diversity was much lower, as 80% of the university students and faculty in the program were White, middle-class, monolingual English speakers, none of whom lived in the Broadway Circle School neighborhoods. UTEC did not want to develop teachers who fit into the usual pattern of urban schooling, where, as Koerner and Abdul-Tawwab (2006) explain, "most teachers in urban classrooms . . . often teach in communities that they have never previously even visited" (p. 37). Issues of race, class, privilege, and community dynamics came into play in all interactions. UTEC needed to consistently consider how people in the neighborhoods might take a racially, economically, and educationally marked view of their students and faculty (Noel, 2010b).

Both Broadway Circle School and the school district in which it is located are in Program Improvement status, indicating that student test scores have not met the target set by the No Child Left Behind standards. Accompanying this fact was an instability in the school's administration. The need for more stable school–community connections was evident as early as 2005, when the principal and assistant principal both resigned just before the school year began. With no time to hire a qualified full-time principal, the district assigned four retired principals to rotate through the school year. Since retirees are only allowed to work for a set number of days during the year, each principal needed to determine how best to utilize those days. While one of the principals served mostly as the solo principal, the remaining principals overlapped their days of responsibility and also sometimes served as co-principals. For the latter part of the year, one principal served on Monday–Wednesday–Friday, while the other served on Tuesday–Thursday. Needless to say, communication broke down. Agreements made with one principal were not always communicated to the following principal. Both the teachers and the community lost trust in the school to effectively serve their children. The result of an inconsistent administration was a breakdown in communication, and a lessening of trust from the parents and neighboring community.

A key principle driving the creation of the UTEC, then, was that by moving teacher education into urban schools and communities, preservice teachers and faculty would better understand the realities of urban education, including the social, political, and economic conditions impacting the lives and education of urban children and their families (Noel, 2006). UTEC operated under the principle that to effectively educate children in urban settings, teachers must learn about and engage in the communities of their students. Becoming part of the daily fabric of an urban community (Noel, 2010a), through collaboration between universities, teacher education programs, urban schools, communities, and community-based organizations, should transform all partners. As Reid (2007) writes, "teacher education embedded within the context of inner-city education" (p. 228) can lead to transformation of teacher education, schools, and communities. For UTEC, an unexpected result was that the community turned to UTEC for some stability, for another voice to represent them at the school, and for both structural and spontaneous joining of efforts to both create and strengthen efforts to educate children.

Community's History of Mentoring Children

The matriarch of the community has lived in the housing complex for nearly 25 years. Her family includes children and grandchildren, some of whom have stayed in the neighborhood with her and others who have moved out but contribute back to the community. However, the family is more than biological connections, as she and her now-departed husband unofficially adopted many of the community's children, helping to guide them toward high school and higher education. The community organization was founded by this family network, and has provided tutoring and mentoring for the neighborhood children for over a decade.

UTEC's key contacts within the community are the matriarch, her son, and one of the other former residents, who was indeed brought into the family. When UTEC moved into Broadway Circle School and its neighborhood, the organization was operating its program with inconsistency in tutors. UTEC provided weekly tutoring, going into the housing complex to work with the children, providing learning experiences for children and student teachers alike. After several years, the organization applied for and received nonprofit status.

The organization's records show that they work with 75–100 children per year, through activities such as daily after-school tutoring, daily homework help, an after-school dance program that has resulted in performances around the city, summer sports sessions, and field trips to colleges and universities. They follow the progress of their neighborhood children through the middle and high school years, speaking with tremendous pride of those who have completed high school and have gone on to attend higher education. For their work, they were nominated and received the Sacramento State College of Education Community Partner of the Year Award, the first such award for this oft-overlooked neighborhood.

Community Strengths and Presence

The development and operation of UTEC was shaped by two theoretical frameworks: (a) community strengths, and (b) theories of presence.

Theories of Community Strengths

An expanding set of literature is defining communities in terms of their assets, or the term used here, their strengths. Theories of community strengths urge teachers to go into the community, meeting and partnering with community members and agencies, to learn about the important community strengths that can then be utilized in a more culturally relevant education.

Funds of Knowledge

The concept "funds of knowledge," introduced by Moll, Amanti, Neff, and González (1992), refers to the sets of cultural and strategic knowledge and skills found within a particular community. Moll et al. (1992) describe funds of knowledge as a family's "development and exchange of resources—including knowledge, skills, and labor—that enhance the households' ability to survive or thrive" (p. 73). Funds of knowledge can include such cultural components as language and traditions, or can include the strategic network of relationships established within and outside the family and community. This community knowledge often does not coincide with the types of knowledge valued in the educational system, but when a teacher takes the time to learn and recognize a community's funds of knowledge, that set of cultural and strategic skills, she can more effectively draw on those to create a culturally relevant classroom (Ladson-Billings, 2006).

Community Cultural Wealth

In a similar fashion, Yosso (2005) developed the concept of "community cultural wealth," which "focuses on and learns from the array of cultural knowledge, skills, abilities, and contacts possessed by socially marginalized groups that often go unrecognized and unacknowledged" (p. 69). Yosso details six types of "capital" held by members of marginalized communities:

1. Aspirational capital: "the ability to maintain hopes and dreams for the future, even in the face of real and perceived barriers" (p. 77), also known as resiliency.
2. Linguistic capital: "the intellectual and social skills attained through communication experiences in more than one language and/or style" (p. 78).
3. Familial capital: "those cultural knowledges nurtured among *familia* (kin) that carry a sense of community history, memory and cultural intuition" (p. 79).
4. Social capital: "networks of people and community resources. These peer and other social contacts can provide both instrumental and emotional support to navigate through society's institutions" (p. 79).
5. Navigational capital: "skills maneuvering through social institutions" (p. 80).
6. Resistant capital: "knowledges and skills fostered through oppositional behavior that challenges inequality" (p. 80).

When urban educators come to realize that many children and their families maintain these forms of community cultural wealth, even through difficult times, educators can learn to build on these to help support students and families.

As González, Moll, and Amanti (2005) write about the funds of knowledge approach, utilizing community strengths is "for educators who are willing to venture beyond the walls of the classroom. It is for those teachers and teachers-to-be who are willing to learn from their students and their communities" (p. ix).

Theories of Presence

There are both real and perceived differences in level of authority and voice between community and university. Communities may not readily accept efforts of
schools and universities to take a community learning approach to their lives. As
Reed (2004) describes,

> Low-income neighborhoods are jaded by the comings and goings of orga-
> nizations that have no grassroots base in the community. . . . Local residents
> are weary of seeing new initiatives come and go. They are tired of the dis-
> ruptions caused by those who live outside the neighborhood who try to
> offer solutions that, no matter how well intentioned, are not grounded in
> the realities of the street. (p. 81)

Recognizing this very real possibility, Murrell (2001) introduces the term "humility of practice," with which he reminds us that educators "have to avoid the
fatal assumption that they know all they need to know about the culture, values,
traditions, and heritages of the people they purportedly serve" (p. 31). When
working to connect with a community, teachers, administrators, and faculty must
come to recognize that they will be working with organizations, groups, and individuals whose lives are different than their own.

These efforts take not only effort but also simply time. Murrell's (1991, 2001)
concept of teacher education programs "being there" in schools and communities is key here. As Murrell (2001) and Reed (2004) both describe, communities
ask that we be physically present in schools to learn, to show commitment, and
to build trust with community members. Community members need to realize
that community oriented educators are there, in the community, for the long
term. Further, not only does a teacher education program need to "be there" on
a consistent basis, it also needs to be willing and ready to address the needs identified by the community. Murrell (2001) is aware of this concern within urban
neighborhoods, when he writes that

> critical pedagogy is a perspective that . . . our research, our theory, and our
> program development must be loosely linked to the everyday practical ac-
> tivities of school and community development. This means the elimination
> of "helperism" in our relationship to our partners in urban communities
> and working with them on *their* enterprises of change. (pp. 32–33)

Rosenberg's (1997) sense of "dwelling" is another way to describe the importance of "being there," of spending time in the community. As Rosenberg
describes, "we need to think about what it means for us to 'dwell' in the institution. To ask our students and ourselves to 'dwell' is to ask ourselves to exist in a
given place, to fasten our attention, to tarry, to look again. We take root, day after

day" (p. 88). With time, commitment, and humility of practice, urban educators can build trust with the community while learning with community members.

Creating the Urban Teacher Education Center

One of the long-standing centers for teacher preparation at Sacramento State was placing student teachers in schools within a local school district. This center was traditional, in that it offered its university courses on the university campus and then placed student teachers into 12–15 elementary schools for their student teaching experiences. The schools utilized for student teaching placements ranged from low to upper income. In the spring of 2004, a group of faculty and administrators from the school district and Sacramento State collaboratively created the UTEC, moving university courses into Broadway Circle School and its community neighborhoods.

Supported by a host of research from that timeframe describing the benefits of school- and community-based teacher education in urban areas (Cook & Van Cleaf, 2000; Delgadillo & Haberman, 1993; Haberman, 2000; Honig, Kahne, & McLaughlin, 2001; Howey, 2001; Mason, 1999; Murrell, 1991, 1998, 2001; Reed, 2004; Valli, 1996; Weiner, 2000; Zeichner & Melnick, 1996; Zimpher & Ashburn, 1992), two faculty and the Department Chair of the Department of Teacher Education proposed UTEC, to be moved into an urban elementary school within the district where we already had a long history. There were three main changes to the traditional center: (a) courses would be moved into the elementary school; (b) the remaining 12–15 schools where students would be placed for student teaching would all be low-income, culturally and linguistically diverse schools; and (c) students would take part in community studies and in the efforts of the community to provide quality education and mentorship for its children.

Because relationships had already been long established in this school district, it only took one phone call and one in-person meeting with district administration to get approval to create UTEC and move it into an urban elementary school. The one caveat: "only if you move into Broadway Circle School." One meeting with the then-administrators of Broadway Circle, and a Memorandum of Understanding was signed, giving UTEC entrée into the school.

Broadway Circle School immediately incorporated UTEC in the structural functioning of the school. We were given Room 7 for our classroom, where we taught 75 student teachers on a weekly basis. To make us feel at home, the school also donated an old refrigerator for our program. We were given a mailbox within the set of teachers' and staff mailboxes, in which we received copies of everything that the teachers and staff received. This allowed us to keep up on both the most-important school events and the most-mundane daily operations of the school. Faculty and student teachers each semester were given Broadway Circle nametags, letting staff, students, parents, and the student teachers themselves know that they are part of the everyday operations of the school. Faculty became integrated into the functioning of the school by serving as members of the school's School Site Council, serving as co-authors on grant proposals, and serving on several planning committees.

Other papers describe the various ways that UTEC was involved in the activities of the school (Noel, 2006). While not detailed here, examples include:

- Creating a Family Resource Center at the school
- Restarting the Mathematics, Engineering, Science Achievement (MESA) program (after a hiatus of several years) by serving as MESA teachers
- Opening the school's library at lunchtime when there was no librarian hired for the year
- Serving as Lunch Buddies to mentor students
- Leading the university field trip for sixth graders
- Helping to plan and facilitate Family Literacy Nights

Of particular importance were three sets of experiences: "community liaison" role, "community studies," and the neighborhood tutoring/mentoring center.

"Community Liaison"

While serving as UTEC Coordinator, the author took a sabbatical during the fall 2006 semester, serving as an unofficial "community liaison," working to connect the school, the university, and the neighborhood community. She spent time building closer connections between Broadway Circle School and the neighboring public housing projects, as well as at the social services serving these communities. She also initiated a Community Outreach Committee at the school to help further the community involvement efforts of the school and communities.

Broadway Circle Community Tutoring/Mentoring Center

This after-school tutoring/mentoring program within one of the housing projects was created and is operated by the matriarchal family of the neighborhood, including the matriarch herself and two men who grew up in the neighborhood, moved out to get their college degrees, and now give back to their former community by running this center. UTEC students were invited to serve as tutors and mentors for the program, which serve approximately 100 children per year. This created a sense of consistency for the program. It also enabled student teachers and faculty who volunteer to learn more about the lives of children, as it is held within the housing complex rather than on school grounds. This developed into a direct partnership between UTEC and the Broadway Circle community organization, and operated somewhat independently of the school. The UTEC Coordinator nominated the program for a Community Partnership Award from the local university, which they received in the spring of 2006.

Community Studies

The culminating project for student teachers in their first semester of the UTEC program was a "community study," in which they got to know the community, the neighborhoods, and the public housing complexes in which the children and families live (Noel, 2011a). Prior to relocating this program into the elementary school, when the program was still taught on the university campus, four students chose to do their community study on Broadway Circle School. Two of these students did not visit the school or community, doing their research online, while one visited the school's preschool and one visited the Head Start program in the community.

However, with the creation of UTEC and the location of the program on the elementary school campus and with work in the neighborhoods, UTEC students conducted their community studies in the Broadway Circle School community. New approaches to this community study undertaken by student teachers included:

- Interviewing the director of the social service agencies complex on-site at one of the housing complexes
- Interviewing and spending time on the job with the "crosswalk lady," and with the "playground aide," who both live in the neighborhood
- Surveying the children in their classes about their views on whether the library should be reopened
- Talking with the workers at CalWorks, the agency that assists in job searches by residents of the housing complexes
- Riding public transportation to meet parents
- Talking with members of a nearby church that has adopted the school to provide service to children, families, and teachers

Learning Through Community: Leading Through Collaboration

What follows here is a discussion of the impact of moving UTEC into the school, with a particular focus on collaborations with the community organization and community members. The impact on community is presented through entries from my journal while serving as coordinator and through the results of a formal fifth-year evaluation of the program (previously published in Noel, 2010b, 2011b).

The key concern addressed in this chapter is how we worked collaboratively with the community-initiated efforts while at the same time bringing in our ideas. How did UTEC support the community's efforts, on the terms of the community members who created and engaged in the activities? How did we offer our collaboration merely as a supplement to their already-operating community efforts to improve the education of the neighborhood children?

Personal Stories

Journal Entry 1

I finally got to meet the matriarch of the neighborhood. Apparently if anything gets done in [housing project #1], it goes through Ms. F. Danced with Ms. F at the Jazz assembly. We were terrible! But we laughed so hard, and all the teachers and other parents laughed so hard at us, that I think we now have that connection I have desired. Ms. F told me that I could visit her neighborhood anytime.

Journal Entry 2

After arriving at the school and learning about UTEC's focus on community, two of the rotating principals asked for my help in learning more about the community. I led the two principals on a walking tour of the housing complex, introducing them to the neighborhood's matriarchal family and showing them the neighborhood's tutoring/mentoring center.

Journal Entry 3

Since there are no buses at this school, all children must walk to school. One of the principals and I initiated the practice of serving coffee to parents outside the cafeteria as they arrived at the school with their children. The principal even decided to do a "drive through" coffee delivery, for parents who dropped their children off at school by car.

Journal Entry 4

Went to Broadway Circle School for the Monday morning assembly. I sat on the bench by the office next to Ms. G., a mom who is very vocal about her views. When it came time for the National Anthem, she looked at me and said "You know, those kids aren't singing . . . Maybe one of those leadership roles could be doing the National Anthem with the microphone." I said "That's a great idea. Maybe you should tell Ms. [principal], or I could." She said "Oh you should, because you have more pull with her."

Preservice Teacher's Story

A UTEC preservice teacher observed a Broadway Circle School student climbing the fence between the housing projects and the road. She stopped her car to talk with the student, and got permission to serve as an unofficial crosswalk guard. A parent who had seen this preservice teacher acting as crosswalk guard asked if she could help him get information on community colleges for himself. She did some research on her own and interviewed two staff members of the school who live in the neighborhood, and prepared a packet for the parent and for the community overall.

Evaluation of UTEC

After five years of collaboration, it was time to evaluate the impact of UTEC within the school and community (Noel, 2010a). Evaluation instruments included Likert scale surveys, open-ended surveys, interviews, and a focus group. Questions asked reflect the themes found in the literature on urban community-based teacher education, and are grouped by the themes listed below. While a previous paper laid out the results from all participants (Noel, 2010a), and a previous article described the impact on myself as a faculty member "other" (Noel, 2010b), the discussion here will focus on the feedback from the community leaders' focus group and the survey of parents:

1. Perceptions of the benefits of the program for children and UTEC students
2. Level of equality in partnerships (whether they feel valued in the process, whether they feel they have a say in the program's activities)
3. Perceptions related to trust and outsider status
4. Communication issues (understanding the purpose of the program, timeliness of information, flow of communication channels, enough effort gathering information from school and community members)
5. Self-efficacy (I feel I make a difference, I will continue this work in the future)

Instrument	Participants	N	% of total in group	Time of data gathering
Likert Scale Survey (LS)	Teachers Support staff (reading coach, library aide, office staff, custodial staff, playground staff)	5 5	38% 38%	Second-to-last week of 2008–2009 school year
	Administrators	1	50%	
Interviews (I)	Administrator	2	100%	Second-to-last week of
	Teachers	2	15%	2008–2009 school year
	Support staff	2	15%	
Focus Group (FG)	Community leaders	3	N/A	Two weeks after 2008–2009 school year ended
Open-Ended Survey	Parents	17	30% of parents attending Open House 10% of school's total population of parents	2009 Spring Open House: a 15-min time period just before event began Raffled two $25 Target gift cards

Benefit of UTEC in the School and Community

Ninety-five percent of all respondents in all evaluation instruments agreed that having UTEC at the school and community benefited the school's children and UTEC students (Noel, 2010a). However, when asked if they felt that UTEC students are adequately prepared to engage in the partnership activities, community focus group members expressed concern over lack of preparation. Interestingly, the concerns were expressed at a higher rate by community members (50%) than by school personnel (20%). The largest number of concerns from community related to UTEC students' preparation for participating in the particular non-classroom-related activities coordinated by the community, and these respondents requested an initial training tied to the specific programs they operate.

Level of Equality in the Partnership

Likert scale questions asked teachers and school staff whether they felt like they "have a say" in what activities UTEC undertakes at the school and community (63% agreed) and in the organization of those activities (timing, number of students involved, etc.) (54% agreed). Interestingly, more teachers perceived a lack of voice in these matters (50%), than did support staff (20%). This is consistent with the interviews and the focus group, in which one administrator described not having much say in the program while the community members felt very empowered to make decisions regarding the particular UTEC/community collaborative program that they coordinate.

Trust and Outsider Status

All school personnel respondents except for one teacher indicated that they "feel comfortable expressing my thoughts and opinions about UTEC to UTEC faculty," and all survey respondents responded either agree or strongly agree that "I feel that I can trust UTEC faculty and students." Participants were also asked if they had any concerns about "outsiders" coming into the school or community. The community leaders in the focus group expressed two original concerns, alleviated over time, related to outsiders. One, they thought that the program might bring in a set of judgments about the lives of the people in the projects (cf. Foucault, 1977). Two, they were sure that UTEC would not "stick around" (cf. Reed, 2004). The community leaders expressed that they were "amazed" that UTEC was still active in their community after five years.

Communication

All focus group members indicated that they feel comfortable and confident in communications with UTEC, with information flowing both ways smoothly and frequently. However, parents did not express such confidence in the level of communications about UTEC. The first question on the parent survey asked "Has your child ever told you about the university students at Broadway Circle School?" 23% of parents responded yes, 76% reported no. The three parents who answered the open-ended question regarding suggestions, all with children in Grades K–1, expressed the desire to have more opportunities available for the primary-aged children (the focus of most UTEC activities was in Grades 2–6). One parent wrote, "Be more available to the children who need it," because, as another parent wrote, "Children in 1st grade etc. should have a chance to go. The earlier the better." The third parent wrote, "I did not know of the program for the university," and expressed verbally that it "sounds great" and she would like to learn more about it.

Self-Efficacy

One member of the focus group indicated that he finally feels like he is able to impact the children of the neighborhood through the full spectrum of their lives. He felt able to "give up" the tutoring/mentoring program he ran at the public housing site to run a similar program at the high school, because he knew his mother, the community's matriarch, in combination with UTEC, could run the elementary school program on their own. Previously, he felt he had to work only with the elementary children, and his impact might end as they enter middle school. Now he is confident that he, and his family, can make an impact across K–12.

Post-UTEC Collaboration Continues

A confluence of events from 2008 to 2010 signaled the end of UTEC as a formal structure for teacher preparation at Sacramento State, yet collaborative efforts continue today. I stepped down as UTEC Coordinator in May 2008, to serve as the Sacramento State Community Engagement Faculty Scholar. UTEC remained committed to Broadway School and its community, through the work of a talented and caring adjunct faculty member, who had served as my mentor and entrée into the role of coordinating within this district. However, with a new superintendent and continuing low standardized test scores, the entire school's administration and teaching staff (except for one teacher) was "turned over," in an effort to start anew. With such a drastic change, the university assigned a new coordinator, the program was renamed and moved into another low-income elementary school within the district, and within one year the entire program moved back into the university setting.

As stated at the beginning of this chapter, the university's partnership developed with the community organization has had a longer life than that with the school. Currently, although UTEC as a formal teacher education program does not exist, I have been able to help the university and the Broadway Circle community develop new relationships. For example, the Sacramento State admissions counselor who works to recruit students from the community's high school has now met with the matriarchal family to share ideas for collaborating more closely with the neighborhood, positing possible events in the community beyond the walls of the high school.

Partnering With Community in Urban Teacher Education

In the effort to create a more authentic teacher education program for Sacramento State students, the UTEC moved off of the university campus and into Broadway Circle School. By "being there" every day, members of the community began to see us as fully committed to their neighborhood. We were invited into neighborhood gatherings, and were trusted to serve as tutors/mentors in community-led programs. The school allowed us to initiate or help facilitate efforts that would connect the school more closely with the parents and the community. Due to the instability of leadership during our time at the school, UTEC became the more stable force at the school. Despite our outsider status, UTEC was afforded personal and structural opportunities to connect with community members. We became a voice for the community. It is clear that our daily presence within the school and community had begun to break through the layers of distrust the community held toward outsiders. UTEC became seen as a source of strength for the community's efforts to support the neighborhood children's education.

Implications for university educators whose work takes them into urban communities are threefold:

1. Be aware of and open up about coming into the school and community as an "other." Be willing and interested in having conversations about privilege and positionality.
2. Build trust through "being there." Be an enthusiastic collaborator and learner, not a judge or expert on life in the neighborhood.
3. Plan to stay awhile, to "dwell." Don't disappoint by moving briefly in and out of the lives of community members.

With these implications in mind, guiding our relationships, we can gain validity within the communities where we do our work. We can move toward more authentic connections and collaborations.

References

Cook, D. W., & Van Cleaf, D. W. (2000). Multicultural perceptions of 1st-year elementary teachers' urban, suburban, and rural student teaching placements. *Urban Education*, *35*(2), 165–174.

Delgadillo, L., & Haberman, M. (1993). *The impact of training teachers of children in poverty about the specific health and human services offered to the students in their classrooms.* (ERIC Document Reproduction Service No. ED367751)

Foucault, M. (1977). *Discipline and punish: The birth of the prison.* New York: Vintage.

González, N., Moll, L. C., & Amanti, C. (2005). *Funds of knowledge: Theorizing practices in households, communities, and classrooms.* Mahwah, NJ: Erlbaum.

Haberman, M. (2000). *What makes a teacher education program relevant preparation for teaching diverse students in urban poverty schools? (The Milwaukee Teacher Education Center Model).* (ERIC Document Reproduction Service No. ED442745)

Honig, M. I., Kahne, J., & McLaughlin, M. W. (2001). School–community connections: Strengthening opportunity to learn and opportunity to teach. In V. Richardson (Ed.), *Handbook of research on teaching* (4th ed., pp. 998–1027). Washington, DC: American Educational Research Association.

Howey, K. R. (2001). *A conceptual map to guide The Great City Universities Urban Educator Corps Partnership Initiative.* Retrieved from http://www.gcu-edu.org/conceptual framework.doc

Koerner, M., & Abdul-Tawwab, N. (2006). Using community as a resource for teacher education: A case study. *Equity & Excellence in Education, 39,* 37–46. doi:10.1080/10665680500478767

Ladson-Billings, G. (2006). It's not the culture of poverty, it's the poverty of culture: The problem with teacher education. *Anthropology and Education Quarterly, 37*(2), 104–109.

Mason, T. C. (1999). Prospective teachers' attitudes toward urban schools: Can they be changed? *Multicultural Education, 6*(4), 9–13.

Moll, L. C., Amanti, C., Neff, D., & González, N. (1992). Funds of knowledge for teaching: Using a qualitative approach to connect homes and classrooms. *Theory Into Practice, 31*(2), 132–141.

Murrell, P. C., Jr. (1991). Cultural politics in education: What's missing in the preparation of African-American teachers? In M. Foster (Ed.), *Qualitative investigations into schools and schooling: Readings on equal education* (Vol. 11, pp. 205–225). New York: AMS Press.

Murrell, P. C., Jr. (1998). *Like stone soup: The role of the professional development school in the renewal of urban schools.* Washington, DC: AACTE.

Murrell, P. C., Jr. (2001). *The community teacher: A new framework for effective urban teaching.* New York: Teachers College Press.

Noel, J. (2006). Integrating a new teacher education center into a school and its community. *Journal of Urban Learning, Teaching, and Research, 2,* 197–205.

Noel, J. (2010a). Weaving teacher education into the fabric of urban schools and communities. *Teacher Education Quarterly, 37*(3), 9–25.

Noel, J. (2010b). A critical interrogation of privilege, race, class, and power in a university faculty–urban community relationship. *The Urban Review, 42*(3), 210–220. doi:10.1007/s11256-009-0131-4

Noel, J. (2011a). Striving for authentic community engagement: A process model from urban teacher education. *Journal of Higher Education Outreach and Engagement, 15*(1), 31–52.

Noel, J. (2011b). School-community based urban teacher education as a voice for the community. In A. Cohan & A. Honigsfeld (Eds.), *Breaking the mold of pre-service and in-service teacher education: Innovative and successful practices for the 21st century* (pp. 189–197). Lanham, MD: Rowman and Littlefield.

Reed, W. A. (2004). A tree grows in Brooklyn: Schools of education as brokers of social capital in low-income neighborhoods. In J. L. Kincheloe, A. Bursztyn, & S. R. Steinberg (Eds.),

Teaching teachers: Building a quality school of urban education (pp. 65–90). New York: Peter Lang.

Reid, C. (2007). The confluence of teacher education and inner-city activism: A reciprocal possibility. In R. P. Solomon & D. N. R. Sekayi (Eds.), *Urban teacher education and teaching: Innovative practices for diversity and social justice* (pp. 227–239). New York: Routledge.

Rosenberg, P. M. (1997). Underground discourses: Exploring Whiteness in teacher education. In M. Fine, L. Weis, L. C. Powell, & L. M. Wong (Eds.), *Off White: Readings on race, power, and society* (pp. 79–89). New York: Routledge.

Valli, L. (1996). Trusting relations, preservice teachers, and multicultural schools. In D. J. McIntyre & D. M. Byrd (Eds.), *Preparing tomorrow's teachers: The field experience* (pp. 26–40). Thousand Oaks, CA: Corwin Press.

Weiner, L. (2000). Research in the 90s: Implications for urban teacher preparation. *Review of Educational Research, 70*(3), 369–406.

Yosso, T. J. (2005). Whose culture has capital? A critical race theory discussion of community cultural wealth. *Race, Ethnicity, and Education, 8*(1), 69–91.

Zeichner, K., & Melnick, S. (1996). The role of community field experiences in preparing teachers for cultural diversity. In K. Zeichner, S. Melnick, & M. L. Gomez (Eds.), *Currents of reform in preservice teacher education* (pp. 176–196). New York: Teachers College Press.

Zimpher, N. L., & Ashburn, E. A. (1992). Countering parochialism in teacher candidates. In M. E. Dilworth (Ed.), *Diversity in teacher education: New expectations* (pp. 40–62). San Francisco: Jossey-Bass Publishers.

10

A COMMUNITY–UNIVERSITY PARTNERSHIP TO DEVELOP URBAN TEACHERS AS PUBLIC PROFESSIONALS

Cynthia Onore and Bonny L. Gildin

A long-standing, vexing issue for teacher education has centered on preparing teachers for high-need urban schools. As long ago as 1969, Robert Farls addressed this issue by making a number of suggestions that still resonate. He recommends increasing fieldwork in the schools and providing on-site course work, and re-quiring course work in comparative culture, human relations, psychology, and the history of the civil rights movement. His central concern then, like ours now, was developing teachers' capacities to work effectively with poor children of color in underserved urban neighborhoods.

Preparing teaching candidates for working with a diverse student body has be-come a central tenet of preparation programs (Darling-Hammond & Bransford, 2005). Course work that attempts to develop new teachers' perspectives on diver-sity and multiculturalism as assets rather than deficits has been woven into teacher preparation curricula (C. A. Banks & Banks, 2004; J. A. Banks, 1994; J. A. Banks & Banks, 2010; Grant & Sleeter, 1999; Nieto, 2007; Ladson-Billings, 1995), while the application of multicultural insights and affirming attitudes toward diversity can be found in the study of culturally responsive teaching practices (J. A. Banks et al., 2001; Gay, 2000; Irvine, 2003; Ladson-Billings, 2001; Villegas & Lucas, 2002). Taken together, such course work offers opportunities for preservice teachers to generate new knowledge about and appreciation of diverse cultures and com-munities and supports deep examinations of their own beliefs and assumptions. At the same time, it provides them with frameworks for developing pedagogy and curriculum for educational equity and cross cultural competency, a commitment both emotional and intellectual, to appreciate difference while recognizing the fundamental unity of all humans (McAllister & Irvine, 2000).

Recognizing that academic courses that focus on pedagogy, no matter how transformative its intentions, may be insufficient to educate teachers of diverse students, courses of study for urban teacher preparation have integrated knowledge of family, home, and community. A "funds of knowledge" approach (Gonzalez, Moll, & Amanti, 2005; Moll & Gonzalez, 2004), for example, adds a critical element to cross cultural competence by demonstrating the positive contributions of families and communities, which can greatly enhance student achievement.

Multicultural service learning is a more robust form of community-based learning. It combines service learning and diversity education to create opportunities for preservice teachers not only to learn about the assets of students' home communities but also about community-defined needs (Boyle-Baise, 2002; Boyle-Baise & Grant, 2000; Boyle-Baise & Sleeter, 2000; Carter-Andrews, 2009; Grineski, 2003). Combined with ethnographic inquiry and action research, these kinds of field experiences can help teachers to interrogate and modify their beliefs and assumptions and even to understand their work as part of an explicit social justice agenda that privileges access to knowledge and equitable education over individual, meritocratic success (Hyland & Nofke, 2005; Tiezzi & Cross, 1997).

Peter Murrell (2001, 2008) offers, perhaps, the most comprehensive and integrated framework for educating effective urban teachers in his model of the "community teacher," one who can "draw on a richly contextualized knowledge of culture, community, and identity" (Murrell, 2001, p. 4). A central component is the "circle of co-practice," a nonhierarchical professional collaboration with the potential to create a new kind of professional community. Of particular note is that these professional communities are reciprocal—community members have a voice in setting the goals and standards of achievement for teachers while educators provide support in addressing community needs.

The power of the "community teacher" framework lies in its central insistence on enhancing the capacities of schools to address the needs of learners through community collaboration. However, its power is diminished, we believe, to the extent that preservice teachers focus their efforts on enhancing school-based, individual achievement objectives alone. Rather, community teachers might align themselves more closely with other, more transformative purposes such as cultivating civic virtue in the young. In so doing, they would be engaging in shared responsibility for community betterment.

Despite all the advances that universities have made to better prepare urban teachers over the past 40 years, concerns remain about their capacities to devote adequate time for discussion and reflection on field-based work, provide enough resources for effective supervision in fieldwork sites, and implement structures to maintain contact between universities and field sites (Carter-Andrews, 2009). Additionally, multicultural service learning and community-based learning have had mixed results. Some participants' negative beliefs about urban children and communities have been unwittingly reinforced rather than transformed (Cooper, 2007; Cross, 2003; Leland & Harste, 2005; McAllister &

Irvine, 2000; Sleeter, 2001; Tiezzi & Cross, 1997). As Sleeter (2001) has concluded in her comprehensive review of multicultural teacher education, "extensive community-based immersion experiences coupled with coursework seem to have the most promise" (p. 102), but she is skeptical that universities will commit enough human and financial resources to these projects. More evidence of this may be found in a recent study of 161 schools and colleges of education in which, despite increased awareness of the importance of community knowledge for preparing education professionals, structural, organizational, and attitudinal factors deeply affect the extent to which institutions are able to do so (Epstein & Sanders, 2006). Clearly, then, the challenges facing urban teacher preparation persist. Equally clear is that these challenges cannot be met by universities alone. Partnerships among teacher-preparing programs, schools, and communities are essential.

Teachers as Public Professionals

One promising direction for meeting these challenges may be derived from Yinger's (2005) call to reconceptualize teaching as a "public profession." To do so would require a vision of schools as sites for educating publics in civic virtues—virtues that center on understanding our rights as individuals alongside of and in balance with our responsibilities to our communities; understanding the interdependences of community members, even those with unequal power; and seeking and finding shared values and goals with others to produce forms of life that benefit the wider public.

If public schools had such purposes, they would not simply occupy spaces within a community, but they would see their work as embedded in the community and, thus, intimately tied to community values and goals. In such school settings, teachers would recognize their work as a connected enterprise, as facets of the same work that is carried out by parents, cultural and religious organizations, and social service agencies. Teaching, then, would be a form of social activism in which teachers engage in collaborative exploration of educational issues, identify mutually valuable social projects, and commit to civic values, all of which would simultaneously serve educational purposes (Yinger, 2005). Such civic values and virtues are an essential requirement in a diverse, multicultural society as they include publicly deliberating contested issues, seeking mutual understanding, a commitment to dialogue over diatribe, and collective meaning making over individual gain (Kymlicka, 2002, p. 293).

Civic virtues of this kind are best expressed through covenantal relationships, according to Yinger, relationships that make it possible to develop mutual understanding and are defined by their reciprocity. Through such relationships, separate purposes are rendered as common purposes and a new context is created. Such a perspective would alter the very nature of teachers' work and would redefine the role of citizens in the work of education. While it is not Yinger's intention to apply this view of the teaching profession to urban teacher preparation, his framework offers a compelling way to frame university–community partnerships for urban teacher preparation.

A conceptual framework for preparing teachers as public professionals in the context of poor communities of color must include complementary notions of student and community identity. One contemporary Black scholar whose work resists categorical and rigid identity definitions is that of Appiah (1997), who has developed the concept of the "cosmopolitan patriot," the individual who is a citizen of their particular country and at the same time a citizen of the world. For Appiah, the idea that one can have more than one cultural identity is an important one, because it means that our individual histories and backgrounds do not define, in a fixed way, who we are. Identity then becomes both multilayered and open to being created and re-created.

Appiah's insights into becoming cosmopolitan have a direct application to educational programs for urban youth. Such programs must make growth through identity reflection and development possible. Narrow identities, from Appiah's perspective, create a tendency to view oneself as a victim of one's circumstances, rather than as a human being with the capacity to create one's life. Cosmopolitanizing practices also have rich potential to construct teachers as powerful participants in social justice and social change while offering enriched opportunities for urban youth to go beyond narrow identity descriptions. Such are the potential contributions of urban teachers as public professionals.

Murrell's (2007) stance on identity development and learning, as articulated in his situated-mediated theory, is consistent with Appiah's. Murrell's suggestion that "school success is achievable when learning is understood as the acquisition of a set of preferred cultural practices" (p. 34) offers a pathway toward creating more effective school environments, especially if the classroom is viewed as a space for collective performance in which the participants roles are created, not given, thus opening up new identities.

The kinds of teacher education practices envisioned by Murrell and which might be inferred from Appiah and Yinger cannot be conducted by teacher-preparing institutions alone. Partnerships with community institutions can situate teaching at the intersection of inside and outside of school. Such a vision is articulated by Howey (1999), who imagines this new space as truly transformative. Of particular interest to us is that Howey also advocates for creating a collaborative, "interprofessional culture" (p. 36). For teachers to enact their roles as public professionals, they would have to understand schools as co-participants in the construction of a new and better community life.

In this paper, we describe a new partnership for urban teacher preparation between a university teacher education program and a nonprofit, youth and community development organization, through which we are attempting to build a new interprofessional culture as we explore how to prepare new urban teachers to be public professionals.

The Partners and What They Bring to This Work

The All Stars Project Inc.

The All Stars Project Inc. (ASP) is a 31-year-old, privately funded nonprofit that sponsors outside of school development programs for poor, urban youth of color. reaching 10,000 youth a year in four cities—New York City; Newark, NJ; Oakland/San Francisco; and Chicago. Completely funded by the private sector, primarily through individual contributions, ASP has been relatively free of bureaucratic constraints and has created a new, youth development model built on theoretical inquiry in psychology and philosophy (e.g., the work of Vygotsky and Wittgenstein). It is grounded in the belief that personal and social growth and development are preconditional for learning—"what you get from development is the need and desire to learn" (Newman, 2010).

As the organization evolved, the understanding that the human capacity to play and to perform can foster growth at any age, has figured centrally in all of its programs. Performance allows young people to stretch beyond what they already know how to do and actively create new ways to be in the world, new identities, reflecting Appiah's (1997) ideas. The All Stars Project established an operation in Newark in 1999 and currently involves close to 1,500 young people a year in its program activities. The Newark organization is supported by 600 individuals and corporations, 250 volunteers, and partners with more than 50 corporations that provide paid summer internships to youth who complete the organization's leadership training program. ASP core programs include neighborhood hip-hop talent shows (All Stars Talent Show Network), and the Development School for Youth (DSY), a leadership training program, provided in partnership with the business community.

At the end of 2012, the All Stars Project will open a 9,000-square-foot center for after-school development, in the heart of downtown Newark. The center is designed to further support the expansion of program activities, partnerships between youth and adults in the business and artistic communities and research and training collaborations with universities.

Concepts of After-School and the All Stars Project as New Spaces for Growth

Community-based, after-school, and youth development programs have the power to engage the social contract in ways that Yinger identifies. In many ways, these kinds of programs are a natural vehicle through which preservice teachers can develop a broader identity as public professionals and participate in a larger social agenda. What can distinguish such programs is not just their location but also their intention to foster the development of youth and their capacity as a force for transformation. Through developmental experiences, young people learn *that* transformation is possible—that they can create their own lives—and also that they can, and need to, develop their communities, echoing Appiah's cosmopolitanizing.

Organized after-school programs have been part of urban America since the turn of the century and have a rich history of service to urban children separate from that of school (Halpern, 2002). Currently, many focus on a compensatory or supplemental roles, particularly those that serve poor and minority youth. For Halpern, the struggle between programs that are driven by children's interests and those that are shaped by adult views of what children need, ironically, has had positive consequences for after-school programs and has created:

> room to be a different kind of child development institution—one that mostly avoided pathologizing low income children and one that can identify gaps in children's lives and try to fill them. It allowed after-school programs to be adult-directed institutions where the adult agenda is relatively modest. And it has allowed them to be responsive to the changing needs and circumstances in the lives of low income children. (p. 179)

In this way, after-school programs establish a different kind of space, one the ASP characterizes as "room to grow."

After-school programs have historically also had strong connections to the communities in which they are located and some, like the ASP, begin from the premise that schools "only have so much success to give," and that "after-school programs can afford to be much more generous in this regard" (Halpern, 2002, p. 203). On the other hand, after-school programs are under increasing pressure to make their activities more school-like and demonstrate that they help to improve test scores.

ASP's conceptual framework has strong resonance with Appiah's (1997) insights into the relationship between becoming cosmopolitan—becoming someone with multiple and layered identities and learning. The ASP has discovered that young people choose to develop as learners and become active creators of their lives (Fulani, 2008). Rather than accepting the popular notion that there is an achievement gap for urban youth, the ASP understands this as "the development gap." Fulani and Kurlander (2009) argue that "these kids are not simply failing to learn. They are failing to become learners . . . It is a development gap" (p. 2).

The ASP emphasis on performance and play and its underlying commitment to development are examples of the "responsive practices" to which Yinger (2005) refers. Participation in these practices is one route for preservice urban teachers to explore "school problems as community problems and [to] seek community solutions" (p. 287).

Montclair State University's Work in Newark, New Jersey

For more than 30 years, Montclair State University (MSU) has had thriving partnerships with the Newark Public Schools, including a professional development school (dismantled in 1995 when the state of New Jersey seized control of the

Newark Schools) and a rich array of professional development activities for teachers through the MSU Network for Educational Renewal. MSU offers the Urban Teaching Academy (UTA), a strand in its teacher preparation program for students preparing to teach in urban schools, has developed the Partnership for Instructional Excellence and Quality (PIE-Q), a consortium of seven Newark schools, the Newark Teachers Union, and the university and, most recently through a Teacher Quality Partnership Grant, the Newark–Montclair Urban Teacher Residency program (NMUTR). In short, the university and the Newark Public Schools have long-standing and well-established collaborations.

Collaboration with community-based organizations has also been a centerpiece of MSU's urban teacher preparation programs for many years. The UTA, PIE-Q, and NMUTR all provide opportunities for teaching candidates to work in community settings as part of their course of study. By including community internships in the urban teacher preparation curriculum, these programs attempt to develop teaching candidates' understanding of, and appreciation for, urban communities, understandings that cannot be filled academic course work alone. However, we have learned that such experiences does not automatically lead to insights about essential inside- and outside-of-school connections.

The Evolution of the Partnership and Its Activities

A few months after the co-authors met at an ASP fundraising event, they met again at a conference on preparing teachers for urban schools. At that time, the university sought opportunities to embed more community-based fieldwork in its course of study, and the ASP was looking for a university partner to advance research and professional training on play and performance in outside-of-school youth programs.

Over time we began to see that our objectives were two sides of the same coin—one side focused on getting young people ready to learn, and the other one supporting young people's actual learning through teacher education. From Yinger's perspective, our partnership became a covenantal one, one that could provide mutual benefits that went beyond being responsive to and supportive of one another's goals. Working together actually helped us to understand our work differently while it simultaneously helped us to develop our individual endeavors. It offered prospects for the renewal and enhancement of our individual and organizational endeavors by situating our work in new space between the university, the schools, and the community, thereby creating a new "interprofessional community" (Howey, 1999).

In exploring what a partnership between MSU and the ASP would look like, we sought to address the limitations of our previous university–community collaborations. In past collaborations, the internships were, in essence, placements where interns filled roles and responsibilities that were already defined by the organizations. In addition, we were concerned that, overall, the majority of the internships ended up engaging the MSU students in school-like activities, primarily tutoring. Since the ASP engages in youth development through activities that are "not school-like," these internships had a different potential. Additionally, unlike many community-based organizations, the ASP has a positive youth development orientation rather than a problem orientation, thus making it possible to avoid reinforcing the beliefs of many teaching candidates that they are "saving the poor children" (Ladson-Billings, 2001). Since the ASP deliberately resists this through offering activities that center on experiencing imaginative possibilities, we believed that ASP internships could engage the preservice teachers in seeing transformative potential in the youth themselves. We also speculated that the students could come to see teaching as a facet of a larger social project in which their roles as teachers would be yoked together with their relationships to communities.

The Initial Collaborative Design

Our initial design for the first cohort of teacher education students had four basic components: an orientation to the ASP; participation in two core activities—the DSY and the All Stars Talent Show; a mid-semester meeting with a group of young people from the DSY; a final, in-class reflection on the ASP with program leaders. The university students were required to keep field notes to use in a paper and a final reflection on the course. Together, we designed several questions about the ASP experiences for them to address. These were the core components for two semesters. We observed and recorded our observations of each activity and event. We also regularly reflected on our work with MSU students and ASP staff and redesigned or created entirely new activities. For example, in response to feedback we received, we convened a gathering of the MSU students and a group of DSY participants. We helped the MSU students to create questions to ask the DSY students, but were surprised when the DSY students arrived with their own questions for the soon-to-be teachers. As we watched the young people take the lead in the Q&A, we realized that not only was this a cosmopolitanizing experience for them but that we could create more opportunities for them to take the lead in their interactions with the teaching candidates. These sorts of experiences and insights led to a redesign of the work.

The Collaborative Redesign

After reviewing the feedback we received from the MSU students and ASP staff, and based on our firsthand observations, we decided to make a number of changes in our work. Several new or enhanced components were part of a "second generation" design that we implemented. First, we decided that the MSU students should visit DSY in pairs or small groups. That way, they would have an opportunity to reflect together on an in-common experience. We also created a mid-semester get-together for everyone involved in the project. In a performance workshop in which directors, professors, DSY students, and MSU students came together, we all participated in movements and skits focused on putting us all in unfamiliar situations. We hoped that in this way the youth and preservice teachers could see each other as human beings and interact in ways that are different from their traditional roles.

An equally ambitious effort at redesign went into the creation of a Student Study. This component drew on our previous experiences where they DSY youth acted as leaders. This project had three settings in which pairs of preservice teachers would participate and gather data. First, the DSY youth were asked to volunteer to buddy with the MSU pairs. The MSU pairs accompanied their buddy to a DSY session and then visited them in their regular school setting for a day. The young person also invited the pair of MSU students to participate in a home- or community-based activity with them. This activity was one in which the young person normally engaged: going to church or the mall, babysitting a younger sibling or visiting a grandparent, for example. This inquiry project had two key elements: the DSY youth were inviting and leading the MSU pairs into their contexts, and the MSU students were posing their own questions about the three settings. Our belief was that through this work, the teaching candidates' understandings of and appreciation for urban youth and communities would be enhanced, and their desire to participate in positive youth and community development efforts would be ignited. We also hoped they come to see their work as teachers differently.

After this third semester, the program itself went through a significant change when MSU received funding to create the Newark–Montclair State Urban Teaching Residency program (NMUTR). Students would now be embedded full-time in Newark school classrooms, starting in the fall semester, which meant that community fieldwork during the school year would not be possible. Before submitting the final version of the grant proposal, we met to design community fieldwork for the summer months before students began their classroom residencies.

The biggest challenge was that we had to fit the All Stars fieldwork into the summer before the MSU students began their full-time residency. As it turned out, the first summer of the NMUTR would, in fact, coincide with the DSY internship program's most ambitious undertaking to date—to place and support 200 graduates in internships in more than two dozen corporations. The All Stars small staff was already stretched, and we needed to be sensitive to designing a program that could be successful.

The first NMUTR cohort was small, which gave us the chance to address these challenges creatively. We decided to build off the Student Study experience and have the residents serve as "relationship managers" for small groups of DSY interns placed together at a single company, with anywhere from 2 to 30 interns. Pairs of residents would be part of the interns' support system, visiting them at their corporate work site, meeting their internship supervisors and touching base with the interns periodically by phone or email about how their professional work assignments were going. The residents would periodically meet with the DSY director on how to best coach the DSY interns on work and personal issues that were coming up for them and also participate in one of the mid-summer meetings the director held to work with the interns as a group. We also asked the residents to spend time with their small group socially and in the community. All the residents would take a turn spending three weeks in the All Stars office, helping with the considerable paperwork and organizing involved in the meetings and end of summer receptions.

With this third redesign, we continued to see the positive impact of supporting preservice teachers to get to know urban youth and developing a capacity to interact with them in a variety of settings.

The Impact of the Partnership on the Participants

At the end of the each year of our work, we reflected on the results of our work in a number of ways. We held focus groups with the residents, and reviewed the written reflections of each cohort of university students and with staff and faculty from both organizations.

How the Teaching Candidates Were Affected

From the anecdotal data and the focus groups, several themes emerged. Among these are reconsiderations of stereotypes of urban youth; new pedagogical orientations and approaches; making connections between students lives inside and outside of school in the classroom; establishing ongoing and committed relationships to students beyond the classroom. In the following section, we relate a few, selected comments by the residents about how they have been affected by the opportunities that working with the ASP has provided.

Many of the residents commented on how their views of urban youth were changed by their outside-of-school experiences with them. One remarked that, "It calmed me down. These were just adolescents . . . my future students were no longer this collage of categorizations and imaginations that I had been forming both in life and at MSU." Another said, "The more contact I had with the people who were my future students, the more textured my understandings of them became and the less likely I was to base those understanding on stuff I read or imagined."

Some commented on the ASP approach to performance as a pedagogical practice. One resident said, "It helps students to see beyond themselves in so many ways. Students are more than individuals, more than their neighborhoods, more than their race, more than what society expects of them."

Quite by chance, one resident had a DSY participant in her one of her high school classes. Recognizing that the very same young people appeared quite different in the outside-of-school setting, he said, "The idea that students who may not have much interest and participation in the classroom setting, do still have interests and things that get them excited, amazed me." But they also recognized that their students might have talents and dreams that can be given expression in the classroom: "Because of the All Stars, I am able to see my students' other side and invite them to bring that side into the classroom." These sorts of inside-/outside-of-school connections are essential to transformational teaching practices. Learning to talk with young people in generative ways is an another essential element of powerful teaching and learning. The summer internships also provided opportunities for the residents to learn about how to have conversations with youth:

> You had to work to create structures to talk with young adults. Communication with young adults was harder than you thought. You had to press harder. I was naïve about that. I didn't anticipate that . . . I thought about teaching and how they're not going to do their homework—and how this experience will directly influence my next experience.

Follow-up conversations with members of the first cohort of residents, now first-year teachers, have given us some further insights into potential impact of these experiences on urban teachers. As you can see, they continue to draw on their experiences with the ASP. One former resident and now first-year Newark high school biology teacher told us that "kids want to be able to talk to you, and you have to be open to their experiences—even in the middle of a lesson—because it's relevant to how they process information." We could see that beyond attitudes and dispositions about urban youth, the residents were also developing responsive skills for teaching.

Another resident demonstrated, through her commitment to an ongoing relationship with one of the DSY youth she coached over the summer, that she wants to continue to learn how to develop her relationships with young people and sees herself as an integral part of this young person's support network. We view this kind of commitment as one of the components of a teacher who is a public professional.

We are also very encouraged by the current and former residents' positive attitudes toward and interest in participating in community-based efforts. All Stars staff was delighted to see a former resident, now first-year teacher, accompany one of his current students to a Development School for Youth Orientation. Another former resident told us how keeping connected to the community supports her, "I feel that I am part of a broader effort when I see programs in the community. It keeps me motivated . . . We can do better . . . with the right guidance from everyone, they [students] can perform." That is exactly the kind of orientation to teaching that we had hoped to engender, based in reciprocity between the needs of urban youth and the needs of new, urban teacher.

Impact on the Community Through the All Stars Project

In reviewing how the partnership has affected the All Stars Project and its work in the Newark community, it is clear that benefits have accrued in both planned and unplanned for ways. These include seeing the residents as resources; developing new programs with the university that benefit the ASP agenda and the university, and new opportunities for leadership development for the ASP young people.

During the summer internships, the residents proved to be a resource to the young people in ways we had not imagined. It had not occurred to us that the preservice teachers' subject matter expertise would have a role to play in supporting the development of the DSY youth. However, while planning for a workshop with them, the summer director and resident pair recognized that they could create an opportunity for the residents to teach the youth about topics and issues of direct relevance to them, ones that were also school subjects of study. In one example, a resident preparing to teach math developed a statistical presentation on poverty in America and led a discussion in which the youth were able to connect their lived experience to the data. Another resident in biology prepared a lesson on nutrition in poor neighborhoods and how the highly processed foods generally available in stores in the poor community contributed to high rates of diabetes. When debriefed, the youth expressed how deeply touched and affected they were by the ideas their "community teachers" shared with them.

The ASP cosmopolitanizing agenda calls for the participants to have experiences that are naturally part of growing up in a more affluent social milieu and that help young people develop sophistication about how the world works and nurtures their interests in and readiness to learn. We had discovered in an early encounter between the residents and the DSY youth that the exchanges between the two groups were reciprocal and mutually beneficial. As a result, the ASP has added visits to the MSU campus and attendance at teacher education classes, where they have the opportunity to meet and talk with preservice teachers. This not only provides a chance for the youth to become acquainted with university life, but also allows them to act as consultants to new teachers. They exercise their leadership abilities though dialogue with teaching candidates as they give them access to the perspectives of urban youth on life inside and outside of school.

In the process of developing the new center for after-school development, we have reached out to members of the first NMUTR cohort and invited them to help the ASP design some of the activities that will be offered through the center for after-school development. The former residents, now teachers, bring their unique perspectives to this work by enhancing the center's capacity to be an educative setting, while simultaneously providing another way for new teachers to connect to the community. In addition, one of the authors is now an adjunct member of the Montclair State faculty, designing and teaching the first course of a potential new undergraduate program at the university focused on the after-school field. The ASP is a resource and research site for students in this course, and the new center will be integrated into the course of study, as well.

Most recently, MSU has invited the All Stars to develop and teach a course on after-school development on campus. Using the ASP as a fieldwork site in this course has provided the students with the chance to connect theory to practice. When the new center for after-school development opens in Newark, fieldwork and research opportunities will be greatly expanded. The response to this course has been so positive that here is discussion about developing a doctoral program through the Department of Family and Child Studies that would develop expertise in and a research agenda for the impact of after-school on urban youth. The ASP sees this outgrowth as a unique opportunity to engage with the academic community about policy as well as practice. The ASP mission is both to directly serve young people in poor communities by creating and sponsoring outside-of-school activities for them and to advocate for "after-school development" to be understood—and adopted—as a new and critical strategy for solving the education crisis in America's poor, urban communities. This aspect of the partnership with the university opens a space to do just that.

Developing Our Partnership and Ourselves: An Agenda for Action

Our work is continuing to evolve. An ongoing challenge is how to design experiences that meet the needs of larger residency cohorts while the ASP itself is going through significant growth and transformation with the new after-school center as a focus of activity. As of this writing, the NMUTR faculty and the All Stars have agreed to continue the summer relationship management experience with the DSY summer interns, and we are exploring how residents can also participate in summer grassroots community outreach for the All Stars Talent Show Network.

Educating teachers to be public professionals offers promise as a way to reconceptualize the knowledge base for teaching. As Zeichner (2010) has recently pointed out, "the old paradigm of university-based teacher education where academic knowledge is viewed as the authoritative source of knowledge about teaching needs to change to one where there is a nonhierarchical interplay between academic, practitioner, and community expertise" (p. 89). We believe our work suggests alternative ways for university-based programs to partner with community-based organizations and to construct a course of study where community learning is collaboratively developed and carried out and where knowledge is situated in an interprofessional space.

Recognizing the importance of sharing our work with other teacher educators we hope to contribute to an agenda set forth by Peterman and Swiegard (2008) to explore how to prepare urban teachers to meet standards that respond directly to the urban context. These include forming identities as partners in the education of urban youth with families and communities, a commitment to urban renewal and community activism, and developing "resiliency, resistance, and persistence" (p. 34), three attributes that, we believe, can be engendered through initiatives designed to educate teachers as public professionals.

These beginning stages of the collaboration between the ASP Project and MSU's teacher education program demonstrate the potential to help teachers to envision their work in new ways and show, as well, how an interprofessional community of educators and community activists can strengthen community development work. We believe that the new urban teachers who are educated in these ways will not only be able to meet the highest professional standards of content knowledge and teaching skill but that they will be different kinds of urban teachers. They may conceptualize teaching as a public profession in which they "play crucial roles in the work of forming persons and forming citizens for democratic nations" (Yinger, 2005, p. 289). Such ways of thinking will be part of their understandings of themselves as educational professionals who are citizens with special purposes—to work together with those outside of school to achieve common goals. Simultaneously, community-based organizations can become integral to a collaborative educational enterprise while they also benefit from collaboration with the institutions of schooling through their integration into this work. These new relationships can engender a kind of hope that can only come from constructing our world together and publicly as a common endeavor.

References

Appiah, K. A. (1997). Cosmopolitanism patriots. *Critical Inquiry, 23*(3), 21–29.

Banks, C. A., & Banks, J. A. (2004). *Handbook of research on multicultural education* (2nd ed.). San Francisco: Jossey-Bass.

Banks, J. A. (1994). *An introduction to multicultural education*. Boston: Allyn and Bacon.

Banks, J. A., & Banks, C. A. (Eds.). (2010). *Multicultural education: Issues and perspectives* (7th ed.). Hoboken, NJ: John Wiley.

Banks, J. A., Cookson, P., Gay, G., Hawley, W. D., Irvine, J. J., Nieto, S., et al. (2001, November). Diversity within unity: Essential principles for teaching and learning in a multicultural society. *Phi Delta Kappan, 83*(3), 196–198, 200–203.

Boyle-Baise, M. (2002). *Multicultural service learning: Educating teachers in diverse communities*. New York: Teachers College Press.

Boyle-Baise, M., & Grant, C. A. (2000). Citizen/community participation in education: Historic change in terms of engagement. In S. Adler (Ed.), *Critical issues in social studies teacher education* (pp. 145–164). Scottsdale, AZ: Information Age.

Boyle-Baise, M., & Sleeter, C. (2000). Community-based service learning for multicultural teacher education. *Educational Foundations, 14*(2), 33–50.

Carter-Andrews, D. J. (2009). The hardest thing to turn from: The effects of service learning on urban educators. *Equity and Excellence in Education, 42*(3), 272–293.

Cooper, J. E. (2007). Strengthening the case for community-based learning in teacher education. *Journal of Teacher Education, 58*(3), 245–255.

Cross, B. (2003). Learning or unlearning racism: Transferring teacher education curriculum into classroom practices. *Theory Into Practice, 42*(3), 203–209.

Darling-Hammond, L., & Bransford, J. (Eds.). (2005). *Preparing teachers for a changing world: What teachers should learn and be able to do.* San Francisco: Jossey-Bass.

Epstein, J. L., & Sanders, M. G. (2006). Prospects for change: Preparing educators for school, family, and community partnerships. *Peabody Journal of Education, 81*(2), 81–120.

Farls, F. (1969). Staffing the slum school. *Elementary School Journal, 69*(8), 408–412.

Fulani, L. (2008, June 14). *Introduction to Professor K. Anthony Appiah.* New York: All Stars Project Inc.

Fulani, L., & Kurlander, G. (2009). *Special report: Achievement gap or development gap: Outliers and outsiders consider an old problem.* New York: All Stars Project Inc.

Gay, G. (2000). *Culturally responsive teaching: Theory, research and practice.* New York: Teachers College Press.

Gonzalez, N., Moll, L. C., & Amanti, C. (2005). *Funds of knowledge: Theorizing practices in homes, communities, and classrooms.* Mahwah, NJ: Erlbaum.

Grant, C. A., & Sleeter, C. E. (1999). *Making choices for multicultural education: Five approaches to race, class and gender.* Mahwah, NJ: John Wiley.

Grineski, S. (2003). A university and community-based partnership: After-school mentoring for low-income youth. *School Community Journal, 13*(1), 101–114.

Halpern, R. (2002). A different kind of child development institution: The history of after-school programs for low-income children. *Teacher's College Record, 104*(2), 178–211.

Howey, K. R. (1999, Winter). Preparing teachers for inner city schools. *Theory Into Practice, 38*(1), 31–36.

Hyland, N. E., & Nofke, S. E. (2005). Understanding diversity through social and community inquiry: An action research study. *Journal of Teacher Education, 56*(4), 367–381.

Irvine, J. J. (2003). *Educating teachers for diversity: Seeing with a cultural eye.* New York: Teachers College Press.

Kymlicka, W. (2002). *Contemporary political philosophy: An introduction* (2nd ed.). New York: Oxford University Press.

Ladson-Billings, G. (1995, Summer). But that's just good teaching! The case for culturally relevant pedagogy. *Theory Into Practice, 34*(3), 159–165.

Ladsen-Billings, G. (2001). *Crossing over to Canaan: The journey of new teachers in diverse classrooms.* San Francisco: Jossey-Bass.

Leland, C., & Harste, J. (2005). Doing what we became: Preparing new urban teachers. *Urban Education, 40*(1), 60–77.

McAllister, G., & Irvine, J. J. (2000, Spring). Cross cultural competency and multicultural teacher education. *Review of Educational Research, 70*(1), 3–24.

Moll, L. C., & Gonzalez, N. (2004). Engaging life: A funds of knowledge approach to multicultural education. In J. A. Banks & C. A. M. Banks (Eds.), *Handbook of research on multicultural education* (2nd ed., pp. 699–715). San Francisco: Jossey-Bass.

Murrell, P. C., Jr. (2001). *The community teacher: A new framework for effective urban teaching.* New York: Teachers College Press.

Murrell, P. C., Jr. (2007). *Race, culture, and schooling: Identities of achievement in multicultural urban schools.* New York: Taylor and Francis.

Murrell, P. C., Jr. (2008). Toward social justice in urban education: A model of collaborative cultural inquiry in urban schools. In F. Peterman (Ed.), *Partnering to prepare urban teachers: A call to activism* (pp. 41–58). New York: Peter Lang.

Newman, F. Developmental Philosophy lecture, February 12, 1010.

Nieto, S. (2007). *Affirming diversity: The sociopolitical context of multicultural education* (3rd ed.). Boston: Allyn and Bacon.

Peterman, F.P. & Sweigard, K.C. (2008). Defining standards that respond to the urban context: A call to activism. In F. Peterman (Ed.), *Partnering to prepare urban teachers: A call to activism* (pp. 21–40). New York: Peter Lang.

Sleeter, C. (2001). Preparing teachers for culturally diverse schools: Research and the overwhelming presence of whiteness. *Journal of Teacher Education, 52*(2), 94–106.

Tiezzi, L. J., & Cross, B. E. (1997). Utilizing research on prospective teachers' beliefs to inform urban field experiences. *The Urban Review, 29*(2), 113–125.

Villegas, A. M., & Lucas, T. (2002). *Educating culturally responsive teachers: A coherent approach.* Ithaca: State of University of New York Press.

Yinger, R. (2005). A public politics for a public profession. *Journal of Teacher Education, 56*(3), 285–290.

Zeichner, K. (2010). Rethinking the connections between campus courses and field experiences in college and university-based teacher education. *Journal of Teacher Education, 61*(1–2), 89–99.

PART VI

Focus on University Faculty

11

SUSTAINING TEACHER EDUCATORS[1] ENGAGED IN PARTNERING TO PREPARE URBAN TEACHERS

Francine P. Peterman

While much has been written about partnering to prepare urban teachers, the structures and resources required to support such work, its institutional impact and that on new teachers, rarely has the impact on teacher educators been addressed. In fact, most teacher educators involved in teacher preparation partnerships selflessly focus their efforts on the quality of the experiences and expertise of the teachers who participate in and graduate from their programs. Tirelessly, teacher educators engage in the ongoing tasks of developing and sustaining partnerships with schools, agencies, and individuals; creating and implementing course work and assessments to support teacher candidate and student achievement; collaborating with school-based faculty engaged as cooperating teachers, supervisors, and/or coordinators; and working as boundary spanners, serving dual roles as participants in the professional activities of two or more partnering agencies, including those of their own university. To complicate the never-ending demands of establishing, negotiating, and reinvigorating ongoing partnerships, institutional requirements for maintaining a robust research agenda are at the forefront of all untenured teacher educators' professional agendas. These bold strokes of the activities for which partnering teacher educators are responsible barely scratch the surface of the time, effort, and commitment they make each day to enacting this delicate yet robust work. One need only to have lived the life of a partnering teacher educator for only a semester to understand the complexity of the roles and responsibilities involved and their competing demands on one's time, resources, and intellectual and physical capacities. Having worked in partnership with local schools and community agencies in a variety of roles for most of my career (Peterman, 2006), I have experienced the delights, struggles, innovations, accomplishments, and challenges inherent in working collaboratively with individuals and institutions to prepare highly creative, talented teachers in school settings. My perspectives as a teacher educator, department chair, and dean inform this narrative of sustaining teacher educators who partner to prepare urban teachers.

Over the last 30 years, I worked collaboratively to establish long-standing partnerships with schools, museum, community colleges, and universities to not only prepare teachers, but also to improve the quality of schoolchildren's experiences and achievement. Across these experiences, certain qualities of teacher educators emerged as distinguishing characteristics of their success and sustainability in a career based on partnership with local schools. As well, specific qualities—or lack thereof—distinguished those teacher educators who chose to leave partnership-based work. Those who stay—and, they are limited in numbers across institutions throughout the United States—experience the personal and professional rewards of self- and institutional renewal, which require resiliency, persistence, and patience in reinventing oneself and the partnership. Based on my lived experience and observations and discussions with colleagues about the sustainability of teacher educators engaged in partnership, this narrative addresses the following questions:

1. Why do teacher educators leave the role of partnering to prepare urban teachers?
2. What are the characteristics of those teacher educators who make a career of partnering to prepare urban teachers?
3. What is the impact of partnerships on teacher educators?

In the late 1980s and early 1990s, school–university partnerships became a significant model for teacher education, as the Holmes Group (1986) began advocating for professional development schools and Goodlad (1994) and the National Network for Educational Renewal called for Centers of Pedagogy, wherein universities and schools work toward mutual renewal while collaboratively preparing teachers. Across the United States, partnerships have developed as a significant means of engaging school and university faculty members, administrators, and community members in thinking deeply about how to prepare the teachers we need for the schools we have, while at the same time renewing practices across and within institutions. While some experts in this field may claim that university, school, and community leaders play the most significant role in the success and longevity of these partnerships (e.g., Howey & Zimpher, 2004), I have found that while administrative support is important for partnerships to endure, at the core of the work are teacher educators whose academic lives are changed and challenged by the nature of the work involved in creating and sustaining school-based partnerships.

Who Leaves?

Interestingly, teacher educators—university faculty members involved in the course work required for the preparation and/or certification of teachers—rarely define themselves as such. When asked what do you do, they frequently respond, "I am a professor of educational psychology," "I am a math educator," or "I teach teachers." Further limiting doctoral candidates view of themselves, there are limited numbers of institutions that offer doctoral degrees in teacher education. The field was not established as a division of the American Educational Research Association until 1988, when Kathy Carter of the University of Arizona was elected Vice President of Division K: Teacher Education. Thus, it is not surprising that when teacher educators are asked to define their work, they announce fields of study (philosophy, social foundations, educational psychology, methods, science education) rather than the preparation of teachers as their main focus. This may seem trivial at first; however, I have found that one's identity as a teacher educator—whether made explicit or implicit in defining one's work—an essential key to the success and longevity in partnering to prepare teachers.

Over the last 20 years, I have been involved in a leadership role that involved selecting and supporting teacher educators engaged in at least seven substantive partnerships to prepare educators for working in local schools throughout Indiana and the Washington, D.C., areas and in Cleveland, Ohio, and New York City. In each partnership, patterns of faculty members' sustainability emerged in relation to their identity as a teacher educator; their patience, persistence and resiliency in balancing competing demands in poorly resourced, highly bureaucratic settings; and the ways in which the university and its leadership value and support program development and implementation. To illustrate these patterns of sustainability, I will provide a variety of stories of teacher educators who left partnership activities to return to other forms of teacher education.

Revisiting Professional Identity

Marcus (all names are pseudonyms) arrived at an urban university, ready, willing, and able to prepare teachers in partnership schools. He had worked collaboratively in several professional development schools during his doctoral work and, for three years participated in a national network of urban teacher educators and school and community professionals engaged in partnering to prepare teachers. Sometimes, however, he wondered aloud if he'd made the right decision to teach teachers when he had always imagined himself as a school leader—a principal, maybe even a superintendent. Hitting the ground running in his new position, Marcus met with the principals of the two partnership schools and quickly began developing relationships with the school liaisons and mentor teachers at each site. A few months into his first year as a college professor, Marcus was reminded by an informal mentor, "Don't forget to find a writing project. Remember, you must publish." Fully engaged with a new cohort of students, meeting regularly with school faculty members, and teaching three courses, Marcus could barely find time for thinking about a research project much less about writing something— writing, after all, didn't come easy for him, and the partnership activities were time consuming. Balancing the demands of developing and sustaining partner-ships with two schools, supervising student teachers, teaching, running a cohort program, and advising students let alone participating in both school and univer-sity service was often overwhelming. Spending time in school and working with two remarkable principals and a set of engaged, enthusiastic teachers reminded Marcus of his initial career goal—to be a principal. By mid-summer at the end of his first year of employment, he accepted a new position as a principal of a local school closer to home.

Reclaiming a Research Agenda

In her doctoral studies and first years of teaching educational psychology courses, Susan really enjoyed her work. She was intrigued by ideas, loved exploring and writing about child development, and enjoyed teaching introductory courses re-quired for teacher certification. But, she wanted to move to a larger community and an opportunity to coordinate and teach in a program that had an urban part-nership focus was intriguing. Having spent very little time in public school class-rooms as anything but a student or a parent, Susan was not fluent in the language and routines of the culture of schools and how to navigate building relationships with teachers and administrators. Further, having taught the required educational psychology course early in teacher education programs, she paid specific attention to covering the content well and making some connections to schools and class-rooms, but she infrequently thought about the trajectory of professional learning through which her students traversed. On moving into the position of coordinat-ing and teaching in a partnership program, a Humanist, Susan devoted most of her time to developing relationships with her students and understanding their needs, and less time to working collaboratively with principals and teachers in ways that worked for them. One principal soon reported concerns about Susan's walking into classrooms seemingly without any awareness of the teachers' willingness to enter into conversation at a moment's notice and about her probing and counsel-ing her adult students in an inappropriately personal manner—calling them at home with advice about how to manage situations outside of school, for instance. Increasing the time she spent with her students in the schools, while teaching and engaging in civic responsibilities at the college, Susan soon realized she had little time left to conduct research on and write about young children's self-efficacy, the focus of her research prior to working in a secondary teacher preparation program. By the end of her second year of employment, Susan began looking for a more traditional role as an assistant professor of educational psychology.

Feeling Valued and Accomplished

Alfonso loved teaching and preparing teachers for urban schools. He rooted every one of his introductory social foundations class sessions in classroom practice, linking complex theory to experiences in local schools where his students would go to work. Often, students lined up at Alfonso's door during his office hours not only asking for professional guidance for their future careers but for explorations of challenging ideas presented in class. When offered the opportunity to coordinate and teach in a program designed to partner the university and several local schools, Alfonso carefully explored the possibility and accepted the position, with the anticipation of learning even more about teacher development and the context of schooling. He would be replacing a faculty member who had accepted a new position as a college administrator and anxiously awaited direction from his department chair to assume responsibility for the program. Culturally deferent to authority, Alfonso waited while the chair and departing faculty member managed all of the planning for the upcoming year, establishing the schedule of courses and instructors and school placements. Alfonso played no role in the decision making. As he assumed his responsibilities in the summer, Alfonso found himself swimming in a sea of challenges: The summer courses were reduced to five-week sessions, the students worried about all the course requirements to complete in a compressed time frame, the previous coordinators departed, a co-coordinator was selected without his input and was rarely available, and the department chair shrugged, "You take care of it." Throughout the year, Alfonso tried to stay focused on partnership activities and teacher development, but with limited departmental support and a sense that the program was not valued by the college, he determined that he could not commit himself to this project and, in the fall, returned to his previous role of teaching introductory social foundations courses across traditional programs.

Aspects of Work Life Related to Sustainability

Although highly simplistic, these stories highlight three aspects of work life that are related to the sustainability of teacher educators engaged in partnerships: professional identity; patience, persistence, and resiliency; and institutional value and support. In varying degrees, each impacts the ways in which teacher educators remain in and resign from positions that require a high level of interaction among university and school professionals in preparing teachers.

Identity as a Teacher Educator

The individuals illustrated demonstrate varying degrees of professional identity as teacher educators. While Marcus studied and participated in many educative experiences related to partnering to prepare teachers, he struggled internally with his professional identity. On finding himself in two highly productive settings led by principals with vision and finesse while at the same time struggling with managing complex, competing demands for his time and efforts, he began to focus solely on his career choice. Not only was serving as a teacher educator working closely in partnership difficult, having to balance teaching and leading partnership activities along with requests for service from both institutions along with writing forced him to confront: What's really important to me? Who do I want to be? While he was highly valued in his professional community throughout his graduate work and in his new position, the demands on his time—especially for conducting and writing about research—forced him to reconsider his career choice. He has served as a school and district administrator now for 15 years.

Susan sense of identity as a teacher educator was fragile—almost circumstantial as she approached her new position as an "opportunity," not necessarily a calling or a commitment. That was clear when she interviewed for the position and evident in the research she conducted prior to and on working in partnering urban high schools. She continued to focus her research on child development, while the schools in which she now worked were full of adolescents. Thus, she needed more time to conduct her research outside of the settings in which she most frequently found herself. In addition, when competing demands for her time arose amid complex cultural norms and structures with which she was unfamiliar, Susan found herself struggling with how her commitment to humanistic psychology did not always play out well in a school setting while working closely with other adults—including her students. Susan determined that her identity as a researcher trumped her identity as a teacher educator, and she returned to a setting in which the scholarship she valued would more easily accomplished.

On the other hand, Alfonso had a strong professional identify as a teacher educator, rooted in his teaching experience and commitment to preparing the next generation of professionals for urban schools like those in which he learned and taught. He wanted to teach teachers and teach them well—that was always evident not only in his teaching and talking about teaching but in his students' enthusiastic interactions with him about their chosen profession. The lack of administrative support and his engagement in crucial decision making, Alfonso felt powerless. When the complexities and demands of the partnership manifested in students' concerns about accomplishing their goals, rather than rebound with his usual resilience and persistence, Alfonso withdrew and resolved to finish one year and return to his prior position.

Patience, Resistance, Persistence, and Resilience

Years ago, I conducted a content analysis of the ways in which researchers defined "urban" to define the context and determine standards for urban teacher preparation (Peterman & Swiegard, 2008). Among the characteristics of urban settings were the presence of highly complex, underresourced bureaucracies offering mixed messages regarding goals, outcomes, and actions and competing demands for individuals' time, energy, and institutional resources. In response to these traits, I recommended that urban teachers address the complexity and demands of urban settings by responding appropriately with resilience, resistance, and persistence.

Over the last four years of working in New York City, I would add "patience" to the list of qualities required—as experience in a highly bureaucratic system has taught me that patience is a far better response than others the frustration of working diligently in such settings can elicit. And if I were to define standards for urban teacher educators, I would ask that we be required to demonstrate patience, resistance, persistence, and resilience in responding to the inherent challenges of the bureaucracies underlying our partnership institutions.

In each of the stories presented, three teacher educators worked in highly complex, underresourced bureaucracies within the school and university settings that continuously presented them with competing demands. In particular, Marcus and Susan found themselves fully occupied with supporting their students, developing partnership, and engaging in service across both institutions. Their most relevant competing demand was the university requirement for scholarship. In Marcus case, the conflict forced him to reclaim his professional identity as a school leader; in Susan case, the conflict—conflated by the complexities of an unfamiliar school culture and a commitment to a research agenda that could not be accomplished in the schools where she worked—led to her returning to a more traditional university assistant professorship that did not involve partnership. When Alfonso found himself working within several complex settings and among structures he had not created and for which he had little support to change or improve, he abandoned confronting competing demands and returned to his more traditional position—in which there was far more comfort and a sense of being valued—at least, by his students. In at least Susan and Alfonso case, I would posit that patience, persistence, and resiliency may have sustained their careers as urban teacher educators engaged in partnership activities. These qualities may have helped them more mindfully respond to the challenges, make different choices, more deeply understand the nature of the contexts for which they were preparing teachers, and collaboratively create settings in which urban teachers thrive. Patience would have allowed them to look past the inconsistencies and inadequacies and focus on creating solutions that work within such complex, demanding settings. Persistence would have energized them, helping them to move through the difficulties and imagine new possibilities. Resiliency may have helped them rebound from the disappointments, barriers, and problems with which they were faced on a regular basis.

Institutional Value and Support

Although not specifically highlighted in each story, the partnering schools and districts highly valued and supported the collaborative work of preparing urban teachers and frequently hired program graduates. The university, college, and departmental support for and value of the partnership varied with leadership and the availability of external funding. In particular, Alfonso found himself in a simple dilemma: Do what I love with few complications and challenges while feeling valued and respected, or do what I love within settings where problems persist and my feeling of being valued is diminished by my leaders' lack of support and interest in my work? This one seems quite simple, from Alfonso's point of view; yet, it raises some clear questions about what is essential not only for partnerships to endure but to sustain teacher educators' involvement and commitment to this important work. In particular, what Alfonso needed was not only shared decision making in determining how the partnership would unfold but also institutional support for negotiating the dilemmas and concerns that will always arise in collaborative work. At least, until he development his own sense of agency within this new, complicated setting, Alfonso needed guidance and mentoring in how navigate the new terrain. Further, given the demands inherent in partnership work and teacher educators' consistent struggle with accomplishing their commitments to schools and university, feeling valued by an acknowledgement of the struggles, of the action research accomplished in the field, and of the resiliency and persistence goes a long way in sustaining academic careers. Valuing the work in the tenure and promotion process as a form of creative achievement means even more for pretenure teacher educators, who struggle with productivity while managing the multifarious tasks of partnership.

Who Stays?

In spite of competing demands, complex bureaucracies, and challenging situations inherent in partnering to prepare urban teachers, many teacher educators sustain long-lasting, substantive careers in the field. The following story of one urban teacher educator incorporates the characteristics of those who remain in partnership work for the long haul, 10 years or more. Rather than tell one person's story, the tales of several urban teacher educators comprise this narrative. In addition to patience, persistence, resilience, and resistance, among their qualities are the following: a consistently renewing identity as a teacher educator strongly rooted in altruism; an ability to develop and sustain relationships and community; integrity; and creativity, creative problem solving, and a disposition toward creating future settings.

Flourishing as an Urban Teacher Educator

Before her four children were born, Claudia taught in a suburban middle school for eight years, completing her master's degree as a means to refine her practice and think more deeply about teaching—a passion. Missing the classroom and interactions in school, she volunteered to serve as a university supervisor, working with six to 12 student teachers each semester, honing her observation and teaching skills and identifying numerous placements for the English education—her field. Her reputation for fairness, commitment to her students and the university, integrity, and excellence in her craft was well known among school and university faculty members, though sometimes critiqued by students who did not fare very well in their field experiences and/or were not used to receiving ongoing feedback about ways to improve their teaching. When asked to supervise clinical experiences and teach courses in as well as co-coordinate a fast-track, secondary teacher education program in partnership with four urban schools, she was taken aback: "Now? Me? Teach classes? I only have a master's degree." Despite her expertise and commitment to quality teaching and teacher education, Claudia needed to be coaxed to say yes. While teaching and teacher education were no doubt important to her, being a teacher educator was not her core identity—being a caregiver and parent were.

Having not only taught in schools but having spent many hours in classrooms observing student teachers and in schools arranging her visitations and being a spokesperson for the university, Claudia honed her understanding of school culture, of teaching practice, and of what works and doesn't work in supporting teacher development. Her keen sense of what needed to be said when and how exemplified her communication style; her positive, engaging manner easily facilitated developing new relationships with students, teachers, faculty members, and administrators. She listened patiently, absorbing and analyzing what she observed, carefully choosing what she would say in every situation. While working in urban schools was sometimes challenging, it was rewarding for Claudia, who believed strongly in doing the next right thing—what is best for self and others, making the world a better place, and creating the conditions for all students to learn and to learn well. Moreover, her actions conveyed these beliefs—as she rigorously applied the same standards to herself as a professional educator as she did to the student teachers with whom she worked. Further, Claudia loved organizing the world, carefully attending to the details of an event, involving people in solving problems, and collaboratively setting an agenda for what comes next.

Claudia found her niche in coordinating and teaching in a partnership program, developing new relationships, new understandings, and even a new language of talking about her profession. As she reviewed her students' portfolio artifacts with them, discussing how the activities represented a commitment to social justice, Claudia's altruism was expressed in new ways. Not only did she collaboratively critique students' work with them but she also began studying social justice perspectives on teaching and teacher education, expanding her research repertoire and determining to write about how these were enacted in the partnership work.

Claudia's emerging sense of self as a teacher educator was expressed in her renewed participation in annual conferences of teacher educators, teacher researchers, and folks who work in professional development schools. Studying and enacting social justice, learning about and implementing teacher research—which was a year-long exit project required of the students in her program—impacted Claudia's identity as teacher educator. Teacher research became Claudia's own methodology; and, as she learned more about it along with her students other school and university faculty members in the program, she worked collaboratively with another faculty member and teachers at one of the partnership schools to implement a study group in which the teachers were conducting studies of their own practice in the same way program interns did during their student teaching experience. That study group shifted the ways in which faculty members at the school and several at the university thought about teaching and learning and enacted research. Claudia began presenting papers at conferences, writing about, and editing a journal related to teacher research and social justice. She was recognized by local, state and national organizations for her expertise in and impact on teacher education.

As in any partnership program, conflicts and problems arose—from students being counseled out of teaching to scheduling course work to allow for more focused attention on student teaching to determining if and when to terminate a partnership agreement and so on. Claudia drew on her relationships to handle each with finesse and support. When a new university administrator determined that there was no need for two program coordinators and terminated Claudia's position and returned her to full-time to supervising student teachers and teaching introductory courses across more traditional programs, Claudia's resistance and persistence came into play, more than ever, as she patiently challenged the decision and worked tirelessly with the union to regain her role as coordinator and urban teacher educator—almost two years later.

Inherent in Claudia's story are the characteristics of teacher educators who sustain careers in partnering to prepare urban teachers. Perhaps, these characteristics helped Claudia to flourish as a teacher educator. At least, they made a significant difference in the lives of the students, teachers, administrators, and faculty members with whom she worked.

Renewing Identity That Is Strongly Rooted in Altruism—Social Justice

Initially, Claudia saw herself as a caregiver—being a teacher educator was not a core element of her multiple identities but emerged and was renewed throughout her professional interactions within the partnership program. Claudia's strong belief in doing what is good for the community—her altruism—was evident in each decision she made, including one to teach in and coordinate the program. Over and again, she expressed her concern to make the city schools better for all children by preparing the kinds of teachers they most need. As she examined her students' artifacts of social justice and began looking more closely at her own practice in light of what she learned, Claudia's understanding, articulation, and practice of a social justice agenda flourished. As she engaged in inquiry about teacher research, at first simply wanting to support her students' completion of an exit requirement of their program of study, Claudia's identity as a teacher educator was punctuated by a new methodology—systematic and reflective examination of classroom practice. A strong identity as a teacher educator—defined in this case by an interweaving of inquiry grounded in teacher research and social justice—most likely describes those professionals who are sustained for the long haul in urban teacher education partnership. Knowing oneself as teacher educator with a commitment to altruism and/or social justice is just the start.

Building and Sustaining Relationships and Community

Throughout her work as a teacher and teacher educator, Claudia consistently demonstrated her skills in building and sustaining relationships within and across school and university settings—at the classroom, institutional, and community levels. Whether interacting with student teachers or their supervisors, planning program activities with college faculty and school liaisons and cooperating teachers, negotiating partnerships with university and district administrators, or collaboratively creating innovative solutions to problems that arose, Claudia communicated clearly, listened carefully, reflected on what was said, and honored everyone in the interaction. Not everyone wanted to hear what she had to say—especially students who were used to regularly hearing "Great work!" and, infrequently, "You might want to think about . . .," or "What was happening when . . . ?" She used silence to engage others and to think carefully not only about what was being said but what was not being said and to allow others a moment of reflection and time to enter the conversation. Whether with a student cohort, a team of cooperating teachers at a school site, or a group of liaisons across school partnerships, Claudia played a critical role in building and sustaining community by providing opportunities for people to get to know one another and to solve problems together.

Using Creativity and Creating Future Settings

Probably the most hidden traits of sustained teacher educators are Claudia's creativity and disposition toward creating future settings—places where a community engages in collaboratively using what they know to solve problems (Sarason, 1972). Beyond patience, persistence, resilience, and resistance—prerequisites for working in any partnership especially those in urban schools, creativity is most essential in responding to the complexity and demands of urban school–university partnerships and the bureaucracies that govern them. Creativity provides the teacher educators with the wherewithal response to each barrier, conundrum, dilemma, challenge, or problem that arises. Being creative allows individuals to think outside the box, imagine new ways of identifying, viewing and solving problems, and respond to conditions with a sense of hope and ingenuity. Such talent is often coupled by a keen sense of autonomy—being able to take on problems rather than be swayed or hampered by them.

While creativity and its inherent abilities to identify and solve problems enables urban teacher educators to continuously reinvent practices and solutions to be responsive the complicated settings and partnerships in which they work, being creative opens the door to one's thinking about possibilities—the creation of future settings where problems are solved collaboratively, new ways of thinking and doing invented. Given supervising teachers' interest in their student teachers' exit projects and her own interest in knowing more about teacher research, Claudia engaged her colleagues in creating an inquiry group to not only study classroom research but to use its methodology and tools to reinvent classroom and school practices. She created a future setting, where the local knowledge and expertise were shared in solving problems of practice. Such creative activities renewed not only individual's practice but also institutional practices across school and university settings, as faculty members and teachers engaged in learning and solving problems collaboratively and shifted the ways in which they taught and interacted as result of what they learned.

Integrity

Perhaps Claudia's most distinguishing characteristic is the integrity of her practice—that is, the alignment of what she thought or understood from research and theory, what she said, and what she did. Not only did Claudia work toward preparing teachers who are socially just—she discussed and enacted her belief that all children deserve to be taught by teachers who care, who promote equity, and who challenge unjust actions and words. Further, as Claudia's beliefs changed—about her core identity and commitment to social justice, for instance, her actions changed. Only through ongoing reflection and inquiry might such alignment occur—as humans, we are simply flawed enough to not always enact what we say we value. Claudia maintained an inquiring mind and a reflective stance, engaging other professionals in collectively reflecting on and learning more about teaching practice, while sharing with each other what they had learned. Her integrity spoke more loudly than words, yet might go unnoticed in the dynamic whirlwind of partnership activities.

How Do Partnerships Impact Urban Teacher Educators

Unraveling the characteristics of urban teacher educators who leave and who stay highlights the specific attributes necessary to strive and thrive amidst the complex, demanding circumstances found within and across school and university settings, especially within partnership. Seemingly, these attributes may not be prerequisites for individuals' endurance and/or success in creating and sustaining partnerships for urban teacher preparation; however, they may flourish and redefine themselves in light of the conundrums, issues, conflicts, and problems that arise in negotiating and enacting the goals and principles that guide such collaborations. Simply working in partnership (as in its simplest form, a marriage) requires skills in communication, collaboration, and creative problem solving that play an essential role in the redefining of self in relationship. Further, patience, persistence, resilience, and resistance play a crucial role in the ways in which problems, barriers, and concerns are negotiated and addressed. These attributes are strengthened, while at the same time supporting individuals in relationship with the time and mindfulness to reflect, the willingness to hang in there even when things get tough, the disposition to bounce back up and land on your feet when things knock you for a loop, and the audacity to resist that which may be unjust, unethical, or inappropriate. Partnerships bring individuals' key attributes to light, place stress on them, and provide openings for them to be examined and strengthened.

In each of the stories told, these urban teacher educators demonstrated varying degrees of these attributes; and each individual encountered many opportunities within their partnerships to use and develop them along with their own professional identities. As described, the quality of seeing oneself as a teacher educator provided opportunities to grow and reinvent oneself professionally; or, if such an identity remained stagnant, it may become a reason for abandoning participation in urban teacher education partnership. By collaborating with other human beings in a common enterprise, partnership provided a setting in which participants mindfully or blindly determine to what degree these attributes would sustain or reroute their professional lives. As with all personal and professional growth, inquiry, reflection, willingness, and intention are the keys to change.

School–university partnerships create the conditions for reflecting on one's teaching practice, research agenda, commitments to social justice and urban communities, and the integrity of our practice. The overlapping, competing demands inherent in these relationships and in light of the purpose of schooling in university and school settings force engaged professionals to feel, see, share, examine, and reflect on the alignment of their theories and beliefs, their teachings and expectations, and their professional practices—as teachers, as researchers, and teacher educators. Because the work is public, authentic, and involves other professionals in inquiry and creative problem solving, it requires teacher educators to look closely at what they know, what they say, and what they do—and to seek the integrity of the alignment of these three aspects of their practice. What is the effect? Mahatma Ghandi said, "Happiness is when what you think, what you say, and what you do are in harmony." Perhaps, then, the long-term impact of partnering to prepare urban teachers is contentment. As urban teacher educators engage in partnerships across school and university settings, as one colleague told me, they "find a home in and across settings," redefining themselves while changing the world in which teachers teach and learn to teach and children learn.

Note

1 Throughout this chapter, teacher educators will refer solely to full-time, tenure-track university faculty members. While school-based and adjunct or part-time faculty members play critical, equally important roles in preparation, they will not be the primary focus of this manuscript.

References

Goodlad, J. L. (1994). *Educational renewal: Better teachers, better schools.* San Francisco: Jossey-Bass.

Holmes Group. (1986). *Tomorrow's teachers.* East Lansing, MI: Author.

Howey, K. R., & Zimpher, N. L. (2004). Engagement in urban school renewal. In N. L. Zimpher & K. R. Howey (Eds.), *University leadership in urban school renewal* (pp. 1–28). Westport, CT: American Council on Education/Praeger.

Peterman, F. P. (2006). Boundary spanning and the creation of future settings. In K. R. Howey & N. L. Zimpher (Eds.), *Boundary spanners: A key to success in urban P–16 university–school partnerships* (pp. 126–141). Washington, DC: American Association of State Colleges and Universities.

Peterman, F. P., & Swiegard, K. (2008). Defining standards that respond to the urban context: A call to activism. In F. P. Peterman (Ed.), *Partnering to prepare urban teachers: A call to activism* (pp. 21–40). New York: Peter Lang for the American Association of Colleges of Teacher Education.

Sarason, S. B. (1972). *The creation of settings and the future societies.* San Francisco: Jossey-Bass.

12

TEACHER PREPARATION FACULTY IN URBAN PARTNERSHIPS

Learning and Leading

Deidre B. Sessoms

Welcome to Sacramento, California, America's most integrated city (Stodghill, & Bower, 2002). Our city earned this designation because its population of about 35% White, 27% Hispanic/Latino, 18% Asian, and 14% Black residents live in neighborhoods that are more integrated, block by block, than any other major city in the country. In addition to being highly integrated, the population is also extremely diverse; fully 36% of our city's residents speak a language other than English at home, while 22% were born outside of the United States. The most common home languages for children in area public K–12 school districts (other than English) are Spanish and Hmong, with a sizable population also speaking Russian, Vietnamese, or Cantonese. Enrollment across Sacramento area K–12 school districts (not including districts in more distant suburban communities) tops 200,000. As is true in most urban areas, poverty affects many Sacramento residents. The city's unemployment rate has hovered around 14% for some time. As a result, the percentage of K–12 students who qualify for free or reduced price meals at school is also high, ranging from 42% to 80% across the same Sacramento area school districts mentioned above.

California State University (CSU), Sacramento (or Sacramento State, its informal title) annually enrolls about 27,000 students, offering a wide range of undergraduate and graduate degrees. It is a "majority minority" campus with about 43% of its students self-identifying as White. Teacher preparation is a primary focus for CSU campuses; about half of all teachers in the state are prepared in the California State University system. Out of 22 CSU campuses statewide that offer

---

Some parts of this chapter were previously published in Noel and Sessoms (2009).

teacher certification programs, in 2009–2010 only two campuses enrolled more students in those programs than Sacramento State (both of these campuses are in the Los Angeles area). While the number of future teachers seeking certification has dropped significantly over the past 10 years in California, Sacramento State still certifies about 500 new teachers each year (http://www.ctc.ca.gov/reports/TitleII_2009-2010_AnnualRpt.pdf).

With this cultural, ethnic, linguistic, socioeconomic, and geographical backdrop, one could reasonably assume that faculty at Sacramento State and the future teachers being prepared here would be deeply immersed in our region's low-income, diverse communities, partnering with schools to improve the preparation of teachers and the academic achievement of students. While this is mostly true today, the path that led to this point was a rough one, strewn with the boulders of past practices, philosophical differences, organizational barriers, and miscommunication. This chapter traces the growth at our university of urban partnerships for teacher preparation—and the enormous impacts that this approach has had on the 15 or so faculty who situated their professional lives in these partnerships.

Changing Teacher Preparation: Supportive Conditions

In an urban setting where no single racial or ethnic group holds a majority, where English is not always spoken by residents and where the majority of public schoolchildren qualify for free and reduced price lunches, how *should* the local public university train K–12 public school teachers? When new teachers still leave the profession in high numbers, despite heroic efforts statewide to provide beginning teacher support, which approach to preparing teachers is most defensible and who gets to decide? A group of predominantly untenured teacher preparation faculty at Sacramento State confronted these questions—not so much "head on," but rather sideways—during the period from about 1998 to 2005. During that time between 10 and 20 faculty from two teacher preparation departments in the College of Education collaborated with each other and with well over 100 K–12 public school teachers, principals, and district administrators to form the Equity Network of Professional Development Schools devoted to training teachers *in* urban settings *for* urban settings. (See Chapter 2 for a description of the Equity Network in terms of types of knowledge, curriculum, and communities of learners.)

The Equity Network was a set of 12 predominantly elementary public schools housed in five school districts in the greater Sacramento region where university faculty and K–12 teachers developed deep collaborative partnerships focused on preparing effective urban teachers—while also enacting the other goals implicit in the Professional Development School (PDS) model. These goals include (a) enhancing K–12 student learning, (b) improving field experiences for teacher preparation candidates, (c) engaging K–16 educators in continuous and targeted professional development in which all partners participate, and (d) using action research and data to inform teaching and learning in schools (Abdal-Haqq, 1998;

Darling-Hammond & Associates, 1994; Holmes Group, 1995; National Council for the Accreditation of Teacher Education [NCATE], 2001; Teitel, 2000). Additional partners in the Equity Network included the nonprofit Area Congregations Together and teacher bargaining units from two of the five districts with whom we partnered (see Wong & Glass, 2009; and Chapter 2 for more detailed information about the Equity Network).

There were a number of conditions supporting the growth of university–school–community partnerships that became the Equity Network. These included statewide changes in requirements for teacher preparation programs; changes at the university in faculty hiring patterns and turnover; funding opportunities and challenges; and other "affective" conditions including building trust and a shared mission to value community strengths and priorities. Ultimately, while the Equity Network of today bears little resemblance to the large network that grew in the early 2000s, the experience of leveraging those conditions over which faculty had control has changed our sense of efficacy. The urban school–community–university partnerships that were fostered in the network have continued albeit in different forms. The growth of the network is illustrative of the challenges implicit in moving teacher preparation into urban settings—and of the opportunities.

In California, teacher certification programs are generally postbaccalaureate, occurring after an undergraduate degree is earned. Programs at Sacramento State during the time period when these partnerships were developing were similar to other programs statewide in length (either two or three semesters), and course work (foundations, pedagogy and field experiences). Where Sacramento State's program differed from others in California was the method by which student teachers were placed with cooperating teachers in public school classrooms. Rather than a central person or office being responsible for recruiting local teachers and making these placements, instead faculty "Center Coordinators" were released from teaching a class to build the relationships required to make effective placements; these same faculty were responsible for the placement of one cohort of student teachers (usually between 20 and 35) in an individual district or geographical region. This division of workload amongst many different faculty (there were between 10 and 20 cohorts running at any one time, in 10 distinct districts or regions) was a unique organizational structure that supported collaborative partnerships. Faculty focused their efforts in limited numbers of "centers" so that, over time, they learned more about the individual peculiarities and culture of the district and its curriculum and built relationships among its teachers and administrators. Prior to the Equity Network, only a small number of tenure line faculty took on the coordinator responsibility, preferring instead to teach their courses and perhaps supervise a few student teachers. Once the Equity Network became established, however, there were nine tenure line faculty and only one or two part-time faculty coordinating the elementary and middle school "centers." Seven of these nine tenure-line faculty were key members of the Equity Network.

Other structural features that supported building the urban partnerships that supported the Equity Network included new standards for professional teacher preparation programs in California that were adopted at the state level and required to be enacted by fall 2004; these standards were significantly different from those that had previously governed teacher preparation (California Commission on Teacher Credentialing, 2001). The new standards encouraged collaboration between university teacher preparation programs and area districts to build "seamless transitions" into the learning-to-teach continuum. New standards also allowed newer faculty to push for substantial change in the philosophy, focus, content, and structure of our programs, which had changed little over the previous decade.

The number of students completing teacher certification programs in California increased dramatically—almost 45%—from 1997–1998 to 2003–2004, due in part to a reduction in class sizes in the primary grades (California Commission on Teacher Credentialing, 2003, 2005). At the same time, Sacramento State hired a wave of new faculty across disciplines. The University of California at Davis, located just 20 min. from Sacramento, had begun a doctorate program in education; many of its graduates were subsequently hired as tenure line professors at Sacramento State during this time. In the two departments that prepare most Multiple Subject and all Single Subject teachers in our college, 10 new tenure-line faculty who were hired during this time period had graduated from the University of California–Davis program. Many had a shared background in sociocultural studies and a shared commitment to a social justice agenda in K–12 schools. The increased numbers of students seeking teacher certification in our programs—with the concomitant hiring of tenure line faculty—allowed us to try innovative approaches in new "centers" where there was not already a long-standing traditional approach to teacher preparation. The influx of new faculty with a shared background and commitment to social justice allowed us to move forward with shared purpose. While there were few senior faculty willing to mentor us, we had each other as we confronted the traditional teacher preparation model—and the senior faculty who supported it.

A final condition that enabled the work of new faculty as we moved teacher preparation into high-needs urban schools was grant funding that supported our efforts. One senior faculty member secured a Stuart Foundation grant in the late 1990s to design and support new ways of partnering in schools. This lay the groundwork for a large federal Title II grant that supported buy-out time for each faculty member in the Equity Network and funded professional development opportunities for K–12 teachers at Equity Network schools, and for university faculty involved. These collaborative activities served a number of purposes. At the beginning, the funding that supported collaborative activities—and the time it takes for faculty to be embedded in urban schools and communities—was a key piece of the trust-building process with our K–12 school and community partners. Without trust, the difficult work of a PDS cannot be accomplished.

Trust Building

A person's or organization's positive intentions are primary in establishing trust. Tschannen-Moran (2004) writes, "Perhaps the most essential ingredient and commonly recognized facet of trust is a sense of caring . . . the confidence that one's well-being or something one cares about will be protected and not harmed by the trusted party" (p. 19). This "affective" approach to establishing trustworthy partnerships between universities and public schools is rarely discussed in higher education, but is critical to engaging urban communities in the work of teacher preparation, and engaging the university community in the work of urban schools (Noel, 2010, 2011).

Collaborative partnerships between institutions are, at their heart, relationships among people. These relationships do not begin with trust already in place; trust grows over time. "Trust is a dynamic phenomenon that takes on a different character at different stages of a relationship. As a relationship develops, trust 'thickens'" (Tschannen-Moran & Hoy, 2000, p. 570). Three stages in the process of developing trust between two institutional partners (in this case, between schools and universities) have been described by researchers (Bottery, 2003; Gambetta, 1988; Hands, 2005; Hoy & Tschannen-Moran, 1999; Stefkovich & Shapiro, 2002; Tschannen-Moran & Hoy, 2000). In the beginning stage when partners do not have a professional or personal relationship, they may calculate the worthiness of a potential collaborative partner based on various factors. Those factors include the amount of risk connected with the collaboration, or whether the activities and partners can be monitored (Gambetta, 1988). Institutions such as schools and universities have an already implied trust since they have similar goals and belong to similar regulatory systems (Bottery, 2003).

As collaborative activities commence, the second stage begins. During this stage, partners move beyond speculation as they assess each other's commitment and trustworthiness based on knowledge of practice in a common realm (Bottery, 2003; Tschannen-Moran & Hoy, 2000). The establishment and growth of this community of practice leads to the third stage of trust formation. At this stage, partners have a shared history of effective collaborative activities. Shared goals, procedures, and beliefs lead to trustworthy relationships where each partner can act on behalf of the other, comfortable and confident in the decisions, activities, and outcomes of the partnership (Stefkovich & Shapiro, 2002).

Over time, all cross-institutional partnerships encounter new community needs, institutional demands, and turnover in personnel. Addressing these challenges in ways that allow the partnership to successfully continue requires the flexibility of a mature partnership that has progressed through all three stages of trust development (Hands, 2005).

In addition to analyzing PDS partnerships based on their progression through the trust-building stages, they can also be analyzed using a PDS framework published by the National Council for Accreditation of Teacher Education

(NCATE). NCATE standards are used to assess the developmental level of a PDS from the "Beginning" (where initial PDS work is at least consistent with the PDS mission) through the "Developing" and "At Standard" levels, culminating in the "Leading" level (where the partnership is sustained, flourishing, and impacts policy, leveraging change in the broader community) (NCATE, 2001). While the five standards focus on various characteristics of a PDS, the foundation of all PDS work is "shared interest, mutual commitment, and trust" (NCATE, 2001, p. 3).

Complicating the trust-building process between urban communities and schools, and the university, is an inequality of roles, with university programs and faculty often setting the tone for interactions (Noel, 2010, 2011). Even when there are multileveled groups involving all stakeholders in the discussions—as there was during the development of our urban partnerships—it is still often the university that provides the impetus and expertise to initiate change rather than the community's own efforts (Kahne & Westheimer, 1996; Reed, 2004; Weiner, 2000). Recognizing this concern, Harkavy and Hartley (2009) urge institutions of higher education to "go beyond the rhetoric of collaboration and conscientiously work with communities, rejecting the unidirectional, top-down approaches that all too often have characterized university–community interaction" (p. 12).

At the beginning of the Equity Network, individual PDS sites functioned at differing levels of implementation on the NCATE rubric, at least in part because they also functioned at differing levels of trust. In some cases, individual faculty had been partnering with area urban schools for years beforehand; these partnerships had gone through the necessary trust stages already and were examples of "thick" partnerships (Tschannen-Moran & Hoy, 2000). Other PDS sites were firmly in the first stage of trust building, still calculating the level of benefit and risk to be had by partnering across institutional boundaries.

The intentions with which university faculty engaged with our urban school educational colleagues and communities were vitally important. Because each of the partnerships was situated in the particularities of the school, children, parents, teachers, and neighborhoods, the emphases within partnerships varied considerably. The needs and strengths of participants determined everything from governance structure to daily collaborative activities. How faculty viewed the partnerships changed over time, from an earlier emphasis (by at least some of us) on the challenges and needs of the children and teachers, to a later emphasis on the strengths within that context. This subtle change in emphasis levels the ground somewhat.

Almost all of our PDSs grew primarily from the ground up. At the beginning, the Dean and Department Chairs at Sacramento State—and the corresponding Superintendents and other district personnel—were unaware of the collaborative PDS work occurring at these sites. In most cases, trust was building between the people most involved at the ground level: teachers, faculty, student teachers, students, and principals. Just one district out of the five involved in the Equity

Network was the exception to this process, the Citrus Heights Unified School District (all district and school names are pseudonyms). In that district, the process for establishing a PDS—and therefore the trust-building process—included extensive involvement from district administrators, in addition to those who worked on the ground level in the schools and at the university.

The Citrus Heights PDS Center

When students begin the Sacramento State teacher preparation program, they request which of many "centers" they prefer to be housed in as they matriculate through the program. The Citrus Heights District Center was requested by many students in the 1990s because they knew of its reputation for excellence and high-achieving students (Noel, 2002). This image, however, obscures the needs of the many low-income, culturally and linguistically diverse students who have a substantially different achievement profile. Many of these students are clustered at the district's borders, especially on its western edge where it abuts the Sacramento City Unified district and the city of Sacramento.

The traditional teacher preparation center in Citrus Heights Unified had a long-standing presence at one Title I school in the district, First Street Elementary, because university classes had been taught for many years in a portable there. However, few preservice teachers were placed at First Street for their student teaching experience; instead the cohort was spread throughout the district, primarily at higher-achieving schools. While university courses were taught in the portable at First Street, most often they were scheduled to begin after the school day had ended. Despite the opportunity to embed teacher preparation more firmly in this high-needs Title I school, our presence at First Street was more for the convenience of university students and faculty (who wouldn't have to wrestle with university parking shortages), rather than for their professional benefit. Consequently, despite the teacher preparation program having been housed in First Street's portable for about a decade, the partnership remained at the first stage of trust building. In fact, a new principal at First Street requested that the university vacate the portable when she determined it could be better utilized in other ways by the school site.

At about this time, the Equity Network was being established across districts in our region. Two faculty and a Department Chair began cultivating an expanded partnership with the Citrus Heights District, with the express goal of forming a PDS in urban sites within the traditional San Juan teacher preparation center. In meetings with district and school administrators, two Title I schools were identified as possible PDS sites, First Street and Harper Elementary, which are within about a mile and a half of each other on the western edge of the district. University faculty members spent months consulting with district and school administrators and teachers to develop a commitment to the PDS approach. This beginning stage of trust building was crucial since the traditional Citrus Heights teacher preparation center had a long history of working "in" Citrus Heights schools rather than "with" them.

The Network PDS at Harper Elementary ultimately involved every teacher in working with student teachers. In the first few years of trust building, the faculty member from Sacramento State collaborated with the principal and several teachers on school-wide curriculum projects that resulted in an academic paper presented to a national audience at the Holmes Conference in Washington, D.C., in 2003. These and other collaborative activities at Harper helped establish a solid shared community of practice at the site, moving the partnership through the second stage of trust building.

First Street School's teachers were understandably more reticent to undertake increased levels of collaboration with the university, since Sacramento State had a history of noninvolved presence at the school. As a sign of its commitment, Sacramento State secured a different portable classroom at the site to replace the one that had previously been used by university students. This became Sacramento State's new First Street headquarters in which to offer university courses and house the faculty member's office. PDS activities at First Street that began in the second stage of trust building included teacher research groups and book clubs. In addition, a large cadre of teacher candidates was now placed in First Street for their student teaching experience. They were included in the professional book club and other professional development meetings. It took this partnership longer to move to the third stage of trust, but trust was solidified through repeated shared professional activities and the commitment of faculty and the principal (and eventually the commitment of teacher candidates and teachers) to its success.

The developing leadership capacities of the faculty members at Harper and First Street, and the support of Citrus Heights District officials and the school community, enabled them to effect a major change in how the Citrus Heights Center for teacher preparation operated. As these faculty and their school partners gained PDS experience and demonstrated success in their efforts, they convinced the university and district officials that PDS collaborative structures and practices would result in effective preparation of successful teachers in the urban areas hiring our graduates. The Citrus Heights Center thus went from being a traditional teacher preparation program focused on a middle-income area—with a PDS option at two schools—to being exclusively a PDS Center, where all 60 student teachers were placed in a Title I PDS setting. The partners added a third Title I school to the program, so those three schools became the locus of teacher preparation in Citrus Heights Unified.

The Citrus Heights PDS Center quickly established a new reputation among Sacramento State preservice teachers. A study conducted when the center was traditional and repeated after the transformation, found that new credential students still recognized the "reputation for excellence" of the Citrus Heights District (Noel, 2002), but in addition they indicated a greater recognition of the district's low-income, diverse student population, and a greater desire to be prepared within that context. There was also an understanding that the center's PDS structure provided "the opportunity to be fully involved with teachers on a regular basis" (Noel, 2006). The study comparison also highlights factors that impacted the preservice teachers' selection of certain centers as their first choice for teacher preparation. When the Citrus Heights Center was a traditional program, only 33% of our students indicated that they selected the center due to its diverse student population, and 20% indicated that they wanted to work with children in poverty (Noel, 2002). As a PDS center focused on Title I schools and diverse learners, 70% of our students now indicated that they selected the center due to its diverse student population, and 48% due to the number of students in poverty (Noel, 2006). This study suggests that preservice teachers who intend to work with low-income, diverse populations will seek out programs they know have a focus on preparation for that context.

Implications for Faculty: Internal Complexities and Challenges

When we formed the Equity Network, only two of 12 tenure-line faculty involved were tenured. While our commitment to challenge our institutional status quo was strong, the challenges were daunting and our responses to them became increasingly complex as we each moved through the tenure and promotion process. Not surprisingly, when we began addressing the central question of how best to design urban teacher preparation programs, we bumped up against long-held departmental and college traditions and values about our programs and how they should operate. We discovered that our efforts to redesign our programs *in collaboration with* urban schools and communities challenged the status quo. Faculty not involved in the Equity Network expressed concerns that collaborating in this way with teachers meant ceding power to schools, which they believed would decrease the effectiveness of our programs. This gets to the heart of the struggle to determine what role a teacher preparation program—and its faculty—*should* play in K–12 public schools.

Marilyn Cochran-Smith's articles describing "teaching against the grain" (Cochran-Smith, 1991, 2001) speaks to the various traditions that inform teacher preparation programs. In an inquiry-oriented program, candidates are encouraged to explore the contexts of teaching and learning. In this view, the prospective teacher is an active participant in constructing knowledge about teaching and learning while critically examining educational goals and practices, in larger contexts (society as a whole or a particular district or school) and smaller (the individual candidate's, and his or her mentor teacher's daily teaching practices). The further subdivision into critical dissonance and collaborative resonance frameworks offers a context for the struggles we experienced within our department.

In "critical dissonance" teacher preparation programs, candidates experience dissonance between the critical university perspective on teaching and learning, and the candidates' own generally less-critical school-based experiences. It is assumed that, without intervention, candidates inevitably become socialized into a conservative school culture that perpetuates inequities. Therefore, dissonant moments are structured into the program to facilitate candidates' development of a critical perspective toward those inequities (of race, class, gender, etc.) to interrupt the cycle. Despite the good intentions of faculty, Cochran-Smith notes that critical dissonance programs have had little overall success, at least in part because programs with this ideology perpetuate the theory/practice split between the ideals of university faculty and realities of schools and teachers.

"Collaborative resonance" teacher preparation programs also aim to reform schools, and they too recognize that candidates' experiences in schools are generally more powerful than their experiences in the university classroom (even when that classroom is a portable at the school site). Therefore, collaborative resonance programs attempt to strengthen the connection between what candidates learn in university course work and in local schools. Critical questioning of school practices or the culture of teaching is still vitally important, but it is done collaboratively, with candidates, host school teachers, and university faculty members together examining practices and goals in joint seminars, professional book clubs, or action research projects. The dominant message of a collaborative resonance program is that school reform is possible when stakeholders collaborate and when power is shared. The knowledge and experiences of reform-minded teachers and the greater school community are as important as those of university faculty members (and sometimes more important).

Our work with PDSs fit best with the collaborative resonance model, and as such, represented an obvious break from paradigms historically used in our college. As tenure line faculty coordinating these teacher preparation centers, we had authority to make program changes, but had to balance this authority with the constraints of being untenured. In implementing changes consistent with our commitments to urban school reform and the PDS goals, we engaged in a public rethinking of key principles undergirding our teacher preparation programs. Our successes and setbacks in this arena ultimately taught us how to act as change agents in our own institutional setting. Given that all faculty in our programs, whether advocating for a critical dissonance or collaborative resonance model, believed that they were acting in the best interests of teacher candidates, schools and the children being served in them, we wondered what motivated faculty to become involved in the Equity Network.

A survey was completed by 15 key faculty in 2005, after the Equity Network was firmly established, to explore the motivating factors that influenced involvement in the project; all but two who completed the survey were tenure line faculty. Of these, one was a Full Professor, and the rest were fairly evenly split between Associate and Assistant Professors. Survey results shed light on the values held by faculty, and the challenges they perceived to the work and their future at Sacramento State. The survey presented a variety of items that were ultimately grouped into three categories when responses were coded: social justice (for example, the level of importance each faculty member placed on the opportunity to work in low-income, culturally and linguistically diverse settings), teachers and schools (the level of importance attributed by faculty to implementing the PDS model or to developing teacher leaders), and professional benefits (for example, receiving assigned buy-out time, or streamlining the faculty focus to one or two schools rather than being spread across many). While our motivations for participating in the Equity Network varied, there was agreement across the respondents regarding the most important and least important factors. All but one faculty member ranked "Focus on low-income students and schools" as a key factor motivating their work and all respondents ranked "Focus on urban school challenges" in the top five most important factors. Those structural factors extrinsic to the work itself—for example, combining our workload—were the least important across responses. All but two faculty members ranked "Receiving assigned time for my work" as one of the lowest motivating factors.

Thus, at least in part due to having so many faculty come from the same doctoral program that emphasized sociocultural understandings of schools and communities and a social justice philosophy, Equity Network faculty began with common values and a shared history. These common values assisted in building trust amongst faculty, an important issue since we represented two teacher preparation departments with a contentious history.

This same survey also asked two open-ended questions regarding faculty experiences with the Retention, Tenure, and Promotion (RTP) process and the role that PDS work might have played in it. A number of complications with the tenure process were described by respondents, as were perceived professional risks, although it is important to note that all involved tenure line faculty who were eligible to apply for tenure eventually were awarded it. A number of respondents noted that their work in a PDS was overlooked, dismissed, or misunderstood by the RTP committee, department chairs, and higher level administrators. Moreover, many PDS projects crossed domains that were evaluated discretely in our RTP process—one PDS project, for example, might address teaching effectiveness, scholarship, and service all at the same time. While there were no written rules, our senior colleagues believed that each domain required a discrete set of activities.

While these obstacles were troublesome, some faculty members noted in the survey that work in the Equity Network provided authentic opportunities for mentoring one another and for building a community of practice amongst faculty. One faculty commented that the Equity Network meetings were the highlight of her professional life on campus. "The meetings are a place where I can bounce ideas off colleagues who will be honest with me, but also know my intentions and trust that those intentions are good." We took comfort in knowing that, while we were junior faculty, there was a critical mass of us. More than once at our monthly Equity Network meetings, someone would say "What can they do, fire *all* of us?"

Over time, there was also an increased understanding and appreciation for the nature of PDS work that has led to radical changes in RTP expectations in our respective departments and in our college. Whereas faculty in 2002–2005 were regularly admonished by RTP committees when their teaching effectiveness, scholarship and service were addressed by common projects in a PDS setting, the opposite is generally true now. Faculty now are routinely commended in RTP discussions when they are able to leverage community service activities (such as serving on a school site governing council) with research and teaching activities (conducting action research with teachers and supervising student teachers at that *same* school, for example). It is now generally understood that we can build relationships, develop trust, and therefore have more impact on both student and student teacher learning, when our efforts are targeted toward a smaller number of schools. In this model, we are more effective.

Implications for Faculty: Learning, Leading, and Leaving

As a result of our participation in urban school–community–university partnerships through the Equity Network PDSs, we became more connected to deeper and broader funds of knowledge, and there were possibilities for being more relevant in a number of struggles for social justice, both in and outside of classrooms. By being physically present and actively engaged in our partner schools, we became seen as persons who were a legitimate and helpful presence in school-based activities and decisions. Due to our participation in K–12 schools, teachers and candidates saw us virtually every day and had more confidence in us. Our courses gained more immediate relevancy as we integrated knowledge of daily school life and classroom structures and practices. We also deepened our understanding of the dynamics of urban school structures and processes. Thus we gained trust and legitimacy within the communities where we were doing the "work" of teacher preparation.

Our involvement in the Equity Network also provided us with opportunities and support to develop practical leadership skills. In the beginning, each PDS was given a small amount of funding from our larger grant to support collaborative professional development activities. Faculty were required to work with partner teachers and site level administrators to craft an annual budget and short proposal, outlining activities to be supported and their connection to Network goals. This low-stakes project evolved into more sophisticated data collection and analyses regarding the outcomes of these activities, and required progress reports. While our partners assisted with these various proposals, data collection, analysis and reports, faculty were tasked with coordinating and completing what was required. A governance committee read through the proposals and reports, analyzing data across sites; faculty could serve on this committee, in addition to serving on site level and sometimes district level PDS governance committees.

The leadership skills we developed were not limited to grant proposals, data analysis and reports. We worked simultaneously within varying complex organizational systems that existed in different cultural contexts. Negotiating across departments and colleges within Sacramento State, and across schools, districts, and various governmental and nonprofit organizations, resulted in tremendous growth in our leadership capabilities. There were continuous opportunities to learn the art of negotiation: from mismatched schedules (the university course schedule never matched the school and each district was different from the others); to unrealistic expectations, regarding everything from K–12 curriculum to university course work assignments; and potentially disconcerting assumptions, about small things (I can't have a key to the school bathroom?) and large (I don't trust your motives). To effectively bring the university, community, and schools together, we employed good listening skills, tact, and perseverance as we were forced to expand on our repertoire of professional knowledge and skills.

It is ironic and unfortunate that many of us found we could not employ these enhanced professional skills—by expanding our sphere of influence in our own institution—without leaving the PDSs. The professional ladder in universities, like K–12 schools, is one of "moving up means moving out." Over the past six to eight years Equity Network faculty have become Associate Dean and department chairs, program directors and Provost's Fellows. One of us retired and established a private school. We regularly write and direct large grant programs (one of us bringing over three million dollars into the university); another will embark on a new role as Faculty Senate Chair this fall while one will begin a prestigious higher education leadership development program as an American Council on Education Fellow. Some Equity Network faculty members, however, have remained in the trenches of urban teacher preparation. The Citrus Heights PDS Center continues to prepare successful urban teachers, flexibly dealing with personnel changes and fiscal uncertainties. Whether intimately embedded in individual urban school sites or leveraging our growing professional knowledge and skills to effect change across broader institutional structures, we continue to apply lessons learned in the Equity Network. We know that authentic partnerships are based on trust, common goals and commitments, shared knowledge, and shared power.

References

Abdal-Haqq, I. (1998). *Professional development schools: Weighing the evidence.* Thousand Oaks, CA: Corwin Press.

Bottery, M. (2003). The management and mismanagement of trust. *Educational Management and Administration, 32*(3), 245–261.

California Commission on Teacher Credentialing. (2001). *Teacher preparation: Multiple and single subject.* Retrieved from http://www.ctc.ca.gov/educator-prep/STDS-prior.html

California Commission on Teacher Credentialing. (2003). *Teacher supply in California: A report to the Legislature, Fifth Annual Report 2001–2002.* Retrieved from http://www.ctc.ca.gov/reports/TS_2001_2002.pdf

California Commission on Teacher Credentialing. (2005). *Teacher supply in California: A report to the Legislature, Seventh Annual Report 2003–2004.* Retrieved from http://www.ctc.ca.gov/reports/TS_2003_2004.pdf

Cochran-Smith, M. (1991). Learning to teach against the grain. *Harvard Educational Review, 61*(3), 279–309.

Cochran-Smith, M. (2001). Learning to teach against the (new) grain. *Journal of Teacher Education, 52,* 3–4.

Commission on Teacher Credentialing. (2011). *Annual report card on California teacher preparation programs for the academic year 2009-2010.* Sacramento, CA: Author.

Darling-Hammond, L., & Associates. (1994). *Professional development schools: Schools for a developing profession.* New York: Teachers College Press.

Gambetta, D. (1988). Can we trust trust? In D. Gambetta (Ed.), *Trust: Making and breaking cooperative relations* (pp. 213–219). Oxford: Basil Blackwell.

Hands, C. (2005). It's who you know and what you know: The process of creating partnerships between schools and communities. *School Community Journal, 15*(2), 63–84.

Harkavy, I., & Hartley, M. (2009). University–school–community partnerships for youth development and democratic renewal. *New Directions for Youth Development, 122,* 7–18.

Holmes Group. (1995). *Tomorrow's schools of education.* East Lansing, MI: Author.

Hoy, W. K., & Tschannen-Moran, M. (1999). Five facets of trust: An empirical confirmation in urban elementary schools. *Journal of School Leadership, 9,* 184–208.

Kahne, J., & Westheimer, J. (1996). In the service of what? The politics of service learning. *Phi Delta Kappan, 77,* 593–599.

National Council for the Accreditation of Teacher Education. (2001). *Standards for professional development schools.* Retrieved from http://www.ncate.org/Standards/tabid/107/Default.aspx

Noel, J. (2002). *Diversity and location in students' selections of teacher preparation centers.* Paper presented at the 2002 annual meeting of the American Educational Studies Association, Pittsburgh, PA.

Noel, J. (2006, November). *Community in teacher education: What do we mean by the concept?* Paper presented at the 2006 annual meeting of the American Education Studies Association, Spokane, WA.

Noel, J. (2010). Weaving teacher education into the fabric of urban schools and communities. *Teacher Education Quarterly, 37*(3), 9–25.

Noel, J. (2011). Striving for authentic community engagement: A process model from urban teacher education. *Journal of Higher Education Outreach and Engagement, 15*(1), 31–52.

Noel, J., & Sessoms, D. (2009). Structural shifts and cultural transformations: University faculty and their work in PDSs. In P. Wong & R. Glass (Eds.), *Prioritizing urban children, teachers and schools through professional development schools* (pp. 155–171). Albany: State University of New York Press.

Reed, W. A. (2004). A tree grows in Brooklyn: Schools of education as brokers of social capital in low-income neighborhoods. In J. L. Kincheloe, A. Bursztyn, & S. R. Steinberg (Eds.), *Teaching teachers: Building a quality school of urban education* (pp. 65–90). New York: Peter Lang.

Stefkovich, J., & Shapiro, J. P. (2002). Deconstructing communities: Educational leaders and their ethical decision-making processes. In P. T. Begley & O. Johansson (Eds.), *The ethical dimensions of school leadership* (pp. 77–87). Dordrecht, Netherlands: Kluwer Academic.

Stodghill, R., & Bower, A. (2002, August 25). Welcome to America's most diverse city. *Time*. Retrieved from http://www.time.com/time/nation/article/0,8599,340694-1,00.html

Teitel, L. (2000). *Assessment: Assessing the impacts of professional development schools*. Washington, DC: American Association of Colleges for Teacher Education.

Tschannen-Moran, M. (2004). *Trust matters: Leadership for successful schools*. San Francisco: Jossey-Bass.

Tschannen-Moran, M., & Hoy, W. K. (2000). A multidisciplinary analysis of the nature, meaning, and measurement of trust. *Review of Educational Research, 71*, 547–593.

Weiner, L. (2000). Research in the 90s: Implications for urban teacher preparation. *Review of Educational Research, 70*(3), 369–406.

Wong, P., & Glass, R. (2009). *Prioritizing urban children, teachers, and schools through professional development schools*. Albany: State University of New York Press.

PART VII

Grow Your Own—A Final Example of Prioritizing Community Strengths

13

TEACHER PREPARATION WITH/ IN AN URBAN COMMUNITY

Elizabeth A. Skinner

> *Yo quiero ser parte de como son los maestros en México y parte de como son los maestros aquí. (I want to be in part like the teachers in Mexico and in part like the teachers here.)*
>
> *[Logan Square Neighborhood Association] me had dado la oportunidad, creo que lo justo es que yo me quede en Logan Square. Es otra forma de demostrar a varias personas que quizás están esperando por una oportunidad que lo puedes hacer. ([Logan Square Neighborhood Association] has given me the opportunity and it's only right that I stay in Logan Square. It's another way to demonstrate to others who might be waiting for an opportunity that they can do it.)*

How can a teacher preparation program evoke from their preservice candidates the above sentiments, that reflect not only a commitment to the culture and people of an urban community but also a commitment to stay and work in the schools of that community? On the surface, the answer is simple: The Grow Your Own (GYO) teachers initiative couples community-based organizations with colleges of education throughout the state of Illinois to prepare community leaders to become teachers in their local schools. Look deeper though, and a complicated, often messy collaboration emerges. For six years, I was the coordinator of project Nueva Generación, the first GYO teachers program in Chicago and in this chapter I will describe and discuss the decade-old initiative and suggest the importance of recognizing GYO as a new and complementary paradigm for teacher preparation.

Community and Organizing Origins

Chicago is a city known for diverse but segregated neighborhoods. In many of those neighborhoods a history of community organizing in the Saul Alinsky tradition, with a focus on participation and leadership lives on through the work of active and vocal community-based organizations (Warren, 2001, 2011). Logan

Square, a neighborhood situated on the northwest side of the city, is one such hub of organizing activity.

Although Logan Square is a multiclass and multiracial community, locals typically recognize it as distinctly Latino.[1] As the community becomes quantifiably more diverse, as a result of gentrification that has resulted in a 31% increase in the number of non-Hispanic White residents since 2000, the majority of the residents in Logan Square, particularly those who live in the western half of the neighborhood, continue to be of Hispanic origin (McCarron, 2011). Within the Hispanic population there is a fair amount of diversity in that nearly 50% of the Hispanics in Logan Square are Mexican and the next largest group is Puerto Ricans, at 35%. (CensusScope, n.d.; U.S. Census Bureau, 2004; Institute for Latino Studies, n.d.).

Within this diverse and dynamic neighborhood, the Logan Square Neighborhood Association (LSNA) has organized and worked for nearly 50 years on a multitude of issues, including housing, health care, immigration, jobs, and more recently, education. LSNA's education organizing work began after Chicago's pathbreaking school reform law in 1988 and continues today through several initiatives designed to improve school conditions and educational outcomes for students and families in the community.

In spite of the increase in the number of non-Hispanic Whites residing in the neighborhood, the student population at the local elementary schools where LSNA is involved remains predominantly Latino. As in many urban settings, a number of challenges converge in the elementary schools in the Logan Square neighborhood (García, 2005). Nationwide, 55% of Hispanic students attend schools where the enrollment is over 50% Hispanic (Llagas, 2003). This trend is exaggerated in Logan Square, where the percentage of Hispanic students is between 83% and 95% at each of the elementary schools in the community. The percentage of low-income students attending the neighborhood schools is at least 97% at each school, and the number of English learners is up to 36% (Chicago Public Schools, n.d.-a). In addition to the data on school population, poverty, and number of students requiring bilingual education, a report on the status of Latinos in the Chicago Public Schools indicated that Latino students are attending the most overcrowded schools in the system and that there exists a large disparity between the number of Latino students and Latino teachers (Aviles, Capeheart, Davila, & Pérez Miller, 2004). Current data shows that while 41% of the entire Chicago Public School student body is Latino, only 15% of teachers are Latino (Chicago Public Schools, n.d.-b).

Based on school data as well as firsthand knowledge of the neighborhood schools, LSNA's education organizers first focused on issues of overcrowding and continue to address the need for bilingual teachers, meaningful family involvement, and a desire to have schools as centers of community. All of LSNA's organizing work centers on "Developing relationships as the foundation for social change, on building a community that can speak for itself and on strong neighborhood based leadership" (Blanc, Brown, & Nevarez-LaTorre, 2002, p. 16).

One of LSNA's most visible efforts in the schools is the Parent Mentor Program, which began in 1995 and is based on the organization's belief in the value of the funds of knowledge, including culture and language, which community members can contribute to the schooling of their children (Moll, Amanti, Neff, & Gonzalez, 1992). The Parent Mentor Program also grew out of a desire to reduce the isolation that many immigrant mothers experience as marginalized members of the broader community. Through the program, at the beginning of every school year, LSNA hires and trains local parents to work with students in the neighborhood schools. The parent mentors receive a stipend each semester, and in addition to the time spent working in the schools, attend weekly workshops that build their skills as tutors and community leaders. Working as a parent mentor expands the networks available to community members and in her in depth account of the program, Hong (2011) explains that "by prioritizing relationships—both creating and maintaining them—LSNA's Parent Mentor Program seeks to change the institutional nature of schools" (p. 119).

Several years ago, after several of the parent mentors expressed an interest in pursuing a teaching career, one of LSNAs lead education organizers began to explore the possibilities. A traditional four-year university program was not a realistic option for the women, because in addition to their family responsibilities, many of them worked outside of the home. The expense of college was also prohibitive. The lead education organizer at LSNA understood the women's desire and believed in their potential as teachers. She began to contact area universities in the hope of finding a partner institution that shared her vision.

Theoretical Framework: Recognizing Intersections

Given their different institutional structures and cultures, community-based organizations (CBOs) and colleges of education may seem like unlikely partners in teacher preparation. However, the theoretical framework that shapes the work of LSNA and other community-based organizations and many colleges of education is the starting point for a successful collaboration. For example, all of the education work, including the Parent Mentor Program, carried out by LSNA is founded on the value the organization places on the cultural capital and funds of knowledge the community members bring to the schools and their capacity to act as change agents within those schools. Funds of knowledge, as defined by Moll et al. (1992), are "historically accumulated and culturally developed bodies of knowledge and skills" (p. 133), and for the parent mentors in Logan Square, include Spanish language, culture, life experience (in home country and Logan Square), and knowledge about raising and caring for children (Brown, 2011). LSNA's desire to change the status quo in their neighborhood schools and to reverse the failing record of school reform, echoes throughout colleges of education. Building off of LSNA's asset-based approach to community organizing and leadership development, the GYO teachers initiative in Illinois frames the movement within a discussion of social reconstruction, critical pedagogy, race uplift, and giving back (Schultz, Gillette, & Hill, 2011). While creating a pipeline of teachers of color is one of the goals of GYO, the underlying belief is that those teachers should also be prepared to resist oppressive schooling and practices that have been perpetuated in their communities and respond yes to Count's (as cited in Schultz et al., 2011) enduring question, "Dare the schools build a new social order?" (p. 9). To do this, the curriculum in the teacher education courses must engage the students in work and discussions centered on a critique of the educational system, recent education reforms, and the continued marginalization of underrepresented groups in public schools (Anyon, 2005; Freire, 1970, 1996; Giroux, 2001).

In the following statement, which also opens the chapter, a GYO student demonstrates Washington's (1901) notion of race uplift:

> LSNA me had dado la oportunidad y creo que lo justo es que yo me quede en Logan Square. Es otra forma de demostrar a varias personas que quizás están esperando por una oportunidad que lo puedes hacer. (LSNA has given me the opportunity and it's only right that I stay in Logan Square. It's another way to demonstrate to others who might be waiting for an opportunity that they can do it.)

This statement is consistent with LSNA's leadership development from within as well as the intentional nature of GYO to prepare teachers who will stay in their communities not only to teach and challenge the status quo in schools but to serve as examples of the upward mobility a college education affords.

When Joanna Brown, LSNA's education organizer, began to look into potential university partners in the Chicago area, the conversation was not about the organization's theoretical framework, but rather about her vision for the former parent mentors and their community. When she contacted personnel from the Bilingual Education Program at Chicago State University (CSU), she soon realized that she had found a partner that did, in fact, share her vision. Historically, CSU has served underrepresented minority students, many from economically disadvantaged backgrounds. The student population is approximately 80% African American, 5% Latino, and 70% female. Many CSU students are considered nontraditional college students, in that they often work full-time while attending school and are older. In addition to a demonstrated commitment to a minority student population, the Bilingual Education Program at CSU also demonstrated a shared mission with LSNA. As the organizer put it, "It was important that from the beginning we shared a common philosophy of education" (Garretón, 2008, p. 4).

The foundation for the original GYO teachers program, called project Nueva Generación, was laid by LSNA's ongoing work in their neighborhood schools. Creating a strong, neighborhood-based leadership that can impact schools requires the development of social capital among and between parents and educational professionals (Stanton-Salazar, 2004). Ideally, the resultant networks reach across class, culture, and language. By partnering with CSU, LSNA increased the social capital of the community members and expanded the breadth of their own network. The remainder of this chapter will focus on the development and implementation of the partnership, including the lessons learned while working within the Logan Square neighborhood, and the challenges inherent in the work.

Implementation: Blurring Institutional and Individual Roles and Responsibilities

The relationship building between LSNA and the Bilingual Education Program at CSU began with conversations about the vision of preparing community members to become teachers. The actual implementation of the federal Title VII grant started in August 2000. After a series of informational meetings in the community, the application and admissions process began. The recruitment of applicants and intake of their materials was initiated at LSNA and potential students received help from LSNA employees in obtaining foreign transcripts, translations of those transcripts, and community college transcripts, as necessary. As the university-based coordinator of the project, I received the students' application materials and reviewed them with an admissions officer on campus. During the review of the applications, it became evident that the university would need to adapt this process. Not all of the candidates that applied met the university's admissions criteria. In keeping with LSNA's philosophy that, rather than solid high school grade point averages and SAT scores, the students were bringing rich life experience and cultural knowledge to the program, bilingual program personnel advocated at the administrative level of the university to allow all of the applicants admission. Bilingual program personnel stressed to the administration that the students would meet all of the same requirements and benchmarks set for traditional CSU students. It was important to both partners that the program provided opportunity but also be held accountable. The university adapted the admissions criteria but did not lower performance standards. As a result, all of the individuals that completed the application process were admitted into the program and received full financial support for tuition, books, and childcare.

During the first two years of the program, the students took all of their classes at the Madison Elementary School in Logan Square, which, as a result of previous work by LSNA, was transformed into a community learning center after school hours. Each weekday evening, the school doors opened to community members for English as a second language (ESL), GED, karate, folkloric dance, homework help, sewing, and other classes. The college classes for the project Nueva Generación students were also held in the evenings at Madison, and the students could access the childcare that was already available on-site and supported through the grant. The facilitator of the Bilingual Education Program invited select professors to teach for the program. Together, we worked at identifying those professors who had experience with students who spoke ESL and/or nontraditional aged college students. It was important that professors recruited to teach in the community setting recognized the strengths of the students, but that they also knew how to address their academic weaknesses. Occasionally, hiring the right professor meant we had to negotiate course overloads and contracts with the chairs of other departments at the university. Once hired, the professors commuted to the neighborhood to teach.

While the students were taking classes in the community they had very little contact with the bureaucracy of the university. On occasion, I drove students to campus for an event but I handled all administrative tasks for them. In addition to teaching a course each semester, I checked in with students and professors on the evenings of their classes. Each semester, I met individually with the students, sometimes at the LSNA offices, to discuss progress and serve as an academic advisor. Forming relationships with the students was important but I also spoke on the phone weekly with the education organizer at LSNA. Most of our conversations dealt with the personal issues students were facing and how they were adjusting to being back in school. This was part of the trust building process between the community-based organization and the college of education but frequent communication also allowed us to negotiate our roles and figure out what we needed to do to foster the success of the students and the program. The initial very high level of communication and support for the students meant that they could adjust to being in college in the comfort of their own community. As one student put it, attending college in her neighborhood "was like a little step. I would just jump on the bus with my kids and be there in half an hour."

Working With/In the Community

Along with the political and geographic notion of community as described in the work of LSNA in the schools and the location of classes, the sense of community created by the cohort model is significant when examining the role of the university in a community-based partnership. The design of project Nueva Generación fostered and influenced an initial broad peer support network. The entire cohort took classes together the first year and got to know each other, while at the same time getting to know the university personnel. Group activities and presentations as part of a low-stress study skills course during the first semester of the program allowed the students to get to know one another in a comfortable environment. When students began to take classes on campus, the fact that the CSU campus is located on the far south side of Chicago posed transportation problems for several students, who either did not own cars or did not know how to drive. When I helped them plan their on-campus class schedules, I made sure they took classes with other cohort members who could provide rides. Moral support on campus and outside of classes was also important. For example, one student relied on fellow students for emotional support as well as transportation. She said, "We are like a huge family that if one falls down, we all help them to get up. I have learned so much from all of them." This peer support, in the presence of personal hardships and family crises that could potentially be barriers for the students, improved their chances at persisting to graduation.

Although it was a little step for the students, it was a greater challenge for the university instructors who commuted to Logan Square to teach. Because classes were held in elementary school classrooms, often the desks and chairs were too small, there were no overhead projectors or smart boards, and often not even any chalk to use on the board. In spite of the fact that the school was considered a community learning center in the evenings, some of the elementary school teachers resented the fact that their classrooms were used by others, and project Nueva Generación students were accused of taking items and messing up the rooms. I was unable to identify the real source of the resentment but it may have stemmed from the perceived threat of LSNA's organizing work in the schools (Mediratta, Fruchter, & Lewis, 2002), or that fact that many educators continue to view Latino and immigrant families through a deficit lens. One such teacher asked me, "Why should these people get everything paid for?" This comment, though startling to me at the time, demonstrates a troubling reaction to project Nueva Generación and the students. First, it suggests that such nontraditional, Spanish-speaking, Latino community members do not deserve the opportunity to become teachers, and, second, I believe it questions their academic ability as college students. This questioning of the GYO students' ability to become effective teachers is not limited to a few skeptics, but is, unfortunately, a doubt repeated in other settings. As alternative certification programs such as Teach For American (TFA), and urban teacher residencies like the Academy for Urban School Leadership (AUSL), and others proliferate and their graduates fill our local schools, GYO is frequently overlooked as an equally viable means of preparing qualified teachers.

Promoting Academic Success

Supporting the academic performance of the students was of the utmost importance to the Bilingual Education Program, particularly in light of the constant questions as to their abilities. Project Nueva Generación was not designed as an alternative certification program; there were no shortcuts for the students. In fact, it was projected that it would take most of them from seven to 10 years to graduate, and during this time the students would be under constant scrutiny by the faculty members of the Bilingual Education Program, employees of LSNA, and the outside evaluators hired to assess the progress of the program. In some ways, the students were expected to exceed the traditional college of education requirements.

Several of the students who started in project Nueva Generación had not been in schools since high school, and others had never attended school in the United States. It was natural that on returning to school, many of them felt apprehensive about their academic abilities and the difficulty of the course work. Several of the students who had attended high school in the United States had experienced firsthand the tendency to track Latinas into nonacademic classes and provide little or no opportunity to access the college preparatory curriculum. Their prior schooling had left some of them ill-prepared for college (Delgado Bernal, 1999; Gándara, 1995; Zambrana, 1994). Other students had started junior college but then left, due to the pressure to contribute financially to the family, which is also a documented barrier to full-time attendance in college for many Latinos (Hugo Lopez, 2009). Understanding the apprehension of the students, as well as their prior educational experiences, meant that providing appropriate academic support was critical for the students to succeed. As such, the program of study began with developmental math and writing courses and ESL classes for those students who needed to refine their English skills. While taking refresher courses, students also enrolled in general education courses, such as history, or art.

One student reflected on the course work and said, "It's not like the book will be read by itself. I had to read it twice." Understanding how hard the students needed to work, I consulted with LSNA to identify tutors for the students. The tutors were available both during class and outside of class hours, and students were encouraged to form study groups. In preparation for the Illinois Test of Basic Skills, required for admittance to the college of education, students attended workshops and had individual study sessions with a tutor hired specifically for test preparation.

In spite of the academic support, not all students that entered the program succeeded. A few students simply were not proficient enough in English to handle college course work and the ESL support we provided was not sufficient, although we tried a variety of teachers and courses. Other students lacked basic math skills and could not pass the developmental math courses. For others, the demands of being at work all day and in class most evenings was just too taxing. The Illinois Test of Basic Skills was also a barrier to some students who did well in their course work but could not pass that standardized test. It is frustrating to note that some of the students who exited the program due to academic difficulties were products of the very public school system in which they wanted to teach. In spite of our best efforts, we could not make up for their academic deficiencies.

As the program progressed, all of the partners in the collaboration (students, LSNA and CSU) had to consider their roles and adapt to new situations and contexts. LSNA and CSU had to keep in mind the common goal, while accepting the different organizational structures and norms at each institution (Garretón, 2008). By the third year of the program, most students were taking classes on campus and at the community center. When the registrar's office informed me that I could no longer complete registration on behalf of the students, I told them that they would need to take a more active role on campus. Concerned that I was removing the scaffolding too quickly, the education organizer from LSNA contacted me. Although we disagreed about the timing, we did agree on the need for the students to become more independent. Following this decision, students began to purchase their own textbooks (for later reimbursement), complete registration, drop and add classes, and request overrides from professors. In many ways, the personal level of support remained with them through graduation, but it was critical at this juncture that the students also learned how to work the system on their own. Adhering to the belief that the construction of self as agent contributes to resiliency, particularly if the students are viewing themselves as active participants in their success (McGinty, 1999), and LSNA's rule of organizing—don't do for others what they can do for themselves (Brown, 2011), the students took on more responsibilities.

Lessons Learned

In December 2006, the first two project Nueva Generación students graduated and accepted jobs with the Chicago Public Schools. In May 2012, there were a total of 21 graduates from the program, and there are currently between 50 and 60 students in the pipeline continuing their studies both in the neighborhood and on campus. As teachers, the graduates' culture, language, and background knowledge match that of their students. Those funds of knowledge, when combined with the pedagogy learned in the college of education, prepared them up for success as urban teachers (Haberman, 1996). Further research will document how long they stay in their current school, and how they impact student achievement and climate in those schools.

In the process of working toward change in the Logan Square neighborhood schools, the Bilingual Education Program at CSU learned valuable lessons about community partnerships that are applicable to all colleges of education engaging in work within urban schools and communities. As the academic partner in the collaboration, the Bilingual Education Program did not limit its role strictly to academics. The professors, administrators, and coordinator attended to the affective needs of the students, and considered not only their life experiences but their life situations. By physically coming to Logan Square to teach, faculty members were integrated into the community in a way that cannot happen on campus. While in Logan Square, professors shared meals with the students, met their children, and observed the conditions of the schools. They also gained an insider's perspective from the students. All of the university personnel essentially became boundary spanners, willingly going from the university to the community and integrating community concerns into their work (Shirley et al., 2006).

The intimate involvement in the community and with LSNA brought new energy to the Bilingual Education Program (Mediratta et al., 2002). I personally felt a new excitement and greater commitment to our mission in the schools when working with our new found ally. From LSNA, university personnel learned the importance of relationship building and witnessed the positive impact that had on the culture within the entire program. The Nueva Generación students also brought a new and palpable energy with them when they came to campus and were integrated into classes with the campus-based bilingual students. Just as the partnership expanded the networks of the students and LSNA, the Bilingual Education Program benefitted from an expanded network. Collaborating with LSNA granted easier access into the Logan Square schools and to teachers and administrators with whom we wanted to work. In other words, the partnership was mutually beneficial. Both institutions contributed to and gained from one another while working toward a mutual goal.

State-Wide Impact

While further research is needed to document the impact of the teachers who graduated with teaching degrees through project Nueva Generación, the program has had a documented impact on teacher education in the state of Illinois. While the Bilingual Education Program at CSU and the education organizers at LSNA were building trust and collaborating to make project Nueva Generación a local success, other community-based organizations in Chicago were also working on issues of teacher recruitment and retention. Action Now (AN) (formerly part of Association of Community Organizations for Reform Now, or ACORN) was one such organization and after learning about and visiting project Nueva Generación, recognized it as a possible strategy for their own neighborhood schools. Thus began the organizing campaign that resulted in the statewide program known as Grow Your Own Illinois. In 2004, the GYO teachers bill was passed, putting into Illinois state law the goals to create a pipeline of teachers of color and to prepare them to teach in hard to staff schools or positions. Only coalitions that include a community-based organization and a college of education as equal partners are eligible for the funding. Presently, the statewide GYO initiative counts 300 teacher candidates in 15 consortia throughout the state (Grow Your Own Illinois, n.d.).

Challenges

While CBOs in Illinois have been actively engaged in working on the effort to tap the resources of community leaders and prepare them to be educators, most colleges of education have also been adapting their programs to better prepare their traditional teacher candidates, who are largely White and female (Zumwalt & Craig, 2005), for the realities of urban schools. In my opinion, the two approaches are compatible and both necessary means to improve teacher preparation. When Secretary of Education Arne Duncan said, "America's university-based teacher preparation programs need revolutionary change—not evolutionary tinkering" (Mathers, 2009, para. 8), many in the field agreed and had already been implementing new programs, including community-based experiences that essentially immerse the teacher education students in a community that is culturally different from their own (Sleeter, 2001). Such programs have merit and it has been demonstrated that the cross–cultural experience "may aid students' cultural awareness and solidify aspirations to teach within such communities" (Gallego, 2001, p. 313).

In spite of such teacher preparation innovations, there continues to be a need for teachers and teacher candidates to understand not only the importance of connecting with the communities where they work, but also the complex nature of the relationship between the school and the community and the marginalized position of the individuals who live there (Koerner & Abdul-Tawwab, 2006; Murrell, 2001). The ongoing quest to more effectively connect teacher candidates with urban communities and schools drives the examination of the role of colleges of education within the school/community context. Given that most community-based teacher education programs originate on campus and then move into communities, it is not surprising that a disconnect persists between colleges of education, their students, and the communities they strive to serve. The GYO teachers initiative in Illinois, as exemplified in the description of project Nueva Generación, offers another perspective and example of community-based partnerships between CBOs and colleges of education.

However, there is an inherent challenge in replicating project Nueva Generación and scaling up such a local initiative. Not all CBOs have the history of organizing in the schools nor do all colleges of education willingly accept the community as a true and equal partner. Without an understanding of the organizational characteristics that made it successful, there is danger in simply replicating or scaling up any program (Payne, 2008). Another danger lies in the possibility that GYO teacher preparation programs like project Nueva Generación remain isolated from the colleges of education and that the students never become integrated into the fabric of the university (Fullan, 2009). To truly transform teacher education and diversify the pool of teacher candidates, community-based programs must be sustained by the university and provided adequate funding.

I propose project Nueva Generación and the GYO teacher initiative as one example of the revolutionary change being called for in Teacher Preparation. However, reform in education does not happen overnight. CBOs know that and work for intermediate gains that will lead to greater long-term outcomes (Mediratta et al., 2002). Likewise, Tyack and Cuban (1995) call for reforms that work to improve education from the inside out and take into account the difficulties inherent in changing the institutional patterns of schooling. Colleges of education have put considerable effort into attempting to prepare White outsiders to teach in historically underserved urban settings and that effort should continue. Following the example of project Nueva Generación and the statewide GYO initiative in Illinois, colleges of education could adopt an alternative and complementary strategy, one that aims to increase the number of teachers of color, but also prepare them to work as change agents in urban schools.

Note

1 *Latino/a* and *Hispanic* have been used interchangeably throughout the chapter. Because *Hispanic* is the term used by government agencies and the Census Bureau, statistics are usually stated in terms of Hispanics, whereas *Latino/a* is used in more general terms.

References

Anyon, J. (2005). *Radical possibilities*. New York: Routledge.

Aviles, A., Capeheart, L., Davila, E., & Pérez Miller, A. (2004). *Dando un paso ¿pa'lante o pa'tras? Latinos in the Chicago Public Schools*. Chicago: Second Legislative Education Advisory Committee, Senator Miguel del Valle.

Blanc, S., Brown, J., & Nevarez-La Torre, A. (2002). *Strong neighborhoods, strong schools*. Philadelphia: Research for Action With Cross City Campaign for Urban School Reform.

Brown, J. (2011). Parents building communities in schools. In E. Skinner, M. T. Garreton, & B. Schultz (Eds.), *Grow your own teachers: Grassroots change for teacher education* (pp. 49–60). New York: Teachers College Press.

CensusScope. (n.d.). *Race and ethnicity selections, 1980–2000*. Retrieved from http://www.censusscope.org/us/print_chart_race.html

Chicago Public Schools. (n.d.-a). *School test scores and demographic reports*. Retrieved from http://research.cps.k12.il.us/resweb/SchoolProfile?unit=3520

Chicago Public Schools. (n.d.-b). *Stats and facts*. Retrieved from http://www.cps.edu/About_CPS/At-a-glance/Pages/Stats%20and%20facts.aspx

Delgado Bernal, D. (1999). Chicana/o education from the civil rights era to the present. In J. Moreno (Ed.), *The elusive quest for equality: 150 years of chicano/chicana education* (pp. 77–108). Cambridge, MA: Harvard Educational Review.

Freire, P. (1970). *Pedagogy of the oppressed*. New York: Continuum.

Freire, P. (1996). *Pedagogy of hope*. New York: Continuum.

Fullan, M. (2009). Large-scale reform comes of age. *Journal of Educational Change, 10*, 101–113. doi:10.1007/s10833-009-9108-z

Gallego, M. (2001). Is experience the best teacher? The potential of coupling classroom and community-based field experiences. *Journal of Teacher Education, 52*(4), 312–325.

Gándara, P. (1995). *Over the ivy walls: The educational mobility of low-income Chicanos*. Albany: State University of New York Press.

García, E. (2005). *Teaching and learning in two languages: Bilingualism and schooling in the United States*. New York: Teachers College Press.

Garretón, M. T. (2008, February). *Restructuring teacher education through collaboration: Reflections on a partnership*. Paper presented at the meeting of the American Association of Colleges of Teacher Education, New Orleans, LA.

Giroux, H. (2001). *Theory and resistance in education* (Rev. ed.). South Hadley, MA: Bergin and Garvey.

Grow Your Own Illinois. (n.d.). *Profile of GYO candidates*. Retrieved from http://www.growyourownteachers.org/index.php?option=com_content&view=article&id=107&Itemid=122

Haberman, M. (1996). Selecting and preparing culturally competent teachers for urban schools. In J. Sikula, T. J. Buttery, & E. Guyton (Eds.), *Handbook of research on teacher education* (2nd ed., pp. 747–760). New York: Macmillan.

Hong, S. (2011). *A cord of three strands: A new approach to parent engagement in schools.* Cambridge, MA: Harvard Education Press.

Hugo Lopez, M. (2009). *Latinos and education: Explaining the attainment gap.* Retrieved from the Pew Hispanic Center website: http://pewhispanic.org/reports/report. php?ReportID=115

Institute for Latino Studies. (n.d.). *Chicago fact finder, area 22—Logan Square.* Retrieved from http://www3.nd.edu/~chifacts/communities.php?alphaorder=22&pag

Koerner, M., & Abdul-Tawwab, N. (2006). Using community as a resource for teacher education: A case study. *Equity and Excellence in Education, 39,* 37–46. doi:10.1080/10665680500478767

Llagas, C. (2003). *Status and trends in the education of Hispanics.* Retrieved from http://nces. ed.gov/pubsearch/pubsinfo.asp?pubid=2003008

Mathers, J. (2009, October 21). Duncan to ed schools: End "mediocre" training. *Washington Post.* Retrieved from http://www.washingtonpost.com/?nid=top_news

Mediratta, K., Fruchter, N., & Lewis, A. (2002). *Organizing for school reform: How communities are finding their voices and reclaiming their public schools.* New York: Institution for Education and Social Policy.

McCarron, J. (2011, March). *NCP and the 2010 census.* Retrieved from http://newcommunities.org/news/articleDetail.asp?objectID=2091

McGinty, S. (1999). *Resilience and success at school.* New York: Peter Lang.

Moll, L., Amanti, C., Neff, D., & Gonzalaz, N. (1992). Funds of knowledge for teaching: Using a qualitative approach to connect homes and classrooms. *Theory Into Practice, 31,* 132–141.

Murrell, P. (2001). *The community teacher: A new framework for effective urban teaching.* New York: Teachers College Press.

Payne, C. (2008). *So much reform, so little change: The persistence of failure in urban schools.* Cambridge, MA: Harvard Education Press.

Schultz, B., Gillette, M., & Hill, D. (2011). Teaching as political: Theoretical perspectives for understanding the Grow your own movement. In E. Skinner, M. T. Garreton, & B. Schultz (Eds.), *Grow your own teachers: Grassroots change for teacher education* (pp. 5–21). New York: Teachers College Press.

Shirley, D., Hersi, A., MacDonald, E., Sanchez, M. T., Scandone, C., Skidmore, C., et al. (2006). Bringing the community back in: Change, accommodation, and contestation in a school and university partnership. *Equity and Excellence in Education, 39,* 27–36. doi:10.1080/10665680500478718

Sleeter, C. (2001). Preparing teachers for culturally diverse schools: Research and the overwhelming presence of whiteness. *Journal of Teacher Education, 52*(2), 94–106.

Stanton-Salazar, R. (2004). Social capital among working-class minority students. In M. A. Gibson, P. Gándara, & J. P. Koyama (Eds.), *School connections: U.S. Mexican youth, peers, and school achievement* (pp. 18–38). New York: Teachers College Press.

Tyack, D., & Cuban, L. (1995). *Tinkering toward utopia: A century of public school reform.* Cambridge, MA: Harvard University Press.

U.S. Census Bureau. (2004). *Hispanic and Asian Americans increasing faster than overall population.* Retrieved from http://www.census.gov/PressRelease/www/releases/archives/race/0

Warren, M. (2001). *Dry bones rattling.* Princeton, NJ: Princeton University Press.

Warren, M. (2011). The school community organizing model and the origins of Grow your own teachers. In E. Skinner, M. T. Garreton, & B. Schultz (Eds.), *Grow your own teachers: Grassroots change for teacher education* (pp. 34–48). New York: Teachers College Press.

Washington, B. T. (1901). *Up from slavery*. New York: Doubleday.

Zambrana, R. (1994). Toward understanding the educational trajectory and socialization of Latina women. In L. Stone (Ed.), *The education feminism reader* (pp. 135–145). New York: Routledge.

Zumwalt, K., & Craig, E. (2005). Teachers' characteristics: Research on the Demographic Profile. In M. Cochran-Smith & K. M. Zeichner (Eds.), *Studying teacher education: The Report of the AERA panel on research and teacher education* (pp. 111–156). Mahwah, NJ: Erlbaum.

CONCLUSION: PRIORITIZING COMMUNITY STRENGTHS IN URBAN TEACHER EDUCATION

Jana Noel

We hope that readers have found both information and inspiration from the chapters in this book. Taken together, the chapters provide the opportunity to build the theory and practice of prioritizing community strengths in urban teacher education. This conclusion highlights the common threads found throughout the chapters that encourage teacher educators, K–12 educators, and communities to transform teacher education contextualized within schools and communities.

As Glass and Lindquist Wong describe in Chapter 2, we need to develop "teachers for communities (not only classrooms)" (p. 24). How can this be accomplished? This volume urges teacher educators to move all or part of their programs directly into urban schools and communities. The underlying belief is that "by moving teacher education into urban schools and communities, preservice teachers and faculty would better understand the realities of urban education, including the social, political, and economic conditions impacting the lives and education of urban children and their families" (Noel, Chapter 9, p. 138). However, this is not enough. Just moving programs into urban schools and communities does not automatically mean a deeper understanding of those urban communities. There must be an intentional goal of participating in communities' efforts to transform urban education. Put simply, the authors in this volume would agree that "we urge teacher education to better connect its work with the social justice work occurring in local communities and beyond" (Zeichner & Payne, Chapter 1, p. 3):

> If public schools had such purposes, they would not simply occupy spaces within a community, but they would see their work as embedded in the community and, thus, intimately tied to community values and goals. In such school settings, teachers would recognize their work as a connected enterprise, as facets of the same work that is carried out by parents, cultural and religious organizations, and social service agencies. (Onore & Gilden, Chapter 10, p. 154)

Shifting Our Perspective on "Whose Knowledge Counts"

How can teacher education become authentically situated within a community? First, those involved in community–school–university collaborative teacher education partnerships need to carefully consider how they perceive of knowledge. Many chapters address the need to shift how teacher educators, and the field of education itself, view knowledge. The groundwork is laid in the first two chapters around what is knowledge, and many other chapters then discuss knowledge in multiple ways. Zeichner and Payne pose the question first: "Whose knowledge should count in teacher education?" (Chapter 1, p. 3). Morgan-Fleming, in Chapter 6, continues: "What knowledge has value? Why? and Who decides?" (p. 90). Even a cursory examination of current national reform initiatives gives us the answer. As a number of authors in this book express, various federal initiatives take knowledge out of the hands of communities and families, and out of the hands of local teachers, and put it directly into external evaluators and standardized tests. Effects of standardization on K–12 schools, such as the structure surrounding No Child Left Behind (NCLB), which requires high-stakes standardized testing, have resulted in takeovers of schools by those external to the communities within which those schools are situated. Fast-track, alternative teacher certification programs that do not encourage collaborative engagement with community contribute to a high turnover of teachers in urban areas, a concern raised by several authors in this book. Prioritizing community knowledge addresses this issue.

"Power is always implicated in judgments of what counts as *knowing*" (Glass & Lindquist Wong, Chapter 2, p. 22). When only the knowledge of university educators and external evaluators counts as acceptable knowledge, community members feel less valued and often develop a distrust of university teacher education programs. The authors in this book propose a democratization of knowledge among universities, schools, communities, families, and children. As Sessoms explains, "the knowledge and experiences of reform-minded teachers and the greater school community are as important as those of university faculty members (and sometimes more important)" (Chapter 12, p. 194). Zeichner and Payne's words exemplify the views of the authors when they write that "teacher education needs to make an epistemological shift in whose knowledge counts and whose expertise must inform novice teacher learning" (Chapter 1, p. 3).

Funds of Knowledge and the Community Teacher

Several concepts prioritizing community knowledge can be seen consistently throughout these chapters. The concepts of "funds of knowledge" (Moll, Amanti, & González, 1992) and the "community teacher" (Murrell, 2001) are at the heart of much of this work. Funds of knowledge, as defined by Moll et al., are "historically accumulated and culturally developed bodies of knowledge and skills" (as cited in Skinner, Chapter 13, p. 205) that community members can "bring to the schools [in] their capacity to act as change agents within those schools" (p. 205). The authors in this volume advocate for teachers, and teacher educators, to learn about and the draw on those community funds of knowledge in their classrooms. Murrell's (2001, 2007, 2008) ideas are heavily referenced throughout the book, including the "community teacher," "one who possesses contextualized knowledge of the culture, community, and identity of the children and families he or she serves and draws on this knowledge to create the core teaching practices necessary for effectiveness in diverse setting" (Murrell, as cited in Zeichner & Payne, Chapter 1, p. 11). How can teacher education participate in the development of community teachers? A number of authors point out that relationships are the key. Sessoms writes that "collaborative partnerships between institutions are, at their heart, relationships among people" (Chapter 12, p. 189). Peterman similarly points out the importance of "building and sustaining relationships within and across school and university settings—at the classroom, institutional, and community levels" (Chapter 11, p. 181). University faculty, as well as their students, need to approach the collaboration as "boundary spanners, willingly going from the university to the community and integrating community concerns into their work" (Skinner, Chapter 13, p. 211).

Learning Communities

Many of the recommendations in this book call for the creation of collaborations, such as "communities of practice" (Lave & Wenger, 1991; Wenger, 1998), "circles of co-practice" (Murrell, 2001), and "interprofessional space" (Onore & Gilden, Chapter 10). According to Catapano and Thompson, "communities of practice [are] groups of individuals who share interests, tasks, beliefs, and practices to accomplish a specific goal" (Chapter 5, p. 79). Onore and Gilden explain that Murrell's "circle of co-practice" is a "nonhierarchical professional collaboration," explaining that if programs developed such collaborations, "they would not simply occupy spaces within a community but they would see their work as embedded in the community and, thus, intimately tied to community values and goals" (Chapter 10, p. 154).

Situated Spaces for Teacher Education

Theories underlying this work highlight the importance of "situated" or "contextualized" spaces for teacher education. Authors use several different terms to describe the importance of this framework of programs "situated" in community, and a number of them cite Zeichner's work (Zeichner, 2006, 2010; Zeichner & Conklin, 2008; Zeichner & Melnick, 1996). "Cultural historical activity theory," as described by Zeichner and Payne (Chapter 1), emphasizes the interconnectedness of culture, history, and learning. Citing Lave and Wenger (1991), Glass and Lindquist Wong describe that "ways of knowing are historically and culturally situated" (Chapter 2, p. 21). Stairs and Friedman describe that "the situative perspective prioritizes community strengths as it puts community at the heart of teacher learning. There can be no learning independent of the context and community in which learners are situated" (Chapter 3, p. 41). Zeichner and Payne, building on Zeichner's (2006, 2010) previous work, have proposed actual new spaces for teacher education, "hybrid spaces" or "third space," "where academic, practitioner, and community-based knowledge come together in new ways to support the development of innovative and hybrid solutions to the problem of preparing teachers" (Chapter 1, p. 6).

Social Justice, Power, and Privilege

Working within these theoretical constructs and practical strategies that prioritize community strengths within urban teacher education necessarily entails a social justice perspective on the work of teacher education. To join in the efforts of communities to transform education for their children, teacher education programs must do the difficult work of preparing teachers who will take on teaching as a political act, as an act necessarily embedded within community, as a commitment to urban children and their communities that will be long term and long lasting. Katsarou, Picower, and Stovall urge us to consider that "teaching for social justice is an act of necessity and solidarity" (Chapter 8, p. 121), in which there is collaboration "among all educational stakeholders (students, families, teachers, administrators, community organizations, community members) with the goal of creating tangible change in their communities, cities, states, nation, and the larger world" (p. 121). The results should impact communities, schools, future teachers, and the faculty who work in these programs. Katsarou, Picower, and Stovall write that:

> relationships that exist between colleges of education and those urban schools/spaces, that are intentional about the work they do with underserved students and communities, are central in our developing teacher candidates that will engage in deeply caring, ethical, and socially and politically relevant teaching. (p. 127)

Sessoms writes similarly about university faculty that "we became more connected to deeper and broader funds of knowledge, and there were possibilities for being more relevant in a number of struggles for social justice, both in and outside of classrooms" (Chapter 12, p. 196).

To develop such relationships, those that are intentional about collaborating to make education transformative for communities, teacher education must recognize privilege, power, and positionality (Noel, Chapter 9). Part of the privilege and power that comes from being a university program in an urban community often comes from demographic differences. Most, if not all, communities described in these chapters are very diverse, while most of the teacher education programs are not (many authors cited Sleeter's, 2001, work to frame this issue). Catapano and Thompson describe the situation: "University–school partnerships are especially important in urban schools, where many of the new teachers are not culturally prepared to meet the unique needs of the learners and families in this setting" (Chapter 5, p. 76). Stairs and Friedman (Chapter 3) and Noel (Chapter 9), among others, describe the importance of developing experiences situated within community that "would provide the mostly White, privileged preservice teachers an opportunity to become part of an urban school culture and community, with which few were familiar" (Stairs & Friedman, Chapter 3, p. 42). Teacher education programs must deal with this distinction directly. As Noel writes, an urban school–community-based teacher education program needs to "consistently consider how people in the neighborhoods might take a racially, economically, and educationally marked view of their students and faculty" (Chapter 9, p. 138). School- and community-based teacher education programs that are intentional about their transformational efforts can provide the impetus for such conversations:

> To paraphrase Freire, *invading* such contested spaces may be the only approach for all concerned within teacher preparation to become deeply cognizant of the communities in which we are working with kids, and families and thus, become truly enmeshed in the local realities and challenges. (Chapter 8, Katsarou, Picower, & Stovall, p. 127)

Identity

Many chapters address identity in one way or another, including student teachers' identities as cultural others (Stairs & Friedman, Chapter 3; Lee, Showalter, & Eckrich, Chapter 4; among others); K–12 student identities coming out through us hearing their voices (Catapano & Thompson, Chapter 5; Morgan-Fleming, Chapter 6); faculty teacher educators developing an identity as teacher educators and not merely as faculty members (Peterman, Chapter 11; Sessoms, Chapter 12); and communities gaining increased self-efficacy and a sense of identity as a guide to learners (Noel, Chapter 9; Onore & Gilden, Chapter 10; among others). Lee, Showalter, and Ekrich (Chapter 4) recommend "cultural mapping" (Murrell, 2007) as a way of understanding the role that culture has on identity. Cultural mapping, they write, helps us "to uncover the ideologies and meaning systems that play a significant role in shaping cultural practices and how young people [and teachers] position themselves in relation to those practices" (Murrell, as cited in Lee, Showalter, & Ekrich, Chapter 4, p. 56). For future teachers, "by participating in the lived community with its complex framework of language, rituals, symbolism, and culture . . . preservice teachers trained in situ are able to take learning to the intersection of meaning, practice, community, and professional identity development" (Lee, Showalter, & Ekrich, Chapter 4, p. 69).

Conclusion

The views expressed in this volume can be summarized from within two sets of literature cited frequently by the authors. An early proponent of partnerships, Goodlad (1994) developed the concept of "simultaneous renewal," defined as "the value of university–school partnerships as an opportunity for simultaneous renewal" (Catapano & Thompson, Chapter 5, p. 78). The importance of school–community-based teacher education is supported by the work of Shirley et al. (2006): "Recent evidence suggests that carefully designed site-based teacher education programs may enhance aspiring teachers' engagement with urban communities" (Jeffery & Polleck, Chapter 7, p. 107). Through shifting our perspective on whose knowledge counts; developing approaches utilizing funds of knowledge and developing the community teacher; developing expanded learning communities; creating situated spaces for teacher education; participating with full recognition of our roles in social justice, power, and privilege; and being aware of how our work affects and shapes identity, teacher education can become a vital partner in the effort to transform urban education.

References

Goodlad, J. L. (1994). *Educational renewal: Better teachers, better schools.* San Francisco: Jossey-Bass.

Lave, J., & Wenger, E. (1991). *Situated learning: Legitimate peripheral participation.* New York: Cambridge University Press.

Moll, L. C., Amanti, C., Neff, D., & González, N. (1992). Funds of knowledge for teaching: Using a qualitative approach to connect homes and classrooms. *Theory Into Practice, 31*(2), 132–141.

Murrell, P. C., Jr. (2001). *The community teacher: A new framework for effective urban teaching.* New York: Teachers College Press.

Murrell, P. C., Jr. (2007). *Race, culture, and schooling: Identities of achievement in multicultural urban schools.* New York: Routledge.

Murrell, P. C., Jr. (2008). Toward social justice in urban education: A model of collaborative cultural inquiry in urban schools. In F. Peterman (Ed.), *Partnering to prepare urban teachers: A call to activism* (pp. 41–58). New York: Peter Lang.

Shirley, D., Hersi, A., MacDonald, E., Sanchez, M. T., Scandone, C., Skidmore, C., et al. (2006). Bringing the community back in: Change, accommodation, and contestation in a school and university partnership. *Equity and Excellence in Education, 39,* 27–36.

Sleeter, C. (2001). Preparing teachers for culturally diverse schools: Research and the overwhelming presence of whiteness. *Journal of Teacher Education, 52*(2), 94–106.

Wenger, E. (1998). *Communities of practice: Learning, meaning, and identity.* Cambridge, MA: Cambridge University Press.

Zeichner, K. (2006). Reflections of a university-based teacher educator on the future of college- and university-based teacher education. *Journal of Teacher Education, 57*(3), 326–340.

Zeichner, K. (2010). Rethinking the connections between campus courses and field experiences in college and university-based teacher education. *Journal of Teacher Education, 61*(1–2), 89–99.

Zeichner, K., & Conklin, H. G. (2008). Teacher education programs as sites for teacher preparation. In M. Cochran-Smith, S. Feiman-Nemser, D. McIntyre, & K. E. Demers (Eds.), *Handbook of research on teacher education* (3rd ed., pp. 269–289). New York: Routledge.

Zeichner, K., & Melnick, S. (1996). The role of community field experiences in preparing teachers for cultural diversity. In K. Zeichner, S. Melnick, & M. L. Gomez (Eds.), *Currents of reform in preservice teacher education* (pp. 176–198). New York: Teachers College Press.

NOTES ON CONTRIBUTORS

Susan Catapano is Chair and Professor of the Department of Educational Leadership at University of North Carolina at Wilmington. Her research interests include preparation and mentoring of new teachers for urban schools.

Lucille L. T. Eckrich is Associate Professor in the Department of Educational Administration and Foundations at Illinois State University (ISU). She was a founding faculty associate of ISU's Chicago Teacher Education Pipeline and the founding advisor for ISU's registered student organization focused on Urban Needs in Teacher Education (UNITE).

Audrey A. Friedman is Associate Professor of Teacher Education, Special Education, and Curriculum and Instruction and Assistant Dean of Undergraduate Student Services at the Lynch School of Education, Boston College. Her research focuses on teacher candidates' development of reflective judgment, cultural competence, and decision making about ill-defined dilemmas of practice.

Bonny L. Gildin is Vice President, Education Initiatives of the All Stars Project Inc., a privately funded national nonprofit organization that sponsors after-school development programs for inner-city youth.

Ronald David Glass is Director of the University of California Center for Collaborative Research for an Equitable California (http://ccrec.ucsc.edu) and Associate Professor of Philosophy of Education at University of California–Santa Cruz.

Jill V. Jeffery is Assistant Professor in the Department of Language, Literacy, and Sociocultural Studies and the Department of English at the University of New

Mexico. Her research focuses on adolescent literacy, teacher development, and transitions between K–12 and college contexts.

Eleni Katsarou is Clinical Full Professor and Director of Elementary Education in the Department of Curriculum and Instruction at University of Illinois at Chicago.

Robert E. Lee serves as Executive Director of the Chicago Teacher Education Pipeline Programs and Partnerships, based at Illinois State University.

Barbara Morgan-Fleming is Associate Professor in the Department of Curriculum and Instruction at Texas Tech University.

Jana Noel is a 2012–2013 American Council on Education Fellow and Professor in the College of Education at California State University, Sacramento. She previously served as Sacramento State Provost's Fellow for Community and Civic Engagement.

Cynthia Onore is Emeritus Professor of Education at Montclair State University, where she served as Director of the Center of Pedagogy and was a member of the faculty in the Department of Curriculum and Teaching. Prior to that, Dr. Onore was founding Director of Teacher Education at the New School University. She also taught high school English in New York City and Newark, New Jersey.

Katherina Payne is a doctoral student at the University of Wisconsin–Madison.

Francine P. Peterman is Dean of the College Education and Human Services at Montclair State University. She formerly served as Dean of Education at Queens College, CUNY.

Bree Picower is Assistant Professor in the Department of Early Childhood, Elementary, and Literacy Education at Montclair State University and a core member of the New York Collective of Radical Educators.

Jody N. Polleck is currently a full-time assistant professor in adolescent literacy at Hunter College and a part-time tenth-grade English teacher in New York City. Her research focuses on differentiated and culturally responsive instruction and curriculum with urban youth.

Deidre B. Sessoms is Professor in the College of Education at California State University, Sacramento.

Brent D. Showalter serves as Research Associate for the Chicago Teacher Education Pipeline. He currently coordinates research and program evaluation for Illinois State University's community-based work in Chicago.

Elizabeth A. Skinner is Assistant Professor in the Department of Curriculum Instruction at Illinois State University. She specializes in bilingual education and urban teacher preparation.

Andrea J. Stairs is Associate Professor and Chair of the Department of Literacy, Language, and Culture at the University of Southern Maine. Her scholarly interests include urban teacher learning over time, choice in the K–12 English language arts/reading curriculum to meet the needs of diverse learners, and teacher research in literacy.

David Stovall is Associate Professor of Educational Policy Studies and African American Studies at the University of Illinois at Chicago.

Candace M. Thompson is Assistant Professor in the Department of Instruction, Technology, Foundations, and Secondary Education at the University of North Carolina at Wilmington. Her research interests include critical multicultural education in teacher education and developing cultural competency and critical consciousness in preservice teachers through school- and community-based collaborations.

Pia Lindquist Wong is Professor of Bilingual/Multicultural Education at California State University, Sacramento and serves as Chair of the Teaching Credentials Department of the College of Education. She is the former director of the Equity Network of urban professional development schools.

Kenneth Zeichner is Boeing Professor of Teacher Education at the University of Washington—Seattle.

INDEX